Published in Great Britain by
L.R. Price Publications Ltd, 2022
27 Old Gloucester Street,
London, WC1N 3AX
www.lrpricepublications.com

ISBN-13: 978-1-91-533015-4

# My Impressions of Travelling in China

\*

## David Colyer

Dedicated to my wife Bai Ling
and her excellent family.

# Introduction

I first started travelling to China back in 2002, but didn't start recording some of my experiences in a diary until 2009.

This book was both written based on my writings in that diary, and also includes real-time extracts. The first extract was dated Thursday 5th November 2009...

THURSDAY 5TH NOVEMBER 2009

After a nine-hour flight, during which I didn't manage to get any sleep, we arrived in Beijing airport. It had been snowing, but the roads and airport had been cleared. Ling's son Qiang Qi was there to meet us and help with our cases: two large ones, weighing about twenty-six kilos each, and two small carry-on bags at about ten kilos each.

We went to a rather basic hotel, which was quite cheap at about 190 yuan (eleven to the pound) per night; it had been arranged by Ling's aunt, who had some sort of special discount card. We weren't too impressed – the paint was peeling off the walls and ceiling, the water was not hot at that time of day, and the duvets were rather second-hand looking – so Ling arranged for us just to stay just the one night, before transferring to our usual place, the Golden Palace Hotel in Silver Street, near Wan Fujing Lu, where we had previously stayed on several occasions, since we married in 2002.

When we went to visit Ling's aunt and uncle, they weren't too happy that we were moving out of the hotel they had arranged, as I predicted, but they took us to a great restaurant, in a fully traditional pagoda-style building. There was good food and a very professional floor show, comprising a Beijing opera singer, a young acrobat girl with about ten hula-hoops, a magician and another girl who balanced a huge clay pot on her feet as she lay back on a special chair lifted by four attendants; they then put a volunteer from the audience inside it, while she spun him around with her feet.

We then had an early night and slept reasonably well, having not slept the night before.

FRIDAY 6TH NOVEMBER 2009

After a quick breakfast of eggs and bacon at a local McDonald's, we moved to the Golden Palace Hotel, just behind St. Joseph's Catholic Church on Silver Street. The place hadn't changed much, and was still priced at about 350 (£35) yuan per night, with a rating of three stars.

We went out to look around the general shopping area, and were surprised to note that our favourite Japanese restaurant had been pulled down and moved to the main shopping mall in Wan Fujing Lu. On the opposite corner, a huge poster of David Beckham had been replaced by one of Wayne Rooney.

In the evening, we had a meal with Qiang Qi's girlfriend Chen Meng (Vicky) at the famous Beijing Duck Restaurant

– the total price was 519RMB. Afterward, we went to take a look at his rather basic flat, which was provided free by his "father's sister" (aunt, surely?). Everybody seems to have one or more homes in China!

Later that day, Qiang Qi took us to a temple, and later a big, famous antique and artefact market, although probably everything was repro – not that we wanted to buy anything, already having too much to carry back to Ling's mum's home in Jinan.

We had lunch at a nice Korean restaurant recommended by Qiang Qi, who seemed to know his way around. Then, in the late afternoon, we visited Liu Pei (Gary) and his new wife.

Liu Pei had his parents staying with him: Liu Lingsheng and his wife Mei. Liu Lingsheng was a former work colleague of Ling's, when they worked at the same hospital in Jinan about twenty years ago. I'd met Liu Pei in London, when he started a delivery business in Feltham, Middlesex, delivering goods to and from China, but the business had only lasted about five years.

Theirs was a lavishly styled two-bedroom flat, rather resembling a marriage suite from a catalogue, with underground parking and a spare storage room. It looked very much like a display showhouse, with large plants and floral displays everywhere. It cost about a million yuan (approx. £100,000), which was the going rate for Beijing, even in zone 4 or 5.

They took us to an excellent restaurant, as might be expected, where we were given a private room and table for about ten, before some other relatives arrived.

SUNDAY 8ᵀᴴ NOVEMBER 2009

I woke at about 11.00 a.m., after twelve hours sleep, getting over the jetlag. I then had a hot-pot lunch with Qiang Qi and Vicky.

MONDAY 9ᵀᴴ NOVEMBER 2009

It was very cold – about two degrees – but we decided to visit Tianjin as planned, which was about thirty-five minutes by train.

This is one of the largest cities to the north in China, with a population of around fifteen million people. We didn't quite know where to go, so we got a taxi to Traditional Street, which was mostly tourist souvenirs, where we had some dumplings at a restaurant famous in China. We then had another look around Number 5

Shopping Street, but as it was so cold and we'd seen enough, we went back to the station, which is quite massive, with a huge public square at the front, beautifully paved, going down to the river. If it hadn't been so cold we would have stayed longer, and maybe booked a walking tour with a local guide, which is one the best ways to find the most interesting parts of a city – as long as you make sure you don't get drawn into buying expensive items on sale for foreign tourists, as the guides obviously get paid commission.

WEDNESDAY 11$^{TH}$ NOVEMBER 2009

I didn't sleep so well the following night, probably due to jetlag, so we stayed an extra half-day at the hotel to get a lie-in. Our flight to Jinan was booked later that day, for 6.00 p.m.

On arrival in Jinan, at about 8.00 p.m., we were met by a chauffeur arranged by Ling's mum, who lived in a retirement flat for ex-China Air Force personnel, who also got access to an Air Force driver once a month.

After settling in and unpacking, we spent some time opening our gifts for Ling's mum, before having a shower and an early night.

## THURSDAY 12^TH NOVEMBER 2009

After a good night's sleep, we got up at 9.30 a.m.

Ling's elder sister Zhang Min, and her husband Lao, came to lunch at 12.00, which was cooked by Xiao Wang, a young lady who cooks and cleans for Ling's mum five days a week. I didn't really like her cooking, though; the food looked okay after she washed and cut up the vegetables, but then she spoilt it all by cooking everything to death, so it looked like a soggy mess.

Zhang Min had given us her office desktop computer, but we had to go out in the afternoon to buy a mouse and keyboard. We nearly bought a new H.P. printer for 590RMB, but Ling's sister said we could have her old one. We then had a rigmarole to cancel the order and get our money back.

A few days ago, I suggested to Ling that we try and get some exercise, and maybe play some badminton, but at the time she didn't know where we could go for this. Then today, strangely enough, there was a sports club next to the Gome computer shop, so we made enquiries. Ling told me that the owner of Gome store was in prison for some offence to do with taking money out of the country, but apparently he was still making money while in prison, as all the stores remained open.

We were told it would cost 1500 yuan to join the sports club as a couple, but we could then play as often as we wanted until the fee was used up. We didn't bother joining, as we didn't think we'd be going regularly. I was sixty-five and Ling fifty-three, and we got enough exercise from walking, which is free.

Stomach was a bit queasy, so I made myself an omelette for dinner. It was cold again today: about two degrees C.


FRIDAY 13TH NOVEMBER 2009

I didn't sleep well, so I took a sleeping pill and got up at 9.30 a.m. Ling and her mum usually get up around 7.00 a.m. I made myself the same breakfast as I usually have in the U.K.: porridge with a banana, followed by a Nescafé, which I'd brought with me. We then stayed in all day, as it was snowing heavily.

I find it takes me a while to get used to eating Chinese food every day, so I usually bring a lot of stuff with me from home, which I can't find in China: namely butter, cheese, Nescafé, English tea, Oxo cubes, curry powder, carraway seeds for making scones, Marmite (which I hardly ever use), wheat bran for roughage and digestive biscuits.

Regarding gifts that we bring for relatives and friends, it's rather hard to find things which don't originate from China in the first place, but we usually fill at least one suitcase with chocolates, sweets and Scottish shortbread, plus a few other things which the Chinese make but are only sent out as exports, and not available there. However, I have noticed that most of the famous Western brands – such as Gucci, Rolex, Armani, Hugo Boss, etc. – have huge shopping malls in most Chinese cities. They probably have their factories in China as well, so no doubt there are a lot of copies being made, for various outlets around the country, at a much lower price.

One of the things which always amazes me is the apparent wealth in China, with luxury goods in the shopping malls and high-rise construction everywhere you go. In comparison, Canary Wharf in London looks almost like a small town.

SATURDAY 14TH NOVEMBER 2009

We went to a very busy hot-pot restaurant with Zhang Min and Lao. The place was like a huge canteen, with steaming food everywhere and everyone wearing their outdoor clothes, as it was pretty cold inside. Lao likes going to these places, where the food is cheap and you get plenty of it. Each party has a large metal contraption on the table, with a brazier underneath, heated by gas or hot charcoal. This heats a large tureen of soup which is divided into two parts: one for ordinary chicken soup and the other hot and spicy – *very* hot and spicy! Then they give you a trolley full of thinly sliced strips of beef and lamb, which you dip into the boiling liquid with your chopstick; it cooks in about fifteen seconds. Added to this, you can get sliced potatoes, carrots and cabbage, which you add to the soup. Then you each get a small dish of peanut sauce, with sliced spring onions, garlic and chopped cucumber, for dipping your meat into. Everyone is chatting and laughing, while washing it down with Tsingtao pijiu (beer). As I can't speak Chinese very well, I just concentrate on my food, while everyone else is chatting nineteen to the dozen around me.

SUNDAY 15^TH NOVEMBER 2009

In the morning, we visited Ling's sister's new flat. It was very luxurious inside, although rather a lot of brown colours, wood panels and old-fashioned furniture, etc., plus a huge T.V. The sofa alone cost 20,000 yuan. There were a lot of traditional Chinese landscapes on the walls. It had three bedrooms and a large sitting room, with windows at each end, one of which led to a conservatory which held their bonsai collection and two birds in cages, where Lao liked to lounge in the sunshine, smoking his pipe, with tobacco we'd bought for him in Covent Garden.

MONDAY 16<sup>TH</sup> NOVEMBER 2009

Still cold, but we caught a bus to the market area, where I bought a cheap practice erhu with a reasonable tone for 400RMB, including a music book, case, resin and an instruction C.D. This instrument is a traditional two-string type of Chinese violin, and I'd had lessons in London for about two years, from a Chinese guy who lived not too far away from our flat in Southwark. I also used to travel to a church in Poplar, where he gave lessons to a group of middle-aged Chinese ladies; there were about ten of us there, each paying £5 for the hour.

We then booked a sleeper train to Hangzhou, to visit Ling's younger brother; it cost 420RMB each for a one-way sleeper. The overnight journey takes about eight hours, and we were to share a cabin with two other people on bunks.

The reason we were going was that the weather there was usually warm all year round, as it is quite far south, with average temperatures of around seventeen degrees in November, whereas Jinan has winters similar to London at the same time of year, but a bit colder.

## TUESDAY 17<sup>TH</sup> NOVEMBER 2009

One degree Celsius. Still a lot of snow about, but it was sunny and bright.

No doubt legions of workers had cleared the main streets. It's frightening enough with these wide roads, where zebra crossings are merely for decoration and the traffic never stops for pedestrians. The road near Ling's mum has five lanes each way, plus one for buses, then there's a sort of kerb interspersed with trees and bushes, before another wide area where pedestrians, cyclists, motorbikes and three-wheelers dispute right of way. The pavement is usually full of parked cars, so it's just a little bit dangerous for us pedestrians!

I bought a tiny 4GB memory stick at an electronics supermarket, plus a webcam – though I don't know who will see us on it, as we would need to connect our P.C. to someone else's phone line. I also got the right sort of

U.S.B. cable for the printer.

After this, we went across the road to a rather swish coffee shop and restaurant, where we bought two lattés and a cake between us. Service was very good. There was a white piano on a small stage, probably for busy evenings.

That evening, Ling's friend Yen Bin took us to a large restaurant attached to the fish market, and the food was accordingly fresh and excellent. The party was made up of ten of Ling's friends, who'd worked together in the compulsory farm labour camps during the Cultural Revolution, which everyone had to undergo for around two years, much like our National Service. They were nice guys who all had good jobs; two of them were policemen. Li Qiang, one of the policemen next to me, could speak a little English, and it was a very pleasant evening.

When we got back, the two new flat-screen T.V.s we'd bought for Ling's mum were working, after some new aerial wires had been connected.

WEDNESDAY 18$^{TH}$ NOVEMBER 2009

We went with Ling's mum to a big exhibition centre, where half a dozen guys were clearing the ice from part of the steps in a rather desultory manner, breaking the chunks of ice with long metal poles. It didn't look very efficient. Inside there was the usual hustle and bustle, with a couple of big fights going on – most apparently people bringing goods back and asking for refunds. Ma was interested in some grey-coloured pearls, and was told they were 900 per necklace, but she ended up paying 380 for two! I bought some dried dates and some excellent salted almonds, while Ling bought a yellow leather wallet.

## THURSDAY 19<sup>TH</sup> NOVEMBER 2009

Everyone was up before me as usual, at 8.00 a.m., including Xiao Wang, the cleaning lady and erstwhile cook. It was bright outside but cold. I finished washing and shaving, to join them for breakfast at 9.00 a.m.

I cooked some bacon, from a joint of salted and smoked pork we'd bought yesterday at the exhibition centre, cutting off a few thin slices; it was okay, but a little bit salty. I cooked it with a fried egg and a few mushrooms. Prior to that I had porridge with dragon fruit, and a slice of bread I'd made myself with my bread machine, brought all the way from the U.K. at great inconvenience, though it worked great. I bought it at Debenhams in Oxford Street for about £50, and am still using it now (in 2020).

We went out at 10.00 a.m. to get our train tickets to Hangzhou, which cost 420RMB each (about £40) for an overnight sleeper, sharing with two other people for the eight-hour, overnight journey. After catching a 35 bus, which cost 1RMB (10p), we walked the rest of the way to the large station building, where we obtained our tickets from a friend of Ling's at the office, and also met her husband there, who was visiting. I had to show my passport, though I'm not sure why just for a domestic train journey.

After that we strolled toward our bus stop, looking for a post office, where I hoped to get cards and stamps. We passed some interesting buildings which were quite massive. It seems to be a mania for the Chinese, building massive new buildings all the time, while last year's constructions tend to start decaying, as if they have already lost interest in the upkeep once the building is finished.

We stopped at a post office, and were served by about four people just to buy a few postcards. There weren't many on display and they seemed a little unsure of the correct prices – in fact, having to go back to the stores to dig out a few scenes of Jinan I'd requested. I eventually bought eight for 2 yuan each. We then had to go to another building to get stamps, which also involved about three people, discussing how much postage was required to send to the U.K. It was like some kind of farce:

"You want to buy stamps? Do we have stamps? I'll have to check with a supervisor. You want to send something to the U.K.? Ah… well, can I see your passport? Hmm, it doesn't look like you – I'd better check with the manager."

A little later, it then seemed it was okay:

"You can have enough stamps to send these postcards; my colleague will help."

The girl then set out the required stamps on each individual card, until she ran out of stock and had to go somewhere to get more, while her colleagues gathered around to watch. It seems the whole process is a lot more complicated than the U.K., where you can buy cards and stamps at most newspaper shops. Maybe they just weren't used to serving Westerners, and wanted to make the most of it?

We then stopped at a centre of traditional Chinese buildings, with a market and department store of good quality, where I bought a new fur cap for 138RMB. It was a little bit expensive really – U.K. prices, rather – but it was worth it to have a comfortable hat for the cold weather, when I usually get quite hot from walking while wearing winter clothes. I find the clothes here get you really warm when you're out walking, and you build up quite a sweat, so feel like undoing all the buttons – you then feel freezing cold again!

Then we went to the shop where we'd bought the two T.V.s to get some money back, as part of a price deal, but were told that the girl who had sold them to us had gone to lunch and nobody else could deal with it.

We walked back home for lunch, as it was so much trouble to get across the busy five-lane roads to catch a bus, where the traffic never seems to stop for red lights, even when it's green for pedestrians; you'll still find motorcycles, strange three-wheeled contraptions and ordinary bikes whizzing at you from all directions. It's bad enough just walking along the broken pavements, as bikes and cars take shortcuts right in front of you, or nudge in from behind; it's a wonder more people don't get struck. I've never heard any police sirens yet, but today I heard the first ambulance flying past.

The streets are a mess of expensive new buildings and higgledy-piggledy shops and houses – mainly apartment blocks with security entrances, with half the tiles having fallen off the walls and the driveway areas all cracked, as if the cement was just poured onto the earth, with no preparation or foundations. Cracks in the paving are everywhere, so it's hard to follow the practice of walking between the cracks. It's also hard dodging the spit, which seems to be normal practice, usually preceded by a vile *"hoik"* sound.

So, home for lunch made by Xiao Wang. It wasn't too bad: rice soup, reheated prawns and a few greens swimming in some liquid.

In the afternoon we caught a 52 bus, costing 2RMB each because it had air conditioning. We travelled about eight stops to a new apartment block – almost a small city, in fact, called Elite City, near the mountains, which would eventually hold about 100,000 people. Some of it had already been completed: rows of massive tower blocks, quite nicely designed. We went to the sales centre, where they had a fantastic model city complete with landscaping, water features, trees, shops and even cars with working lights. First, we were shown the proposed plan of the new city surrounding the mountain area, and the individual models of the various flats to be sold. Then we were shown examples of two-bedroom flats, at 88 square metres and 96 square metres, with a price tag of about 6500RMB per square metre. We could pay a holding sum of 20,000 yuan, which would metamorphose to 50,000 when it was time to pay the full deposit; the extra 30,000 yuan was to be deducted from the full price. The deposit was twenty per cent and the monthly mortgage would be about 3400 per month. The difficulty would be getting a mortgage, as Ling didn't have an income and they probably wouldn't accept mine, which is only my U.K. pension. It seemed we may not proceed.

Returned home at 5.00 p.m., after getting my 400RMB from the T.V. shop. Ling's sister Zhang Min had bought me a new jumper, and she stopped for dinner of chicken, rice and vegetables.

Ling was a little bit depressed re. the mortgage issue, but eventually decided it was okay not to buy a flat here, as we could always stay with her mum anyway. Plus, we still had our unwanted flat in Lushan, on the coast, plus the flat in London as well. I breathed a sigh of relief at not getting too involved in property development.

## SATURDAY 21ST NOVEMBER 2009

Took the sleeper train from Jinan to Hangzhou – a twelve-hour journey starting at 5.58 p.m. (we were told it would be eight, but the train stopped somewhere for four hours). We travelled first-class in a four-bed sleeper compartment, sharing with two guys. The one opposite me, on the bottom bunk, was annoying me with his constant mobile phone activity, and the one above with his *hoiking* noises, which seemed to be a precursor to spitting – but with nowhere to expectorate, he had to keep repeating the loop.

The train was okay, but very hot so I couldn't sleep. Halfway through the night, Ling flung a jumper at me from her top bunk, diagonally opposite. She's always had a mania that I'll catch cold, but all this extra clothing makes me sweat. With a couple of toilet breaks, I passed the night with about two hours' sleep, from 3.00 a.m. to 5.00 a.m.

The train was due to arrive at 6.35, but was delayed at Gonshanmen for nearly an hour, while we waited in the heat of the train, not knowing the reason. I stood looking out of the window, at the usual depressing sights you see anywhere in the world from a railway track, where people who live by the railway have no conception that people from the trains can see into their back gardens and houses; to them the train is just flying past. The main views were of half-finished buildings everywhere, already occupied, their outside just plain concrete, now decaying, streaked with dirt and damp patches, while others nearby looked finished and well cared for. One five-storey block looked quite luxurious, but was surrounded by muddy tracks, piles of broken bricks and dust surrounding muddy pools. It looked like a bombsite, from which a new building had just been parked. In fact, there were so many piles of broken bricks, from demolished buildings, that they could all be joined together to make new mountains to replace the natural ones, which are disappearing to make cement for highways, bridges and housing blocks. Soon all the mountains will disappear and be replaced by high-rise buildings and artificial mountains, made from rubble and broken bricks.

The best views of the countryside were unfortunately blocked, by avenues of trees lining the railway lines. But there were glimpses of cultivated fields, rivers and – here and there – stagnant ponds mixed with wastelands of weeds and wild shrubs. I saw some new housing blocks which looked quite presentable, but extensions had been latched onto them, made of plastic bags sewn together, to make rudimentary shelters or lean-tos. Also beside the tracks there were neat rows of crops, such as cabbage and spinach, but alternating with piles of rubbish waste, in pink and blue plastic bags.

There was an unmade road running alongside the track, where an old man had hopefully set up a market stall, selling a few paltry wares, with no sign of any passing trade. Another man was performing some strange ritual at the edge of a field, taking some liquid, stretching out his arms and spitting the liquid out onto the field. While the train was stopped, another example of these people's unawareness of train passengers was a man urinating in a corner, with his back to the train, blissfully unaware there were rows of people watching him from its windows.

We arrived eventually at Hangzhou, at 7.30 a.m., and I was surprised to see so many people leaving the train, as I hadn't really noticed that many during the journey.

Ling's younger brother Zhang Feng and wife Zhou Xue Qing (Betty) met us at the station, having waited there for us during the one-hour delay. He was a very nice man, tall and well educated. His wife spoke good English and the daughter seems very bright.

For about 24RMB we took a taxi to their block, which was very nicely arranged, with a security gate and landscaped with trees, shrubs and well-kept paths. The three-bedroom flat was on the eighth floor, and they'd lived there for six years; it was worth about four million RMB. It was very cold inside, though, as Ling warned us it would be – even warmer outside, although they'd just had ten days of rain. I was told winter in the city only lasts for about two months, so none of the homes had central heating; most people had to sit around indoors wearing their overcoats. It gets very hot and humid in the summer. Their daughter Duowar, aged eleven, was in bed when we arrived.

I managed to get a wash and shave, before we went to a local café for a breakfast of fried egg, rice soup and the long, doughnut-like bread (youtiao), which all cost about 14 yuan for the three of us. We took two takeaways for Betty and Zhang Xinyiao (Duowar), then went to a local supermarket to buy milk, yoghurt, shaving cream, etc. This was quite expensive, at 143RMB. When we returned to the flat we found the daughter up, vacating her room so that we could use it for the next nine days or so.

While sitting writing this, in her room, sunlight was coming through the windows but I was wearing two jumpers, a hat and two pairs of socks indoors, as there was no central heating.

We had a takeaway for lunch at about 11.30 a.m.; I had spaghetti and meatballs, which tasted quite authentic. After that, we went to the Century Hypermarket and did a bit of shopping for the week: Lipton's tea, bread, butter, parmelos (Chinese name "youze"), two bottles of Australian wine (buy one get one free!), some garlic sausage, sugar-free marmalade and some custard tarts. I paid the bill, which came to about 520RMB.

I made some English tea for all in the afternoon, then later we walked about twenty minutes to dinner. The place was quite clean and we ordered various dishes, plus a bottle of Xaoxing wine to drink with the meal; this was mainly used for cooking, like sherry. My stomach survived the meal, and the last dish – sweet and sour fish – was the one I enjoyed most.

When we got back, it was too cold to sit around, so we went to bed at 9.30, after Ling had a shower.


SUNDAY 22ND NOVEMBER 2009

Slept until 7.30 a.m., but didn't get up until about 9.45, as most of the others were quite late, as well. Had porridge for breakfast, with a banana, bread and marmalade, and coffee made with hot soya milk – not very successfully.

Betty had to take Duowar to the hospital, to get a certificate to go back to school, and was then going on to an English lesson, so Zhang Feng took Ling and I to West Lake Park. It was a very impressive area, the size of Lake Derwent, but with better landscaping on the shores, and mature trees hundreds of years old. There were several traditional dragon-top buildings, pagodas, boats in Chinese design, water lilies and lotus flowers in masses, though not in flower at this time of the year. It was quite busy.

Feng took us to a tea museum, amidst a tea plantation leading up to the mountains, which was quite interesting. We walked from here for about half an hour, and stopped for some green tea at a wayside teashop. I used the outside toilet here, which was very clean with sitting facilities.

Then we took a taxi to another part of the lake, where there were lots of restaurants and temples. We stopped at a jetty area, with shops, promenades, boat trips, lovely views of the water and distant mountains. We took a few pictures, then Feng took us to a famous restaurant overlooking the lake, with excellent toilets and delicious food, which Feng paid about 600RMB for. There were a lot of sweet and sour dishes of freshwater fish and prawns, plus some crispy tofu invented by this restaurant, famous for the past hundred years. It was very well decorated in traditional style, with a huge, red, washed silk carpet, which would have taken about ten men to roll up and carry.

We then separated from Feng, as he wanted to go somewhere to buy crabs. We decided to walk along the lakeside. Ling bartered the price of a boat down from 180 yuan to 120, and we took a nice, gentle ride on the water for about forty-five minutes, around a small island then farther along the shore. A wedding was just coming to an end, for which they'd hired a hundred of these boats. We could hear the wedding march in the distance, as we came near the shore.

We spent a long time looking for a taxi, then stopped at a small children's shop to buy a gift for Douwar: some coloured gel floating in clear liquid, for 25 yuan. We then had to wait about half an hour before we could get another taxi; we didn't know which direction was home or which bus we might catch, plus it was getting very busy at about 5.30.

Ling's brother had been waiting outside for us for about half an hour, as he'd given Ling his key. We got back inside and had a wash, etc. We were not really hungry, but Feng had been busy cooking, even though I didn't think I could eat any more tonight. I was forced to eat two small crab legs – which were delicious, but I had no appetite – plus a small bowl of marrow soup.

Then we went to bed at about 10.00 p.m., covered with two duvets.


MONDAY 23ᴿᴰ NOVEMBER 2009

Ling's official birthday. I'd already bought her a pair of brown boots in Jinan, costing about 1000RMB; prices seemed to be getting closer to that of the U.K.

Feng, Betty and Douwar were out at approximately 7.30 a.m. and I got up around 8.30, after twenty minutes of meditation. Had a simple breakfast of porridge and banana, followed by Nescafé, bread and marmalade, after trying to find my way around the kitchen. All the windows were open, although it was cold, though sunny. It seems that they close the windows during the stifling heat of summer, so the air conditioning can work effectively, and open the windows in winter, as it feels slightly warmer outside.

We went out at about 10.00 a.m. and took a taxi to Lingying Temple and Park, passing the football stadium, where China beat Lebanon 1-0 last night. It was an average game, which I watched on T.V., with no one confident enough to get goals. The streets were tree-lined and gave an impression of Regents Park or Brighton. It was very pleasant driving through the avenues of trees.

The taxi cost about 20RMB. The taxis were Honda in Hangzhou, Volkswagen in Jinan, in a blue-and-white two-tone. Drivers were very impatient, zig-zagging about as they changed lanes looking for the shortest queues, but somehow managing to avoid accidents.

The park was very pleasant, with tourist shops, information centres and clean toilet areas, though of the stand-up-over-a-hole variety. We bought tickets at the office for 45RMB each. It was very pleasant walking a wide, well-paved pavement, which must have cost huge amounts of time and labour – no cracks in the wide stone paving; all were perfectly straight.

We clambered through some rock formations and a large cave, to admire old stone carvings of various Buddhas, with streams and waterfalls winding through the trees and rocks nearby.

In order to visit Linying Temple, we had to pay another 30 yuan each for tickets, but it was worth it to see the large temples and huge, gold Buddha statues inside. I was not sure if they were made of clay or wood and covered in gold leaf. These were alongside amazing accompanying statues of various angry-looking minor gods. We burned some incense and Ling said some prayers, as we were treated to monks praying while sounding drums and bells.

Having finished with the temples, we decided to explore gardens leading up the mountain, which Ling hadn't visited before. We took a fairly easy upward incline, resting on a seat near an ornamental gate. Having rested there, we went farther up, enjoying excellent views of the mountains with a blue-sky backdrop. Finally we came across a tea place, where we found clean toilets, and stopped for a glass of chrysanthemum and pomelo tea. We were given dishes of crisps, popcorn and kumquats free, as they were serving a meal, which was usual. This was very restful, sitting outside in the warm sun, served by monks, beside a pool full of goldfish.

We went farther up some immaculate stone steps, beside running water with trees overhead, which we felt would give good shelter from the heat of the sun in summer. We then visited a smaller temple, dedicated to the Hall of Heroes.

From here we retraced our steps downhill, looking for lunch, which we found near the exit. We had a plate of noodles each for a total of 75 yuan, including a glass of beer. I noticed another European sitting nearby, with a Chinese girl; I overheard him saying he was staying at the Ramada Hotel, and guessed he was Dutch or German. He was a bit like Peter Ustinov.

We took a taxi toward town, where Ling suggested we look for a silk market. We were dropped off at a rather expensive establishment called Silk Depot, and had a brief look around before deciding that the prices were rather high. I was looking for a gift of a silk nightdress for Veronique (my friend Trev's wife), but the price was over 1200 yuan. So, we took another taxi to a different place called Silk Palace. They had better prices but we couldn't agree on what to buy, so we waited for another taxi.

Ling soon became fed up with the difficulty of catching one, so we stopped in at a French croissant café I'd noticed, where we had nice cakes and a rather dodgy latté, which smelt of toilet fumes, possibly because of the cardboard holders being stored near the toilets! The prices were better, though, at 12 yuan for a coffee and 5 yuan for oolong tea, as opposed to 50 yuan back at the temple.

We decided to go back to Feng's home at 4.00 p.m., first going to buy some vegetables, including potatoes, at a small market area across the road. Then we waited around the flat for a while, debating what we should cook for dinner.

Douwar came home first, at around 6.00 p.m., so I made her and myself an omelette and baked potato. Feng had gone out for a meal with business colleagues, so the rest of us finished off a few leftovers and watched T.V. up until 8.30.

Due to some unfortunate problems with the family finances, Zhang Feng had been on bad terms with the rest of the family for some time. But all seemed to be forgiven now; he was sort of back with his wife and daughter. But still he tended to disappear every now and then – like a couple of nights ago, when he didn't get home until 2.00 a.m. He and his wife didn't seem that well suited, as the wife was a serious Christian – not exactly conducive to his playboy life expectations. He worked in the sales department of a mobile phone company.

I hadn't been able to use the computer today, as it was packed away, apparently to stop the daughter using the internet; instead she was doing piano practice. She studied quite hard, with various lessons after school and at weekends. She would start studying as soon as she got up, go to school, then take more lessons after school and at weekends. She had one piano lesson per week and practised for half an hour a day, though was not prodigy material. Anyway, now I found out that I could have used the computer. It was an Apple Mac, and the processor seemed to be built into the monitor.

## TUESDAY 24<sup>TH</sup> NOVEMBER 2009

Feng didn't get back until 2.00 a.m., and had to phone his wife to open the door, as we had his key and security entrance card. Then, after four hours sleep, he had to get up at 6.00 to go to work, while Ling tried to find him a hangover cure.

It was a bit warmer today, and Ling managed to persuade me to have a shower, which turned out not to be as bad as my imagination of it being freezing cold. We had breakfast and put some clothes in the washing machine, then didn't get out until about 11.30, so that we could hang them on the eighth-floor balcony.

We took a taxi to the town centre, to look around and find a good silk shop. However, by the time we were dropped off, we felt it was time for an early lunch. We stopped at a Pizza Hut, where I ordered spaghetti Bolognese and Ling some chicken dish, which we swapped, as there was too much cheese on mine.

Then we made our way to Wanshang Lu (the equivalent of Oxford Street) and had a look around a department store, seeking a silk nightdress for Veronique. The prices were quite high, and the shop looked like something of the sort of Selfridges. Indeed, there are so many expensive shops in China now it's becoming as expensive as London, Paris or New York. I don't know how the local people can afford these prices. There were loads of huge designer shops; Gucci, Armani and Cartier, etc., all had their own exclusive stores.

We tried another place along the road and found a nice silk dress, reasonably priced at about thirty-eight pounds. I also bought Ling a silk scarf, which she liked.

As it was getting so warm in the afternoon, I had to go into the toilets to remove a padded undervest and woollen jumper I'd been made to put on before going out. When we arrived a couple of days ago, it was only two degrees, but today it had jumped to seventeen.

Ling was feeling fractious for a while, but improved when we managed to get a taxi to a large pagoda overlooking West Lake (Xi Whu). It was a very interesting building and the original part, built about a thousand years ago, had been preserved to a height of about twelve metres, plus underground chambers, foundations, etc. Then, in 2000, they put a glass barrier around it and built a brand-new pagoda over the top, supported by huge steel girders and reinforced concrete struts. The pagoda on top was huge, with a commanding view over the lake and for miles around, with a lift to take you to the third floor, so that you could walk all the way round to get amazing views. Plus, there were two further floors above, reached by marble stairs. On the way down we noticed some fantastic wood carvings, depicting a local legend about a woman who became a snake, but wanted to go back to mortal life to meet her lover.

One of the views revealed a sort of harbour, where some

interesting vessels were moored, so we took a walk along that way once we'd reached ground level. We found a fleet of pleasure boats and were talked into taking a trip around the lake. Luckily, there were two ladies already on the boat, a sort of Chinese gondola, who shared the cost of 160 yuan.

It was getting dark by about 6.00 p.m., and there didn't seem any prospect of us coming ashore, although we were enjoying the relaxing and interesting journey. It soon became apparent that we were being taken to a silk factory to have a look around. The two ladies bought a load of stuff and Ling bought a silk cover for her brother's sofa, as it could be a bit cold at night sitting on the shiny leather.

It was dark by the time we left there, and the boatman took us to a place where we hoped to get a taxi. After waiting for ten minutes, we decided to walk on a bit. He told us we could get a 527 bus to Wanseng Lu, which saved us a bit, as it only cost 2 yuan instead of 20 by taxi, and we only had to wait five minutes more.

Near Ling's brother's place, we had a look around for somewhere to have dinner, and decided to try the café where we'd had breakfast on the first day. I ordered seafood fried noodles, which were delicious and only cost 10 yuan. Ling also enjoyed her chicken and rice dish, so we decided to come here again tomorrow, rather than go to the more expensive places, which usually cost about 100 yuan, instead of the 36 we paid here, which included a bottle of beer.

Feng and his family were waiting outside the flat when we arrived home, at 8.00 p.m. We came in and showed them some photos of Ling's mum, from when she stayed with us in the U.K. We then went to bed early, at 9.15 p.m., as we hoped to get up early tomorrow and take a coach trip to Xiaoxing Village, where they make the wine/sherry used in most Chinese cuisine.

WEDNESDAY 25$^{TH}$ NOVEMBER 2009

Managed to drag myself out of bed before 8.00 a.m., and we left the house at 9.15.

We took a taxi to the bus depot, which cost 25RMB – about £2.00. The driver was mad, as usual, changing lanes like a looney, although I suppose this must be normal, as not many motorists sounded their horns. The roads were really quite busy, even by U.K. standards, bearing in mind that most of the roads here are based on a one-way system and square grid pattern, with six-lane dual carriageways and taxis weaving in and out of lanes – like queues at a supermarket checkout; you never know which queue to join.

The buses left for Xiaoxing every ten minutes, for the one-hour journey, and we caught a bus at 10.19 a.m., at a return fare of 48RMB each. Nothing much to remark about the journey, except that I took some footage of the well-tended hedges all the way along the central reservation, showing neat, symmetrical patterns, which probably uses a lot of manpower. There were the same haphazard building areas outside the cities, with run-down hovels next to new, luxury four-storey blocks, in Sino-European designs. I saw what I first thought were some allotments with garden sheds, but then realized these were people's homes, each with a small piece of land allocated to grow their own crops. Eventually, I suppose, all these new high rises would be occupied, so the locals wouldn't have to continue living in this way – although probably some of them would be reluctant to leave, and have to be forced into the new flats.

At the bus depot we were met by the usual array of people shouting, trying to sell us goods and/or services. I was surprised when Ling stopped to listen to one of them, as she usually brushes past these kind of salespeople. We finally agreed a price of 240RMB (about £24) for him to drive us around for a few hours on his three-wheeled bike, with a sort of canopy for two passengers. I guess this was a development of the rickshaw, and quite a good way to see the sights, although a bit bumpy. The bus depot was a long way from any recognizable places of interest, and we wouldn't have known where to start on our own. *Next time,* I thought, *we'd be better going with a group package.*

We went through some really primitive areas, with people washing clothes in the semi stagnant canals – a little bit like Venice, but not so grand. Washing was hanging everywhere and the water didn't look too clear, but it smelt fresh enough and the clothes looked okay.

The first stop was the house of famous writer Lu Xin, who apparently falsely accused a Buddhist monk of stealing a pearl, which had in fact been swallowed by his pet goose. The monk was so distraught by the accusation that he hung himself. Later, when the goose died, they discovered the pearl when preparing a meal of the roasted bird. The writer was so shocked and remorseful that he converted his large house into a shrine to Buddha, in which capacity it remains today.

Next stop was a small street running alongside a canal. It was very narrow, with people's open doors right next to us, and felt like we were almost intruding as they went about their daily routine squatting, washing clothes in the river, sweeping the path and preparing food. Various kipper-like fish were hanging from a wooden shelter along the path, as we dodged through the washing hanging to dry. We bought some quite delicious, sweet cakes from a chap along this path, made of rice and bean paste with a peppermint flavour, all very clean and wrapped up nicely, at about 6RMB for ten.

An old man stopped us along the way and said: "You're here!"

"That's right," we replied, "just having a look around."

"Having a look around," he nodded, then walked on.

When back with our driver, he took us through a slightly better part of canal life. Although the people were all friendly, while we were watching them they were watching us. It all felt a bit like going back three-hundred years, and probably hasn't changed very much – except that now they've got running tap water and electricity. There were various new housing blocks looming overhead, but this particular area was protected from development by the government.

Included in the price was a short boat trip along one of the canals, probably by arrangement with one of the driver's cousins. This was quite good and I took some video recordings of the leisurely journey, gently drifting through the water – a little like the punt trip we took in Cambridge a few months ago, though the surroundings were makeshift houses, falling apart in places. But others were well looked after, with established plants and flowers, and even a few chickens grubbing about, in about one square foot of space at the water's edge.

Back on land we asked the driver about lunch, and he said he would show us a place; if we didn't like it we could try somewhere else. However, once inside we didn't like to leave, so I was happy to order my usual Kung Po chicken with rice. Ling deliberated as usual, before choosing some fish soup and cabbage cooked with bacon, the same as we do it at home. We washed it down with half a bottle of Xiaoxing wine, called huan jiu ("yellow wine"), as it was necessary to try the local brew. It was okay, though I'd prefer to stick to red or white in future.

After lunch, which cost 100 yuan, while the driver dozed outside in his cab or chatted with some of his cronies, he took us to a local provider of Xiaoxing wine – a sort of working museum, showing how it was made from rice with yeast, and left to foment in clay flagons for several years. I bought a small souvenir bottle, which we could see being hand-painted upstairs. Apparently this wine has been used for about 2000 years, although there are now several different varieties. The driver had been giving us a good running commentary along the way, and I suppose he would have been on some commission for whatever we bought, although he wasn't too pushy.

After lunch he showed us a famous local drinking place, featured in a book by the local well-known writer, and we had our pictures taken by a statue of one of the characters from his books. He was going to take us to the writer's house, as the final destination, but the road was closed, so he simply pointed out where we needed to go. We paid and bade him farewell. A slight con-trick in one of his offers was that entry to this house was supposedly included in his price and he gave us a complimentary ticket, but when we got there Ling noticed that entry was free anyway – probably why he didn't want to take us all the way. Still, not bad for three-and-a-half hours of service.

The house was quite large, and previously belonged to the writer's family. There was a bewildering number of rooms and courtyards, with a well-preserved kitchen which looked quite primitive, even though the house itself must have been owned by pretty wealthy people. In his bedroom were a four-poster bed and his writing desk.

Halfway through the tour of the house we visited the Bai

Cai Garden ("One Hundred Plant Garden"), and were delighted with the varied birdsong. But we didn't see any birds, so maybe it was a recording – or perhaps birds in cages on the other side of the wall.

When we came to the end, we followed signs to the exit, but there were about four different rooms we had to pass through first, with various products for sale. We weren't tempted, even though there were some excellent embroidery pictures in frames, produced by a resident artist and family. Not too expensive, but: a) we didn't want to spend too much of our travel money, and b) we couldn't be carrying all this stuff around with us. On the way out, though, I did buy a local conical (or is it *comical*) hat made of some rough fur, for 15 yuan (about £1.50).

At about 4.00 p.m. we decided to return to Hangzhou, but had our usual luck in (not) finding a taxi. A rickshaw/cycle driver offered to take us to the bus depot for the same price of 25RMB, but we declined this and eventually managed to find the right bus, which only cost 2 yuan. We got our tickets and only had to wait five minutes for the bus. We dozed all the way back to Hangzhou in the rather stifling bus, but otherwise quite comfortable. Then we got a taxi back.

Douwar let us in, then the three of us went down to

dinner at the place we visited yesterday. I had fried noodles again, at a total cost of 38RMB – about £3.50. Betty came back from a business trip and helped us eat the leftovers at around 7.30, when we came home.

Ling's brother was out again, no doubt pursuing his hotel-visiting hobby.

## THURSDAY 26TH NOVEMBER 2009

I don't know what time Feng came back last night, but he didn't get up until 11.30 a.m. today.

Meanwhile, I had a shower, as it was warmer today, at about twenty degrees. After breakfast we washed some clothes and hung them out to dry on the balcony, before leaving at about 11.45 a.m., to go and buy our train tickets to Nanjing. Feng knew a place where we could get them at 187RMB each, just around the corner, and we waited ten minutes for the office to open, to buy our tickets. I noticed how impatient a lot of the locals were to get tickets, or getting on and off of buses and trains. Even when there was a queue already and the place was closed, a couple of people came along, hopping about and fidgeting as if they couldn't wait to get their tickets, even though they could see the place wasn't open... and there were about ten people in front of them. What was the point of all this fuss? It wouldn't make things happen any quicker.

After this, we walked along the road a bit to get a taxi, as Feng decided not to go to work today, but instead take us to visit a wetland park. I'd seen it mentioned in one of the tourist maps we'd bought, so I was quite happy to go. As usual, the taxi driver took us at breakneck speed. I found that the best way to travel as a passenger was not to look where we were going, as I would get too nervous that we might crash or knock somebody over. It wouldn't really matter to me, as such, because I wasn't driving, but I couldn't help feeling nervous.

The wetland centre used to belong to a rich family of landowners, who owned a large area of land with about a thousand lakes, where they bred freshwater fish for sale in the city, with a population of approximately ten million. This business had been in the family for five generations before they finally sold it to the State, to turn into a visitor park and conservation area. There was a large visitor centre at the entrance and a good, metal-reinforced road leading to the main area of interest, along which we were driven by an open minibus, for 5 yuan each.

We stopped at an area of small shops, tearooms and restaurants, then had a pleasant walk through the pathway and small bridges, as the temperature warmed up in the sunshine. There were large areas of water plants, rushes, etc., and they had even constructed two-metre-wide wooden platforms, so that you could walk through all the plantations of large water plants growing in the water on either side. The only thing missing was that there weren't many birds – except for a few sparrows and one magpie – considering that it was a custom-made wetland area. There weren't even any fish that I could see, which was strange as the place used to be a fish farm. I did, however, see a few people fishing, so they must have been somewhere.

Feng wasn't hungry but we stopped at a small café, and ordered a couple of dishes of noodles and a glass of tea each. The prices here were quite high, and this simple meal cost us about 100 yuan. I've been generally surprised at the high price of a cup of tea in the country, when I thought it was supposed to be one of the cheapest drinks there are, even usually given free with meals. I asked for fried noodles, but Ling said they didn't serve the dish at this place – however, after the meal, when we passed a few other restaurants we discovered that I could have had fried noodles at these places.

We went to have a look at a sort of gallery, which sold paintings and hand-embroidered pictures, similar to the ones we'd seen in Xiaoxing yesterday – there were even two or three showing exactly the same scenes. But here the price of a picture about two feet long was 800RMB, compared to 360RMB in Xiaoxing.

After a pleasant walk around the well-constructed and clean raised areas between the large freshwater lakes and channels, over which they'd built replica bridges of the willow-pattern design, Feng purchased tickets for a two-hour boat trip, for about 200RMB. This was a long wooden boat or large canoe, with a canopy above, and was propelled by an ingenious form of oar, which also served as a rudder. This was mounted at the back of the boat, on a metal pin about four inches high, with a metal ball on the top, which fitted into a shallow hole in the oar. The boatman manipulated the boat with little apparent effort, and we glided silently along with hardly a ripple. It was so peaceful drifting through the willow-lined channels, with pagodas and traditional Chinese-style buildings on either side, mostly empty now, but kept in repair for the benefit of future generations. We could see where the banks had been constructed everywhere, to reduce the thousand or so lakes to about twenty large ones, connected by winding canals only a metre deep; I noticed the boatman using the oar like a punt pole whenever we got stuck near a bank.

Halfway through our allotted time we stopped, in order to go ashore and visit the mansion or villa belonging to the previous owner, Hongzhong. This was a complicated edifice, built in a traditional manner, with the sloping tile roofs surmounted by ornamental dragons, and wooden verandas interspersed with open courtyards and outdoor passages, which allowed for a free flow of air to keep the building fresh in the hot summers, when the temperature can get up to thirty-eight degrees, plus humidity. In the middle of the housing complex was a large ornamental pool, with huge, crazy shaped volcanic rocks brought from Yilong area, which must have cost a fortune to ship in, making a sort of grotto area around the pool. All of this was intended to please the eye and help with keeping the occupants cool.

We spent some time here, then our driver had to come and fetch us as we were using up our time. We took about another half an hour to get back to the start.

Back at the visitor centre, I was pleased to find a clean sit-down toilet, then at 4.30 we caught a number 86 bus back toward town. Ling and I got off first, to go and do a bit of shopping at the Century Hypermarket. We bought Duowar a combined rucksack and trolley for her schoolbooks, etc., which cost 260RMB, then we went back home by taxi, as Feng was cooking dinner.

This consisted of some marrow soup, fish in brown sauce, various vegetables with rice, plus a cooked chicken Ling and I had bought, washed down with some Australian Chardonnay at 45 yuan a bottle.

Betty came home from work halfway through dinner, just before Feng was setting off to meet another colleague, coming from another city, to take him to his hotel. There followed a bit of an argument about this, the wife wanting him to take some photos for her work's magazine, to which he demurred as it was unpaid. But he was persuaded to do it, as it was his hobby anyway, and one never knew if it might lead to some paid commissions.

We stayed up watching Ling's favourite new soap, about some married guy having an affair – this might have been more appropriate for her brother to be watching, but he was off, out and about with too much to do, juggling his various activities. We went to bed at about 9.45 p.m., after watching depressing medical programmes. One of these was about three generations of a family all having some mysterious muscular problem in their legs, which made it difficult for them to walk without crutches. The next was about an eighteen-month-old baby girl born with a huge stomach, which turned out to be her unformed twin mixed with a tumour, all of which had to be removed. The operation was delayed though, because hers weren't the real parents; they had found the abandoned baby in a field, and had to go through various adoption procedures before they could sign a consent form for the operation, which was being paid for by donations from everyone in their village. I'm happy to say that the operation was a success.

FRIDAY 27$^{TH}$ NOVEMBER 2009

Arose the next morning before 8.00, though I usually wake up at about 6.30. My excuse was that I delay getting out of bed here, to give the family a chance to wash, have breakfast and get ready to go to work/school.

All except for Feng, of course, who was sleeping off another late-night hotel experience. He did get up at 9.30, however, and headed out to his wife's workplace to do the photo assignment. Ling explained to me that he was a manager of his department, and it wasn't always necessary for him to go into work every day, as his instructions could be given over the telephone.

A few years ago he wanted to go and visit his elder brother Yan, over from the U.S.A. and staying with his parents in Jinan. Feng decided to take five days off of work to go visit, taking the overnight train, which in those days took about fourteen hours. But he did so without advising his work, which resulted in him being sacked. However, his mother pulled a few strings and contacted a few people to get his job back.

Also a few years ago, he had wanted a divorce, due to an expensive mistress who had cost him the sale of his two-bedroom flat and one belonging to his mum, plus some stocks and shares. When it was all spent he came back to the wife and daughter, having nowhere else to go. This would provide plenty of material for another one of these Chinese soaps which seem so popular. There wasn't much else on T.V., although maybe I was only seeing the soap channels. The only channel I could watch was CCTV9, which is in English; I watched for business news and China travel documentaries, but nobody else wanted to watch this.

Not much to report today, as we decided to relax and not rush about too much – maybe cut down on spending for the day, too. We did take a taxi (15 yuan) to West Lake (Xi Lu) though, and had a walk around. Eventually we found it a little boring, not having a real purpose, and the views weren't so good today, being rather misty or polluted – not sure which. One street was lined with expensive car dealerships – Rolls Royce, Bentley, Porsche and Mercedes

– and farther down I even saw a branch of Gieves and Hawkes from Savile Row, which should give another idea of the condition of the Chinese economy.

Searching for a restaurant, we had a look at one Chinese coffee bar, which was charging prices similar to Starbucks (i.e. 40RMB for a tea or coffee), so we found a restaurant not far away, which looked expensive, but found we could get a meal for the same price. We stopped here, even though we were the only customers – whether that was because the food wasn't good or it was too expensive, we found it okay. It had an excellent, clean sit-down toilet, complete with warm water, soap and paper. There were several cats playing in the bamboo bushes nearby, and when Ling saw one of the waitresses stroking one of them, she asked her to go and wash her hands before serving food to us. I had very tender fried beef with cashew nuts, vegetables and rice, and a hot and sour soup, which was very tasty. Ling ordered boneless fish fried in batter. The bill came to 183RMB. When Ling asked to have a look at it, the girl tried to pull it away. When Ling grabbed it back, she noticed that we'd been overcharged 25RMB, for a jasmine tea instead of the bottle of local beer we'd ordered. Apparently this is something you have to look out for, which was a pity, because otherwise it was quite a nice place. The girls wore neat grey uniforms in a sort of Thai style, and the decor was all wood and bamboo panelling, like a scene from *Tea House of the August Moon.*

We had a further walk along the lake, fairly aimlessly, and Ling started getting depressed again, because I hadn't paid for six months' worth of lottery tickets before leaving. I thought I'd be able to do it online, but apparently it's illegal to buy lottery tickets or receive prizes if you're living or staying in another country, in case you infringe local bylaws. Then her funk was about neither of us working or earning money, in spite of the fact that we were earning more now than when I *was* working, taking into account that we were renting out our flat in London. But, of course, we had to be paying for travel or living elsewhere. Hopefully we could establish a routine in China, to reduce our living costs. This should be possible. For example, the restaurant we'd had evening meals at for the last two days only cost about 35RMB for a perfectly good meal, and fruit and veg from the shops or supermarkets was cheap enough. Dragon fruit, for example, was 3.5 yuan – about 30p – as opposed to £1.95 in Asda, in the U.K.

A breeze blew up at about 3.00 p.m., and there were waves on the previously placid lake. We decided to make our way home as, although we didn't have a key to get back in, Ling's brother was due home early. We planned to buy the family dinner tonight, as we were leaving tomorrow morning – hopefully not to somewhere too expensive, as we'd been spending a little over our travelling budget.

This should be rectified if I could establish that the agents in London had actually paid some rent into my account. I received a management statement online from them this morning, stating that there was a balance due to me of about £1400, but no mention of when I was going to get it. I fired off an email to them.

It was 5.30 now, and we should be going out somewhere soon to get dinner. Ling sounded a bit more cheerful. The weather was supposed to be turning cold again tomorrow, which in some ways wouldn't be too bad, because I'd have to wear a lot of my winter clothes, and there wasn't enough room to pack them all in the small cases we brought with us.

We took Douwar to a place just across the main road: a Chinese version of McDonald's or KFC, serving Chinese food. I ordered Kung Po chicken, but it wasn't very Kung Po – more like a stew; still, it was okay. All the dishes came in plastic containers and, after paying at the counter, we took them to a table to eat. Betty joined us a bit later and had some pork dish with broccoli, in a sort of Yin-Yang-shaped dish, with some other chopped greens. Ling had some vile-looking pork belly dish, which was mostly fat, with some black stuff which looked like the scrapings of a burnt saucepan – but apparently it was quite tasty. Douwar had rice and mixed veg, with a sort of junket-style mushroom soup, as she wasn't allowed to eat fried chicken; based on some theory of her mum's, because she doesn't want the child to grow too quickly. Feng didn't have any dinner, as he'd already eaten, and he stayed in for a change.

We watched some celebrations of an Olympic-style stadium being opened in Jinan, attended by Hu Jin Tao, which took two years to build. It was a fantastic display, along Olympic Yimou lines, with light displays, mass dancers and acrobats moving in unison. There was seating for about 100,000, eclipsing the new Wembley Stadium.

Halfway through this there was an electricity short of the whole block – about ten floors – together with some other blocks, though not all were affected. This lasted for about an hour, and was caused by a vehicle colliding with electric lines across a low bridge.

We went to bed at 10.00 p.m., as we had to get up early to catch our train to Nanjing. Though I didn't sleep very much.

SATURDAY 28TH NOVEMBER 2009

Woke up at 4.30 a.m. and dozed until 6.00, when we got up. Had a quick wash and grapefruit for breakfast, to a dull morning of rain and cold.

Feng saw us off at the place where we usually got a taxi from, and we caught one at 6.40, the roads still fairly quiet. It was a thirty-minute drive and cost 25 yuan. We had bought first-class tickets, but there was only one waiting room, so they let us on the train fifteen minutes before leaving, at 7.49.

The train was a lot cleaner than the one we took coming down, although we only had seats, which we could recline. But it was quite comfortable, and in my opinion a better time to travel. Ling opines the belief that it is better to travel through the night on a sleeper, so as not to waste daytime. But, if you're like me and can't sleep on the train, you then arrive at your destination completely shattered and spend the rest of the day wandering about in a daze, feeling unkempt and unrefreshed, just waiting for the evening so that you can get a good night's sleep. Whereas, if you travel by day, you can have a few snacks to eat, read a book, listen to a C.D., look out of the windows, close your eyes occasionally, or take a leisurely walk down to the loo. Then, when you arrive at your destination, you still have time to settle into your hotel and go for a meal, do a bit of sightseeing, then go to bed in the normal way. On the sleeper you feel compelled to sleep, whether you can or not, and you constantly worry about it, checking each hour as it passes. And you worry about having to get up to go to the loo, just in case you disturb other passengers who have somehow managed to get to sleep – switching lights on and off, putting on your shoes, opening and shutting doors. Then, when you get back to your bunk, you sit worrying if you'll ever get to sleep, due to the rocking of the train and the snores of your travelling companions. It's strange how people who snore are always those who drop off to sleep first.

The tickets we bought were again not synchronized so that we could sit together, but we were able to swap with another passenger. We had tickets 31 and 32, but 31 was next to 30 in front, while 32 was next to 33 behind.

Had a few things to nibble which we'd brought with us, including tea and some mini walnuts, which are about one-third the normal size and they call smallnuts – quite logically, I suppose.

I didn't have any paper to write notes during the journey,

so instead used some sanitary envelopes provided (not used). I don't know why the train had to start at 7.49, to arrive at 12.07 – presumably a computerized timetable, to synchronize with other train services, crossing lines, etc. – but in fact the train arrived at Nanjing station at 12.20 in the afternoon.

Sitting in my seat, I had to keep reminding myself of everything we'd brought with us, and where it was: *Did we remember teabags? Yes, packed a few spares in the carrier bag, in some paper cups. Where's my passport? Oh, yes, Ling's got it in her handbag, along with the tickets.* And so on.

But we did forget to bring a carton of milk – or, rather, there was no more room in our bags. While travelling you have to be continually aware of what you can carry, and whether items you think you need to buy are really necessary.

As we left Hangzhou, we passed interminable new housing blocks being built, along with new motorways, reservoirs and flyovers leading who knows where? Somebody somewhere must have an overall plan, although at present it all looked rather a mess, in spite of all the men in hard hats swarming all over the place like ants, knee-deep in mud, or working with oxyacetylene cutters, in what looked tiny pieces of the massive jigsaw of reinforced concrete blocks. I was thinking that, if you stood in a certain place at a certain time, that spot would remain the same, but if you stood there at a different time, the whole aspect would be different. Today I might be standing at the side of a busy road, waiting for a taxi, but two years ago I' might have stood next to one of those workmen, knee-deep in pre-construction mud. Five years before that, there might have been cows grazing on the grass nearby. Fifty years before that it might have been covered in marshland. A million years before that I might have been crushed by a passing dinosaur. You could go to sleep on the top floor of a high-rise block, but if you woke up a couple of hundred years in the past, you might be in the middle of a battle between Chinese warlords across a blasted heath.

And, by the way, where does all this concrete and cement come from? I think the process involves baking and slaking limestone, etc., so somewhere there's a huge natural mountain of the stuff, being broken down and carried away by huge fleets of lorries, to the cement factories. Packed into the brown paper sacks, like those you see from the Portland Cement Company – though in China it's probably twenty-tonne containers at a time. So this mountain, wherever it is, will one day be below sea level and the stuff redistributed across the whole of China, creating a flattened landscape, apart from the high-rise tower blocks. It's happening already; when you're travelling by train, the land is as flat as a pancake for hours on end – they're already running out of mountains.

As I looked out of the window, I saw a moribund river oozing alongside the track, with a few wooden boats moored here and there. Makeshift homes were dotted about, all put there without planning permission, probably, and destined to be pulled down or pushed into the river, to fill it up for a new motorway. Then, *hello*, there's a new tower block being constructed: a huge skeleton structure of rusty metal framework, waiting for a few million tonnes of reinforced cement to be poured into it. Alongside these were rows of huge pillars of cement, about fifty metres high – like Stonehenge in a straight line – all waiting for a new six-lane motorway to be balanced on top, or maybe a railway. And then more neat rows, or acres – hectares, even – of cabbage and greens, with a neat square of garbage sacks, like garish synthetic minestrone.

By this time, the lady in front of me was trying to stretch out to sleep across two seats. She had a small hole in one sock. When this didn't work, she had another go at trying to get her seat to recline. I didn't have the nerve to point out that she had to push the little metal button on her armrest. So, she decided instead to buy a sack of popcorn, and sat crunching this to the very last grain.

I beat her to the toilet, though, and managed to squeeze myself in before she was able to barge past. An excellent toilet it was, too: a sit-down one with paper provided. A sign written in two languages gave directions on where to find soap, drying paper, sensor-operated water and a waste bin. I found out that one way to alleviate the unpleasant smells emitting from loo areas is to flush before you go, as well as after, so you get a fresh stretch of water below you.

One-and-a-half hours later, we entered the environs of Shanghai. Now, that is what you call a city!

The new mighty flyovers, and six-lane motorways being constructed, make Spaghetti Junction look like pot noodles in comparison. A million new cars a year need lots of motorways, and they're winding about all over the place here, on top of each other, in and out and disappearing into the polluted skyline, like giant Lego put together by ants. It's really amazing; you hear about the strength of the Chinese economy, but you have to see it to believe it. They don't care how much something costs, as long as it's new. They don't just build a bridge over the railway line, but a new motorway about half a mile long, so that the incline isn't too steep. It only takes a couple of weeks, so no problem.

Next we passed through Wuxi, where I seem to remember having bought a teapot before, a few years earlier. But I couldn't recognize any of the scenery as the train passed by. I did see a half-demolished (or maybe half-finished) building, which in any event had been forgotten about, except by people living up on the top floor, judging by the washing hanging out to dry. It was just bare concrete, streaked with white salts and damp stains, with no glass in the windows, surrounded by piles of ubiquitous broken bricks.

We arrived at Nanjing at 12.20, and queued for half an hour amongst a seething mass, waiting for a taxi for Nanjing. These were mostly VW Santanas, dark green in colour, with a few Citroens and Kia, just to rub it in when you realize what the U.K. car industry is missing.

Previously known as Jinling, Nanjing has signs of human occupation going back to Homo Erectus, 300,000 years ago. The main city was begun in 472BC by Emperor Gou Jian. In 229AD the place was controlled by Emperor Sunquan, when it was classed as a capital city. He was followed by Langya, then Song Dynasty, Qi, Liang and Chen, all of which gave the city its title: "The Old Capital of Six Dynasties". Zhu Yuan, founder of the Ming Dynasty, used it as his capital city when the whole of China was united. It was a capital under Sun Yat-Sen in 1912, and also a capital under the Republic in 1927. I'm not sure when Beijing or Peking took over this role.

It was about a twenty-five-minute drive to our four-star hotel, Yishiyuan, built in 1920 and favoured by Chang Kai Shek. Priced at 368 yuan per night (£35) it was a really nice place – after all, if it was good enough for Chang...!

Across lovely marble floor, a walled reception and luxurious carpets, we were escorted to our rather small room: perfectly formed dark wood panels, a desk, chair and armchair, in addition to the immaculate bed, heating at our control, T.V., of course, and internet connection. The ensuite bathroom was a delight, with taps and controls which didn't hang loosely out of the walls, and no cracks in the marble floor. Freshly laundered towels, a selection of shampoos, foams and a bar of soap of household proportions – not the one you usually get, which disappears after the first use.

After settling in, we went out and decided on a KFC, for the sake of simplicity. Then we did a little bit of shopping therapy, and found that the department store here was very reasonable. I bought Ling a new black jacket for 98RMB, which made her happy (worth its weight in gold!), and myself an aubergine pure-wool sweater for 71 yuan – excellent value. Bought a map at a newsagent's then, upon returning to the hotel, found a free one in one of the drawers, in addition to a couple of postcards and writing paper.

With evening setting in, at 5.30 we decided to sample the Kung Po chicken of the hotel restaurant, adding 38RMB to the room-service charge.

After a week of sitting around Ling's brother's flat, wearing overcoats, we were now luxuriating in a heated room.

SUNDAY 29$^{TH}$ NOVEMBER 2009

We had paid 250RMB each to take a group tour today. As it started at 7.45 a.m., we got up at seven and just had time to grab breakfast before the bus came. This was a twenty-seater minibus and, by the time we'd picked up everyone from different hotels, it was full. The bus was a bit smelly from condensation and damp, but we got used to it, after about ten hours through the day! The tour guide was a young Chinese girl wearing a yellow yaya (feather padded overcoat), who spoke into a microphone at breakneck staccato speed, which I couldn't understand, of course, and Ling only remembered to translate a few salient points here and there.

The first stop was a rather shabby museum, with the entrance gate badly in need of painting, in the bright colours of red, gold and blue which usually adorn public buildings and monuments. It was pretty cold everywhere we went, through the courtyards of buildings undergoing repairs; even inside there was no heating.

The main exhibit, though, was quite interesting. It was a sort of mini pagoda, made of metal and gilded with silver, studded with precious stones and complicated carvings, which was supposed to have contained one of the Buddha's hairs, including follicle. It was only very recently found, during excavations on 22nd November 2008, in a granite coffin in an underground Changgan Temple, having been there undiscovered for 927 years. There was a whole room dedicated to this artefact, with brief histories of Sakyamuni before he became known as Buddha. Some of the translations were rather amusing, such as in one story about how his brother had wanted to kill him and so borrowed a rogue elephant and "drank it" – which I think was supposed to read "make it drunk" – so that it would attack the Buddha. But he pacified the beast, having, in a previous contest among five-hundred athletes, thrown an elephant over his shoulder, making a big hole. Well, it would!

The pagoda was one of 84,000 distributed around the world by King Ashoka (spelt "Asoka" on the info), nineteen of them in China. I've a feeling this may have been an exaggeration, though, caused by the translation into English; Ling also sometimes gets mixed up between her hundreds and thousands.

In addition to this, there was some info about a wall which had surrounded the city during the Ming period. All of the bricks had the name of the brickmaker imprinted on them. If any were found to be below standard, the whole family of the maker would be executed, so quality control was pretty good. I suppose if you wanted to get rid of somebody, all you had to do was stamp their name on a duff set of bricks.

That was about it for this museum, possibly because there was a lot of work being done on it, but there was a good statue of Confucius ("Qu Fu", as they say in China) just inside the main entrance, as well as an antique market, which we didn't have much time to explore. Though, just to briefly mention that there was a photo of an old royal palace, which was even bigger than the one in the Forbidden City, but it was destroyed by the Japanese during

WW2. They obviously have a lot to answer for, having murdered 300,000 civilians during their time of occupation.

On the way to the next place, while waiting at the lights, I saw a few girls waiting on motorcycles at the other side, with long, flowing, black hair like Valkyrie. Farther along, two shopworkers were playing badminton in a busy street to keep warm, passers-by dodging the shuttlecocks.

During the rest of the way, we visited three estates owned by General Xui Da, given to him by the Ming emperor. Apparently this general was an expert Wei Qi player (Chinese chess, or "Go", as we call it in the U.K.). In this game, two players have white and black stones each, and play on a board of about 128 squares, placing the pieces at the intersections of adjoining squares. The object is to surround your opponent, take away their pieces and establish your territory. The emperor added an extra element to the game, that if the general beat the emperor he would be executed for treason, but if he let the emperor win he would also be executed, as this would be a token of disrespect. They played all day, while the general deliberated how he should proceed, and finally came up with the perfect solution of establishing a position whereby the game ended in a draw. As a reward, the emperor gave him the three large estates that we visited, with lakes similar to West Lake in Hangzhou, with houses and gardens, etc.

Unfortunately, over six hundred years later, there were no funds left to install proper heating, and we were freezing during our visit, quite anxious to get back on the minibus and looking forward to lunch. Like Hangzhou, they have hot summers here for about eight months, with a couple of months of warm weather either side, for spring and autumn, so they don't make too much provision for heating in the winter.

This first place was dedicated to a maiden named Moucho, who was happily married with a child, but a corrupt statesman fell in love with her and arranged for her husband to be sent to fight in some battle, hoping that he would die during the campaign. Still, just to make sure, he paid criminals to murder the husband along the way. When Moucho found out she hung herself, rather than dishonour her husband.

The second place we went to was a similar establishment, with temples to Buddha, lakes with quaint boats for hire and ornamental gardens. There was a 300-year-old lucky wisteria tree here, trained over a pergola, which was supposed to bring good luck if you touch the tree and make a wish, but we forgot. There were also ornamental ponds and grottoes made out of the Yilong stone formations. This particular feature contained three-thousand stones, which took six years to assemble, and we took a few photos.

One of the commercial enterprises of the tour guide here was to show us some lucky ornaments made of sandalwood, depicting the sign of the tiger, representing Yang, which is supposed to bring good luck and safety if put in the home. The opposite, Yin, is represented by the lion, which is used outside the home. This is why you see two lions outside a lot of big houses, hotels and restaurants. This piece of good luck cost us about 50RMB. This garden was also home to the first tingzi (ornamental pavilion) to be heated by electricity.

When we went outside we went to a rather bare market, where there were sealed bags of Nanjing duck, which is supposed to be delicious, so we bought one for Ling's mum.

The last one of these gardens was pretty much the same, but we were expected to buy some lucky gold Buddhist tokens, which we declined.

When we returned to the bus early and sat inside, where it was warmer, I felt sorry for some of the street vendors, selling fruit without much success. It was quite sad; every time a tour group came over they perked up, as people milled around their displays, but no one ever bought anything while I was watching. Eventually they packed up and left with full loads, just before another large coach party arrived, probably bursting to buy fruit.

Before proceeding to the next place, we were told we simply must go and visit this new German shop selling the world's sharpest knives, made in Germany and on special promotion. Most of the party laughed, as it didn't seem to quite fit with the culture of Buddhist temples and museums, but we trotted along dutifully. Actually, the guy who made the biggest fun of it himself bought a complete set for 180RMB – one of only two people who bought something. The salesman kept up an uninterrupted patter for about twenty minutes, quite frightening us with displays of how sharp the "Sharply Knife" was, slashing sheets of paper and chopping up bits of rubber – although I couldn't see why anyone would want to buy these fantastic knives for such activities. He then hit the blade against metal pipes, just to show how strong it was. But I'd already bought "the sharpest knife in the world", at a similar demonstration in Asda, a couple of years ago – and those knives were made in China (still got them in 2020; great for slicing bread). On the way out, we did buy a cigarette lighter for 15 yuan, for Ling's son, and a useful little item in a sort of spectacle case, containing two screw-together chopsticks and a mini knife and fork, for travel use. Also, we'd already been given small, sharp fruit knives as free samples.

The best place was the last: a park and mausoleum called Kuomintang, dedicated to Sun Yet Sen, who got rid of the last emperor and created the Republic. The way it looked to me, though, he just got rid of the emperor because he wanted to be emperor! His tomb was every bit as huge and elaborate as those from the Ming Dynasty. We arrived at 4.30 and were allocated one hour to spend here. There were a number of tourist shops and restaurants, which we avoided and repaired to a point of interest: a series of massive tombs with stellae dedicated to the great man, similar in design to the emperor's establishments, though with blue-tiled roofs instead of red. There were three of these buildings, the main one at the top of a flight of 392 steps, bordered by rows of evergreen trees, from which we could hear birds singing.

The thing we debated was: "Is it worth going up all those steps, just to turn around and come back?" The trouble is, once you're there, you have to go up all those steps, whether you like it or not. They sit there, beckoning: "Come on up and have a look. You won't be disappointed." It's like when you're at the top of the Eiffel Tower and you want to throw yourself off, but just manage to stop yourself. This is not quite so dangerous – except for the risk of a heart attack – so you look up the steps and think: *We might as well, now we're here.* So, we made the effort and joined the rest of the party at the top, to go and look at Sun's stone coffin, then walked back down again. The ascent wasn't so bad, to be honest; I guess it took about ten minutes, with a couple of rests.

It got dark as we reached the bus, and several of the party came back late again. As it was pitch dark by then, at 5.30, we were considering sending out search parties, before they all turned up carrying purchases from the gift shops.

The bus dropped us off in the city centre, which certainly looked in better condition than most of the places we'd seen today. We'd been in the freezing cold from 8.00 a.m. until 6.00 p.m., and the lunch – while cheap at 20RMB – was a bit of a joke, although I finished off the soup, sweetcorn and steamed rice. The humorous guy who bought the knives quipped that Nanjing is beautiful, the people are great, but the food is terrible! It was more like a canteen just outside the main tourist centre, and we all kept our overcoats on while eating.

In contrast, the evening meal – which we found around the back of the lady's fashions in a department store – was excellent. It was very clean and modern there – all-white décor and comfortable, white leather seats, decorated with imitation jewels – and the service was first class. I had roast New Zealand lamb with rice and Ling had fried prawns, with a free bottle of beer, tomato soup and a sweet bean and cream dessert, all for about 100 yuan. We found the store quite expensive, though, so decided to go shopping at a place near our hotel, where I bought a jumper for 70 yuan and Ling a new coat for 98RMB.

We then had a bit of a job finding the right stop for the number 100 bus we needed, so eventually gave up and caught a taxi, the driver asking Ling: "Is he American or English?"

We freshened up at the hotel first, then went to the store, where I bought some smart, blue trousers for 128 yuan, which they altered for me on the spot.

Finally, we decided to call it a day and go back to the hotel for a shower and a sleep, having first collected our rail tickets from reception.

Arsenal were thrashed 3-0 by Chelsea that day.

## MONDAY 30<sup>TH</sup> NOVEMBER 2009

We got up before 8.00 a.m. and had a leisurely breakfast, but while we were getting ready to leave our room, Ling had a panic attack and imagined we'd be late for our train. We hurried down to check out of the hotel, and found they had charged us 80 yuan for booking our rail tickets, plus 40 yuan for booking yesterday's trip. The total cost for our semi-luxury hotel stay was 946RMB, for two days.

We caught a taxi and the driver mentioned he would be going by back streets, as some of the roads had been blocked, to allow Wen Jiao Bao to go to a meeting with representatives from the European Union. The taxi driver was great, however, and got us there in fifteen minutes – well in time for the train; Ling took nearly as long to buy a magazine and newspaper!

We had second-class seats, but they were quite good and we managed to sit next to each other, in a triple seat, without having to swap with anybody. It was a little bit hot on the train, so I removed all my jumpers and stowed away my new feather-lined overcoat, which felt like stowing away a tent or sleeping bag. It was a five-hour journey, but quite relaxing, although I couldn't hear my MP3 player, due to the noise of travelling companions constantly shouting across the aisle to each other.

I couldn't see much from my aisle seat, but I noticed there still weren't many birds about – probably a throwback to the Cultural Revolution, when Mao had all the birds killed; perhaps the word had got around, and not many came back over the past thirty years. It was sad to see groups of fifty or so poplars, with only one nest for a solitary resident of detached premises and vast country estate – or sometimes none at all. Occasionally you would see two in a larger copse of trees, and sometimes two in the same tree – perhaps from the same family; two generations living in the same house.

The meal on the train was of the British Rail variety: beef, rice and assorted vegetables, all the same brown colour.

We passed through Taishan, of *"Famous Mountain at Sunset"* fame, and reached Jinan at about 3.10 p.m., where we had to fight for a taxi in a rather disorganized crowd.

It was nice to be back with Ling's mum, and further exciting to find our four boxes of about 100 kilos had arrived from the U.K. already, having only been sent by sea on 26th October, and estimated to arrive by 5th December.

I repaired some holes in the wall, created by electricians when fitting new T.V. connections, then had a baked potato and cheese for dinner. We did some unpacking, in between me writing this to get up to date. An email from cousin Chris and my agent in London confirmed that they would be paying rent into my account today, as of 12.30 U.K. time. Then I packed away my book and DVD collection from the U.K.

Tomorrow we would go to see Ling's policeman friend, to get an extension for my three-month visa, if possible.

And so to bed at about 10.00 p.m. Seemed a lot warmer here now, with very efficient heating.

TUESDAY 1ST DECEMBER 2009

5 DEGREES

Awoke this morning with a sore throat – not surprising, I suppose, after all the changes in temperature: you wrap up warm to go out and find yourself sweating after a while; then, still in the cold, you start to get cold again. Unless it was just someone sneezing on the train yesterday. Anyway, Ling was dosing me up with several different remedies: antibiotics, herbal medicine and paracetamol – and finally, in the evening before I went to bed, acupuncture.

As I needed to extend my ninety-day visa in China, as we were not leaving for Australia until March, the first step was to get registered with the local police in Jinan, just a short walk around the corner from Ling's mum. We were now there, in their cold office, with everybody sitting at their computers wearing overcoats. It took about half an hour of filling in forms, etc., just to establish that I was officially here. We were then given some kind of certification and left. But, as I was having a look at it, even though it was all in Chinese, it appeared that the dates were wrong, and Ling agreed: they'd put that my current visa was due to expire on 1$^{st}$ Feb 2009, instead of 2010. So, we had to go back in and get it put right, as it was also incorrect on their computer system. Having done this, we would then have to go somewhere else later to get the extension.

Bought some nuts at a local street market on the way back, and special nails to hang some pictures. But when we got back home, one of our pictures had all its glass broken. Zhang Min and Lao then arrived and, as they liked this picture and another that goes with it, we gave both to them.

I got an email from Hastings International, our letting agents, to say they would be paying us our rent today, but when I checked (and then again on Thursday morning) it still hadn't reached my bank. I supposed they would say it takes five working days to reach my account, so I would just have to wait until next Monday. Ling agreed with her mum that we would pay 2000 yuan a month toward our living expenses, plus we would buy whatever food we need.

Just to explain our finances a little bit, I retired in September 2009 and decided to go on a world tour with Ling, using a lump sum I'd taken from my retirement fund. In addition, to put toward travelling costs, we rented out our flat in London for twelve months, fully furnished, to a lady from Australia. So now we had to stay away. I call it a "world tour", but in fact we only went to America to visit Ling's older brother Yan, Australia to see my best mate Trevor and his wife Veronique, and the rest of the time would be in China.

Went to bed early with this cold.


WEDNESDAY 2ND DECEMBER 2009

5 DEGREES AND SUNNY

Stayed in bed most of the day, taking repeats of the various concoctions. Not that I was particularly ill, but I wanted to get rid of this cold before it developed into something which would stay with me for weeks. Our plan was to go to Weihai next Monday and check out our flat, so I wanted to be okay to do more travelling, plus a lot of cleaning when we got there.

Not much to report about today, as I didn't go out, just read a Judge Dee book, *The Chinese Bell Murders*, and watched an Alan Ladd DVD, *This Gun for Hire* – although, top of the bill were Robert Preston and Veronica Lake. Must have been one of Ladd's early big roles, made in 1942, when he had dark hair.

Ling went out early with her mum to the supermarket, and I stayed in bed until they got back, cold slightly improved, but still took loads of medicine. Would like to go out later, as it was looking sunny. Lunch would be about 11.30 as usual and I'd only just finished breakfast! I'd made some cabbage and bacon soup last night, which tasted okay, so we'd probably have that again.

After lunch of soup, we went out to Silver Plaza supermarket, to look for cashmere cardigans, but couldn't find exactly what we wanted. We then went through the underground shopping area toward the street market. This place was built initially as an air-raid shelter during the war and is now a brightly lit, seemingly endless underground street of shops, cafés and stalls. We didn't buy anything here, though, but took one of the exits to the street market, which is where I prefer going anyway. They had displays of goldfish and other tropical fish, for sale at only 5 yuan a pair, plus water plants, bowls and also some exquisite birds in cages. But, as we were looking for a china pot for the kitchen, we decided to defer our purchase of pet fish.

We went to the end of the market, where they had a large display of pots, of all sizes and designs, including some about two metres high, but settled on a flower design on a white background, for 30 yuan, and a smaller vase with a small crack, for a reduced price of 10 yuan.

Caught a taxi home, as I felt my cold coming back after I'd ventured out, because it was a nice day. But we had been out in the cold long enough, so we got back home in time for tea.

Phoned brother-in-law Pete at 7.30 p.m., when it would have been 11.30 a.m. in the U.K., as I was waiting for some info from the inland revenue to complete a tax return, but he was in a bit of a rush to go out. He mentioned that he was going to forward a lot of post soon, but now couldn't get the car to start. He thought the battery must be flat, but I thought the car might be in gear or he hadn't deactivated the immobilizer properly. Would try and call him again tonight.

SATURDAY 5<sup>TH</sup> DECEMBER 2009

## 4 DEGREES

Nothing much to report for the last couple of days. Been mainly inside with a cold.

Ling bought ten goldfish for 9 yuan (about 90p), but we would now have to get an aquarium plus various other life-support stuff. On Friday Ling's sister came over, but I was still in bed at 4.00 p.m., trying to get rid of this cold. I got up just as Lao was leaving. Zhang Min tried to tempt me outside with a promise of pizza, but I said I'd rather stay in and get rid of this cold, so went to bed early, while Ling's sister stayed overnight in the spare room.

Got up about 8.30 this morning, feeling a little better, but stayed in until lunchtime, when we were going to meet some of Lao's friends.

One guy I was sitting next to was quite pleasant. He came from Qingdao and spoke a little English. I'd met the guy a couple of years before, with his wife, at a large, expensive restaurant outside town, which had fountains and streams running through it, with fish swimming, waiting to be caught for cooking.

I get a little nervous about being invited out for a meal, so that people can meet me, as they seem to order so much stuff I don't particularly like. I've managed to convince most people that I'm type-2 diabetic and I dislike pork, especially when it comes in piles of grease and fat. Still, they will insist on putting stuff on my plate I don't want. The thing is, I've been eating Chinese food on and off since 1962 in the U.K., and I know what I like and what I don't. I know the cuisine in the U.K. is not the real McCoy, but it's near enough. The dishes I like are sweet and sour chicken or prawns, which I can't eat anymore because of the sugar content, plus Kung Po chicken and chow mein, which is basically a Cantonese dish you don't always get here. There was a place in Hangzhou last week, where we had a simple meal costing 35 yuan for three people, and I was perfectly happy with the chow mein they served there, at a cost of 10 yuan (just under a quid); I could eat it almost every night. But they keep wanting to eat at different places, and even the expensive ones don't serve up stuff that I can transfer my affections to. When people ask me what I want, I say "chow mein," but they reply that this place doesn't do it, then go and order mountains of stuff I can't really enjoy. One benefit is, though, that I'm losing a bit of weight! The above meal was an example of this.

The place was arranged by Lao, who is usually quite good at choosing restaurants, but on the other hand I reckon he would eat anything, and seems to enjoy scoffing and boozing. He is also a diabetic, but doesn't seem to bother about any diet, etc., and has quite a paunch; he was actually sweating the other day, from the amount of food he was packing away.

I didn't play the game at this place regarding the *"gambei!"* thing, where you drink a toast to someone at the table, and you're expected to empty your glass in one go and show them it's empty; nowadays I just take a swig and smile.

Regarding the food, there wasn't much I could enjoy, and I noticed that not many of the dishes were getting emptied, so it clearly wasn't just me. There was a sort of exploded fish served, covered in sweet and sour sauce, which I'd had before and was quite nice, but this was a little bit dry underneath the batter, and I couldn't find any soft white fish to eat. This fish looked like it had been blown up from the inside, frozen in batter and served up hot with sauce. There was also the usual dish of greens, like pak choi, which I always find hard to chew, unless it's the fresh, small ones – otherwise it goes a little like grass and stringy. There was also a dish supposed to be sweet and sour lamb, but it didn't taste like lamb meat and not many people were eating it; probably a lamb's innards of some kind. Then there was "beef" – but no, it was actually beef tendons, which of course were also a bit chewy, but supposed to be very good for your own tendons. The only thing I liked the taste of was the hot and sour soup at the end.

If you don't want to drink too much beer or tea, it's best to leave your cup or glass full, otherwise someone will keep coming to fill it up, just when you think you're finished.

Then I went to use the toilets, as I didn't know where we were going next, but this was rather disappointing; it was next to the bustling kitchen, and used the same basins for washing your hands. I usually make for a cubicle, even if it's just the stand-up variety, but this one didn't have a door, so I thought I might as well just use the urinal. While I was there, out of the corner of my eye I noticed a man enter the cubicle, roll down his trousers and squat over the hole, to go about his business, so I was glad I'd prepared myself by going before I came out, as I'd never have survived this public display. It's bad enough having people looking at you all the time when you're just walking about.

We ordered Trev's cardigan to be made up especially, as we couldn't find his specifications in the shops; it would take about two weeks. Then we went home with Ling's sister Zhang Min, who stayed the night again. I made an omelette and potatoes with carrots, but the others seemed to prefer the leftovers from yesterday: salty vegetables and some limpid dish of sliced carrots and cabbage, and either pork or chicken slices. They seem to want rice soup every night, which has no taste; just rice soaked in hot water, and not even any salt.


## SUNDAY 6<sup>TH</sup> DECEMBER 2009

Still with a cold, but not so bad today. Had lunch of some takeaway stuff from yesterday, and tomato and egg soup.

Ling's friend from the countryside days, Yen Bin, came to pick us up at 2.00 p.m., to show us a new school he had opened, where he had a couple of teachers giving traditional Chinese lessons. He trained to be a lawyer, but hadn't passed the final exams yet, so worked at a legal firm as a lawyer's assistant. I really liked Yen Bin, who was so helpful, but we couldn't really talk much to each other, as we don't speak each other's language. A few years ago I had a touch of food poisoning, which came on at about three o'clock one morning, so Ling phoned him up and he came over, to take me to a hospital in his car. He has an older brother – Su Bin – and a sister whose name I still can't remember. When they were kids, Ling and her siblings used to go and stay with Yen Bin's parents while their own parents were working – Ling now calls his mother her second mum.

Now he wanted to run his own school, on a private system, and so far had about twenty pupils aged about seven, for which their parents paid about 40RMB each for a one-and-a-half-hour lesson.

I was introduced to a small room, with six or seven kids in it, who all screamed at the sight of me and started jumping up and down, laughing, except one girl who came and stood next to me. But when I said hello and tried to shake her hand, she started crying. Another couple of more enterprising kids came over and tried out a few English phrases on me. Gradually, I joined this class and tried them out with a few English words they had printed on cardboard, but it was difficult to turn it into a proper kind of lesson, as they kept running about. After about fifteen minutes, I looked at the door for a way of escape, to find it full of their parents looking on.

However, they finally said goodbye. It seemed that their time was up, and they had to go to the park with one of the teachers. I don't know what they did for the rest of the time. Maybe they had to attend State schools as well, and this was just some extra tuition.

Ling and Yen Bin talked for about an hour, I don't know what about, while I nursed a paper cup of bitter tea, which

Yen kept trying to fill up even when it was already full. We left here at about 3.30 p.m. and he took us home.

Later, Ling explained about his school project. There was a possibility he might add English lessons to his curriculum, as they had advertised for English teachers recently, but had no applicants. I didn't know how good I would be at teaching English to seven-year-olds, but thought I might give it a try if they hadn't anybody else.

We had more leftovers from lunch for our evening meal, at 6.00 p.m.: mushrooms, veg, some prawns and, of course, rice. We went to bed at about 9.30, and I watched the Travelogue programme on CCTV9, which was in English. They'd been covering Taiwan this week, and its ethnic minorities.

MONDAY 7TH DECEMBER 2009

Had a bit of a flurry this morning, as Ling had noticed a few ants in the bathroom. I'd seen some earlier, but they were so tiny – about a quarter the size of ones we see in the U.K. – that I didn't mention it. But now we found quite a few more in the bathroom, in the second bathroom and the kitchen, going up and down in lines on the walls. There weren't enough to call it an infestation, but there were still

quite a lot, and because they were so small it was hard to
find where they were coming from. I eventually traced a
few tracks coming from a hole in the ceiling in the kitchen,
where a hot-water pipe had been installed. So, I plugged
this up with some filler, then went around plugging up any
other holes I could find. I was not sure if this would be
effective, as we didn't know where they were coming from
(other than upstairs, generally), but somewhere between the
walls and ceiling spaces, where wires and pipes go. Ling
wanted to buy some ant killer, but I wasn't sure how this
would work, as we didn't know where to put it; all the ants
were on the walls, not on the floor. So, she went around the
whole flat with a Hoover while I continued plugging holes.
Meanwhile, Ling's sister was around again, working on the
computer.

Afterwards, it was lunch at 11.30 a.m., of rice,
vegetables and fried fish, which tasted okay apart from the
bones. The Chinese like to cook their fish whole, complete
with head, tail and bones, not like in the U.K., where the
fish is usually skinned and filleted, so you can eat it,
covered in batter, without the hassle of looking for or
spitting out bones. They say they do this because you get
the whole flavour of the fish, but this is contradicted, in my
opinion, by their smothering it in soy sauce and loads of

other ingredients.

Ling gave me her dad's watch today, a Swiss-made Roamer which was a bit small for me, so we took a bus to the larger Silver Plaza supermarket and went to a repair shop she knew. The guy fixed it on the spot in about five minutes, and charged 50RMB, plus extra for some spare batteries we asked for (though not for this watch, which was self-winding). We had a look around the supermarket, but prices were a bit high, so we just bought a few odds and ends.

We then took a taxi to what we thought would be a car exhibition, but when we arrived it was all over. It was a large place, like Earls Court, and we had a quick look around the current exhibition of jewellery and jade, but this was also very expensive, as we didn't have Ling's mum with us to get prices down – besides, I'm not interested in jewellery anyway.

There was another, cheaper supermarket around the corner, so we went to that next. There was a huge crowd of people waiting outside, of several hundred, apparently queuing up to buy eggs, which were being sold for about 20 yuan a kilo, instead of 35. We went into the other part of the market and bought a cooked chicken, some noodles and beansprouts, so I could make chow mein tonight!

When we reached the checkout there were massive queues everywhere, like Ikea. I waited in one queue, which didn't move for about twenty minutes, and Ling was in another, so she eventually got served before me. It was totally ridiculous and I don't know why they were so slow. Apparently this queue was part of the "egg rush", where people had to queue and pay for their allocation; then, once they had their receipt and ticket, they had to go and queue somewhere else to pick up their purchases. We passed hundreds of people on our way out.

Got home by taxi, just in time for tea at 3.45. I had one of the custard tarts I'd bought, and we brought up some dragon fruit and pomelo from storage downstairs. These custard tarts were the same ones the Portuguese call their "speciality", and you can get them in the U.K. as well. But they all pretty much taste the same.

At 5.00 p.m. I decided it was my turn to do some cooking, and as I hadn't yet found a place which makes chow mein, I decided to make it myself. In the afternoon we had bought some egg noodles and a whole cooked chicken, though rather small, which had been cooked over a rotisserie; its limbs had been spread out in the manner in which they prepare Beijing duck, rather than whole, like they do in the U.K. There wasn't much meat on it, being rather an underfed example, but it looked as much like roasted chicken as I've yet seen here.

I boiled the noodles, put them in a strainer, ran cold water over them and left them to dry. Next, I sliced a rather aged onion, along with a carrot, some ginger and garlic, and also removed as much meat as I could from one side of the chicken. While the veg were frying, I prepared a sauce/thickener with flour, an Oxo chicken stock cube, Xiaoxing wine and dark soy sauce. When the veg had been cooked enough, I added the noodles and some beansprouts, then mixed in the sauce. I'd obtained the recipe from Youtube, prior to coming to China, where that site is blocked. I must say, it turned out okay, and was the only dish I've really enjoyed in Jinan, washed down with a glass of red "Great Wall" wine, costing 24 yuan. Even Ling's mum had two helpings, and did the washing up afterwards.

We played the Chinese card game "booker" afterwards, until bedtime at 9.00. Ling's mum loves this game, which you play with two packs; the winner is whoever gets rid of all their cards first. I usually lost, and had to stick a strip of paper on my forehead every time.

Checking my Bank of China account online, I noticed the rent had at last been paid into our account. I tried to transfer £1100 to my Jinan account, but couldn't quite work out some of the instructions, so I eventually had to ring the branch in London for instructions; it was about 1.30 p.m. over there. One of the questions was: "Put in your Chinese name", and, as I don't have one, I just had to leave it blank. Where it said "reference number", this was just a number I had to make up myself, to check against the transaction. Finally, under "I.D. number", this was to be my passport number. When I went back to try it, I was gratified to see that the transaction was successful.

## TUESDAY 8TH DECEMBER 2009

Woke up at 7.30 a.m., still with a cold, but to everybody's surprise I got up.

Before I forget, I must just add something which had been amusing me since I first came to Jinan, in 2002. This was about seven years ago, when I first came to meet Ling's family. In the car, on the way to their flat in Liu Li Shan Lu, we passed a three-storey building, which was rather grandly named in English, "Jinan Large Building", which I thought amusing: one, because of the slightly incorrect translation and two, because it was surrounded by several much larger buildings, over twenty storeys high. So, when we returned this year, I looked out for it as we passed, and noticed that someone must have pointed out the anomaly to them, because the name had been changed to "Jinan Building" – although you could still the ghost of the word *"Large"* where the red letters had been removed. I wasn't here a year ago; maybe last year they had briefly renamed it "Jinan Not-So-Large Building". Next year it might be called "Jinan Quite Small Building". I await developments.

In the morning, at about 10.00, we set off to order a new telephone system for the home, plus faster internet service, which was being offered at 86 yuan per month, as part of a new package. Ling tried to explain it to me, but after the bit about 300 free minutes per month, for calls up to 200km between 9-5, and broadband of 300 megabytes per second, I tended to lose interest. Anyway, it was a better deal than the existing one, for which Ling's mum was paying 140 yuan per month.

The large new building for Unicom was within walking distance, so we enjoyed a brisk walk in the fresh air. For once, we could see blue skies in Jinan, which you can't usually see in summer, due to the pollution caused by excessive traffic, and the fact that the city of six million souls is surrounded by mountains, which tends to stop the air from circulating.

We were quickly shown to a desk, where a young man explained the deal to Ling. I just sat there for about twenty minutes, not understanding anything, but vaguely amused by the young man, who had a plastic sign on his desk which, whenever he got up to go and ask someone a question, he turned around to show the words *"Business Suspended"*; when he came back, he then turned it back to read *"At Your Service"*. He did this about six times during the consultation, except on one occasion, when he sat down and forgot to turn it back to *"At Your Service"*! I was deliberating whether I should turn it around for him, when he suddenly remembered and did it himself.

Eventually a deal was struck for 110 yuan per month, including a free mobile phone. Ling agreed the contract, which involved signing her name about eight times on different sheets of paper. Every time she signed her name she put the pen down, before he asked her to sign another document. This went on until I said: "You'd better keep the pen until he stops." Although everything seemed to have been done on computer, there were still masses of paperwork created, and Ling filled her bag with copies given to her.

We walked back home and it was soon time to have lunch, cooked by Xiao Wang. I managed a couple of pieces of fish from yesterday, with some rice and a mixture of peas and sweetcorn, explaining that I don't usually eat a big lunch anyway.

Ling's mum went out for a walk after that and I went for a lie-down, to see if I could get rid of this lingering cold. We eventually went out to the bank, where I was anxious to get my passbook up to date and to change yesterday's transaction from GBP to RMB. We were debating which buses to take and, as it required two, the cost would be 6 yuan, whereas a taxi was only 6 yuan (60p) dearer. So, we took the taxi to the Central Bank of China, where these kinds of transactions were dealt with.

This again was a red tape affair, involving three people, several forms to be filled in, putting my name three times on each page, and even having to go and sit at a different desk after I'd thought the process was coming to an end. Eventually, I got 11.14 yuan to the pound and my book was returned to me, up to date.

We then took a leisurely walk toward home and found a 36 bus, which took us all the way home for 2 yuan. However, we continued for an extra stop, as we were going to do some shopping for food, at a supermarket near Ling's home. We spent 160 yuan here and got quite a lot of "treasure", including Diet Coke, crisps, spicy sausages, cheese, butter and some steak for frying. While we were here, Ling also bought a travel card, which gives even cheaper travel by bus.

It was getting dark when we got home at 5.00 p.m., and I started another beef chow mein, which Ling didn't really enjoy as the beef was a little bit hard; I had forgotten to add "softening powder". Anyway, I enjoyed it, washed down with a glass of red wine, and with enough left over for my lunch tomorrow.

Having finished writing this up to date, at 8.00 p.m., I then went back to reading my book, *Dr. Thorndyke's Famous Cases*, before watching a CCTV9 travel programme at 9.30, about Xian and old city architecture.


WEDNESDAY 9TH DECEMBER 2009

Got up at 7.45 and had a shower, still with a slight cold, though mainly just a cough now and then.

The electrician came at about 9.30, to do something with lights – not sure what. He also checked the water tank, in order to be ready for possible freezing conditions later on.

Made some bread at 10.00 (three-hour cycle) and practised playing the erhu. I couldn't remember so many of my lessons, as I'd left my notes in the U.K.

I didn't go out today, so not much to write, except that Ling went out to renew her Chinese passport. But after waiting for about three hours, she was told that they couldn't do it yet, as it still had eight months to run. She was concerned that she might not be in China when the expiry date was due, but they insisted that she come back later. However, after lunch she phoned a friend at the office, and they arranged for her to go back and try again. This time she was successful, in spite of another three-hour wait, and moving from one desk to another.

## THURSDAY 10<sup>TH</sup> DECEMBER 2009

Got up at 7.40 and had a shower, as I sweated quite a lot in bed last night. The trouble is that we had the heating on, which is controlled by the city council for all houses in the city, and I had a winter duvet.

Xiao Wan phoned to say that she couldn't come in today, as it was too misty in her area and there were no buses. Apparently she lived quite a distance away in the countryside, but bus rides were only 1 yuan for a single journey.

We went out in the morning, to make up some tonic medicine Ling wanted prepared at a local pharmacy. This was a ridiculous place in terms of the number of shop assistants there: about thirty in a normal-sized shop; two to every counter, outnumbering the customers.

Then we walked to a large ornamental gate (Damen), to meet Ling's mum for lunch. We were supposed to meet at 11.10 but she didn't arrive until 11.45; not sure why, but she came on a different bus to the one we expected. We then walked to the Pizza Hut near the football stadium and enjoyed a nice lunch of minestrone soup and pizza, in a nice, clean restaurant. Although, Ling's mum preferred the place we went to nearby last week, which I pointed out only served offal dishes – or, as I called them, "awful" dishes.

We then went to explore a new supermarket which had just opened up, and found some good bargains. I found a good, feather-lined, short winter jacket for 129 yuan (about £11), and a red wine alleged to be cabernet sauvignon for 9 yuan – less than a pound.

We got a taxi back and had a rest, after our lunch and shopping. There wasn't much to have for dinner, but I was content to make myself a cheese and tomato sandwich with homemade bread. Ling complained about me having a glass of red wine, so I didn't indulge – as if I'm somehow becoming an alcoholic!

After dinner, I trawled through the internet for some teaching material, in case called upon to do a lesson next Sunday. I didn't really look forward to it, but would give it a go and at least make some preparations, using old nursery rhymes and Burl Ives songs, to try and make it more interesting for the kids, as I understand they like to learn songs: "Old McDonald", etc. I got quite nostalgic looking through some of them: "Jimmy Crack Corn", "Sing a Song of Sixpence", etc.

Sent Pete a birthday email – hoped it was the right date! Also emailed Bi Chen (Ling's cousin in the U.K.), as her son Kevin was not well.


FRIDAY 11<sup>TH</sup> DECEMBER 2009

Got up this morning at 8.00, and had the usual porridge and dragon fruit. You can buy three for 10 yuan here, whereas in the U.K. they cost £2.95 for one, which is also a lot smaller. It was very dark outside and looked like it had been raining; temperature was about six degrees.

Ling had a brochure for some 37-square-metre flats in Weihai, selling at 140k yuan, so we arranged to take a 52 bus to the company offices, about seven stops away. It was near some big motorway bridge, close to a restaurant we'd had a meal at with some of Lao's friends last week. It was very wet and muddy everywhere, and we had difficulty crossing the road, across six lanes of traffic near a large crossroads – so there were four sets of six-lane traffic, seeming to come at you from all directions, including bikes and motorcycles seemingly coming the wrong way, and lights changing when you're halfway across the road. Anyway, we made it across and entered a building diagonally opposite the bus stop.

We went up to the eighteenth floor, where Ling had a long talk with the salesman. He showed us brochures and a video showing the building work still incomplete, as well as a large-scale model of the complex, built by the beach and surrounding an inshore lake. Then she handed him 400 yuan, before finally explaining to me that we were going to look at the place; we were arranged to leave by bus at 7.30 tomorrow morning – first I had heard about it! – with a group of about thirty prospective buyers. The 400 yuan also included B-and-B at a hotel for one night. This was okay, as we'd planned to go to Weihai next Monday, anyway.

We had also looked at some four-seater electric cars on the internet, which looked quite impressive, at prices around £2000, or 20,000 yuan.

So, tomorrow we would go to look at this block of flats and then would probably stay independently for a further two nights, to check for other properties and also find out about ferries to Korea. Then it would be off to Lushan, to inspect our flat, which we bought a couple of years ago for £15,000. We would probably have to stay at a hotel there, as there wouldn't be any clean bedding or heating.

On the way home, we bought some baked sweet potatoes from a street vendor, an electric pump for the fish tank and some crystals for dechlorinating the water, as we'd be away for about a week, and didn't want to give Ling's mum the inconvenience of cleaning out the fish tank. One fish was on its last fins, but the others seemed to appreciate the improved environment, which I'd looked up on the internet. The tank wasn't really big enough, at about three gallons: the web recommends fifty gallons, which seems a bit excessive; we would need a mini-swimming pool in the flat.

So, we did some packing and got ready more warm clothing, as it is quite windy in Weihai. Then Ling went out to get her tonic/medicine, while I continued reading *Dr Thorndyke*.

It was getting dark again at 5.00 p.m., and would be time for dinner soon. I decided I'd have another sandwich –

probably sausage and tomato.

Not sure how we were going to buy another flat, unless we could sell the one in Lushan/Rushan (whatever). Personally I liked the place, with its three bedrooms, dining room, living room, balcony and two bathrooms; the new places would only be two bedrooms and cost nearly twice as much. However, it did suffer a little bit from condensation.

After dinner, I had a shower and we went to bed early (at about 8.00 p.m.), to get up at 6.00 a.m. tomorrow.


SATURDAY 12$^{TH}$ DECEMBER 2009

Actually, we woke before the alarms and got up at about 5.30 a.m.

Another fish had died, leaving nine grieving goldfish, but the rest looked okay, and hopefully would survive until we got back.

It was cold and damp when we left at 6.50, with our small suitcases well packed, and a bag of fruit and crisps to eat on the bus. We got a taxi and were at the meeting place for the coach at 7.10, which finally left at 7.30, as per schedule, with about thirty of us on board. Although quite clean, there was no ventilation and the windows steamed up a lot during the journey; I spent most of the day wiping off condensation. We stopped for a short toilet break at about 9.00, then for a rather early lunch at 10.30. This was included in our payment of 200 yuan each, which included the coach trip (about eight hours), lunch, dinner at the hotel, a night at the hotel, including breakfast at 6.30 a.m., and travelling during the day, to visit the apartment building site, a couple of scenic spots and lunch, so it was quite a good deal.

Along the way I shot some film of miles and miles of polytunnels, along the roadside and all the way into the distant horizon, and also the same on the other side of the road – like it's going to feed the entire population of China. When you consider it, that is pretty big, at 1.3 billion, compared to 65 million in the U.K.: about twenty to one. If you imagine your one-bedroom flat housing two people in London, that would be forty people living there in China.

The first lunch was at a service area on the motorway, but was quite good, although I noticed it was mostly vegetable dishes. We had a section reserved for our party, and the buffet-style food was lined down one side of the room. We were given metal plates, rather like the kind army personnel use. I had some fried bread, a steamed roll, a piece of fish fried in batter, complete with bones, boiled cauliflower, pickled cucumber, tomato and egg soup, rice, mouli and sweet potato. I had a good fill-up, with no space for slices of orange and melon.

While visiting the toilet area, we were attracted to some rather interesting toy parrots. Okay, they looked a bit cheap (cheep?), made of garish plastic, but the mechanism was really quite good. The heads bobbed up and down, the wings flapped and the tail also moved; with the recorded birdsong, the whole movement looked quite realistic. So we bought one for Ling's mum, at 38 yuan.

We drove on, ever onward, until about 1.00 p.m., when there was another toilet break. I was mortified to be the last person to get back on the bus, while the driver was sounding his horn; Ling had to come and fetch me, to see what the matter could be. But we soon settled into the drive again. It was quite sunny and bright by the time we reached Yantai.

We finally reached Weihai. Part of the arrangement was to take us to the Korean shopping centre near the ferry port. We'd been here before and I'd bought a great screwdriver, with about eight attachments for different kinds of screws, plus a light which I could never get to work. Ling had bought some scarves. We were allocated one hour here, but were finished in about ten minutes. It was quite disappointing really, as there were about a hundred shop units, but only selling about four different kinds of product: clothes, toys, knick-knacks and food, on four floors.

We were waylaid by two charming Chinese salesladies at a knick-knack shop, and spent all our time in there. The agents had warned us the prices might be listed at, for example, 150 yuan, but you should only offer 15, so we tried our best. Having already bought a screwdriver set, I was intrigued by a hammer set in the manner of a Swiss Army knife. It had a reasonably-sized hammer in stainless steel, with the handle making up a pair of plyers, which would also act as a nutcracker. At the other end were a penknife attachment, a bottle opener, a small screwdriver, but alas, nothing for getting stones out of horses' hooves. I thought that, of all the items displayed in a hundred shop units, this was the only one I was interested in. The price was 150 yuan, but we managed to get it down to 70 yuan, although I probably should have paid about 25. But I was quite happy with my new toy. They tried to tempt me with the screwdriver set again, but I was able to explain that I already had one – and nor did I want an electric razor. Ling managed to get talked into buying an electric eyebrow trimmer, originally for 40 yuan, bartered down to 20 yuan. They also wanted 25 yuan for an electric light/torch used to check for earwax, but Ling got two for 15 yuan. These were a treasure for Ling, as she's always checking my ears. As a joke, I shone the light in one ear and got Ling to look in the other one, which the sales ladies enjoyed. They would hardly let us go after these three purchases, but I showed them I only had 1 yuan left and started to cry, so they let us go.

It was still too early to go back to the bus, so we found a travel centre, to ask for details about going to Korea. The upshot of this was that Ling would need to get a visa first, which would take a week or so. I didn't need a visa to go, but would need one to get back into China – so that put us off a bit. I would have to tell Soonok, a Korean girl I'd met in London (on a platonic basis), while learning Chinese at the School of Oriental and African studies, as she was looking forward to us going to visit her, near Seoul. The five-day round trip wasn't a bad price, at £150 each for five days – two days at sea, one night in Seoul and two nights back – including food, but the visa scenario made it a non-starter.

It was pretty cold by the time we reached our next stop at 5.30, which was nearby, at the large, ornamental gate overlooking the bay, called "Enjoyment Gate". There is a café at the top and it's about 150-feet high, in a sort of upturned rectangle shape. We took a few photos here and chatted to some of our fellow travellers, one of whom was the sales manager of the sales company, who said that he understood a bit of English, but was too embarrassed to try saying anything. There was also an old gentleman of seventy-two who was quite friendly. He said he'd learnt English at school when he was about three, but had forgotten all of it, so had become a boxer instead. He was born in Qingdao but said that he preferred Weihai, and wanted to move there from Jinan.

We had left Jinan in fairly muddy and wet conditions, where all the cars and buses were covered in mud splashes to their waistline, whereas all the roads and cars in Weihai looked remarkably clean. There was obviously less pollution here, blue skies, etc., and everything looked pretty clean. The minimum taxi fare was 6 yuan, compared to 7.5 in Jinan, 9 in Nanjing and 10 in Beijing.

As might have been expected, Hotel Jinlang was pretty basic and the room was cold, even with hot air blowing. When we went to bed, we shared a single bed to keep warm, adding a spare duvet and blanket to the bed.

We went down for our dinner at 6.00 p.m., where another basic meal had been set aside for our party. Some of us complained about their assumption that we were all vegetarians, as the only meat involved was a few small fish, mixed with shredded mouli and scrambled egg, with tomato. When we finished, I joked that we should go outside and get something to eat, but I was full enough with rice and steamed bread.

After eating our meal, still wearing our overcoats, we repaired to bed at about 7.00 and watched a bit of T.V., before deciding to turn in at about 8.00 again – one, to keep warm, and two, because we had an early breakfast, due at 6.30 a.m.


SUNDAY 13$^{TH}$ DECEMBER 2009

Slept okay, in spite of the cold, and got up at about 5.30, to wash and pack our cases, ready for breakfast at 6.20. Again this was a separate package for our party, with what looked like some leftover vegetables from yesterday, plus two boiled eggs, semolina soup and more steamed bread.

So, we were off again at 7.00 a.m.

It was twenty-three kilometres to the site, which comprised about fifty-six tower blocks plus a five-star hotel, arranged around a lake; they would hold about 10,000 flats, near where the new city council buildings were to be situated. It was rather a long way from the city centre, which took forty minutes to reach, past some attractive park landscaping, along the beach and through some scenic hills. Although all the grass was brown in colour, maybe it would go green in the summer. It reminded me of parts of Greece or southern Spain.

When we reached the site, the bus stopped at the side of the road, overlooking a beach, where some hopeful soul had arranged some white plastic seats and beach umbrellas, in spite of a biting cold wind. We walked down toward the site, where I could see that six of the fifty-six tower blocks were near completion. It looked like a very tidy building site, with four tall cranes in use. To the west there was a hive of activity, as they were laying foundations for the hotel, although it didn't look like a full contingent of workers were there, maybe because it was Sunday. We were given hardhats to wear but mine was a bit small, and I spent the time there changing it with my fur hat or trying the two together, stooping to pick it up every time the wind blew it off. The whole caboodle was not due to be finished for another three years; I suppose the idea was to buy a flat at about 4000 yuan per square metre, then maybe sell it at double the price in three years' time.

After about twenty-five minutes of sightseeing, we went to have a look at the nearby beach and took some photos, then got back on the bus as it was still quite cold. However, as we were driving to the next part of our tour, the sun became quite hot through the bus windows. I think we had decided by then not to go ahead with this deal as: one, it meant having to raise the money ourselves, maybe with Ling's sister and mum, then nothing happening for three years, and we would have no flat until then; and two, it was too far from Weihai, which after all had been our main objective. In fact, this place was too far from any shops, transport, etc.

However, we decided to enjoy the rest of the trip, and were taken to a couple of photo opportunity areas, one of them being a Daoist temple, where Ling had been persuaded (conned) to part with 666 yuan about a year ago. We had visited this place with Mr. Meng and his wife, along with Ling's brother Yan. While Yan was advising me not to buy anything at the temple, or listen to any of their sales pitches, Ling had been drawn aside by a monk, as a special opportunity to pray for good luck with one of the high priests. After the prayers she was taken aside, "chosen" by the high priest for a special consultation. While he was talking to her, and saying that she was in for several years of good luck for herself and family, he suddenly said: "999."

Ling said: "What do you mean?"

"Yuan," he said.

"I haven't got that much on me," she protested.

"666 will be okay," he responded, holding out his hand.

Ling, mesmerized, handed it over to ensure good luck for the whole family.

So, this time we avoided the temple and just took some pictures of the cliffs.

We'd met Mr. Meng and his wife on a previous visit to Yintan, about an hour's drive from Weihai, where we'd got Ling's sister to buy us a flat while we were still in the U.K. After she'd paid the money for us, I'd taken out a Natwest bank loan and transferred the £15k to her.

We returned to China a year later, and went to have a look at the Yintan flat, along with Ling's brother Yan, his wife Ang Li, Ling's sister Zhang Min and her husband Lao. As the flat was unfurnished, we'd gone to stay at a hotel nearby, but after registering we were told I couldn't stay there, as they don't accept Westerners, because the hotel belonged to the army. While we were standing around outside, debating what to do next; Mr. Meng drove up and offered his services as a taxi driver, saying that he could find another hotel for us, which he did. After that, we paid him 100 yuan the next day, to spend the whole day driving around looking for decorating materials and tradesmen, to do some work for us. He was an eccentric driver, who tooted his horn every hundred metres or so, especially when he saw pedestrians walking on the pavement ahead of him – and even once when two butterflies flew across the road in front of him. Since then, we'd met him and his wife a few times during annual visits.

Lunch was to be another early affair, at 10.15 a.m. I thought we were in for another vegetarian repast, when we were driven to a small, quite neat village just off the main road. When the bus was offloaded, we were taken in groups of ten to separate houses, as I thought, but it turned out to be a small B-and-B. We washed our hands in cold water and soap, and sat at a round table. The food was served by the lady owner, and I must say it was a pleasant surprise – one of the best meals we've had so far: local, homemade steamed bread of excellent quality; a huge plate of clams and mussels, which were absolutely delicious; some fried, sliced potatoes with seaweed; homemade fish balls, soft and delicious; grated mouli and cucumber in vinegar; and a large sea bass as the main course, with the usual rice, spring cabbage and onions. All was as fresh as can be, and served up so quickly, piping hot, straight from the cooker.

Several people, including Ling, took the phone number of owner Mr. Chai, as they had four rooms available upstairs and did full-board hotel service at 100 yuan per person, per night. That was really the highlight of our trip, and all was included in the 200-yuan package (£20). They also had a clean sit-down loo, most importantly.

From here, we were driven back to the city, to the main object of this package: to sign contracts, which most people seemed prepared to do – except the elderly man of seventy-two, who was debating whether it was worth waiting another three years before he could move to somewhere far away from medical facilities. We'd already forewarned the manager that we had a property to sell in Rushan/Yintan before we decided, so he wasn't too disappointed when we said we'd seen enough for the time being.

We parted company on good terms, at about 12.30, and caught a very clean taxi to a hotel we'd booked online: the Qiming Hotel, just outside the town centre. It was in a good part of town, with tree-lined streets, and sea and mountain views. The taxi driver was also a fountain of knowledge regarding local house prices and which area to choose, etc.

Arriving at the hotel, we were very pleased to find an excellent contrast to last night's place; it was as good as, if not better than the hotel in Nanjing. The room was about as big as our flat in London, even with a small kitchen unit, plus underfloor heating, free internet use, a special tap for drinking filtered water, a writing desk and chair, plus a dining table with four chairs at one end. Near the window, overlooking the bay, with great sea views, there was a smaller table and two chairs, with tea-making facilities. We had plenty of wardrobe space, a fridge, a safe and bedside tables, so we were very pleased with this choice, at only 186 yuan per night.

After settling in, we went out and took a taxi to Golden Bay Beach, via the mountain route, which was a bit more expensive at 32 yuan, but worth it for the great views. When we alighted, there were some barriers erected, with warnings about oily deposits found on the beach. These had fortunately solidified in blocks along the strand, so were reasonably easy to avoid, but nevertheless spoilt an otherwise immaculate sandy beach, with clear blue water similar to the Mediterranean.

Because it was Sunday, most of the local shops were closed, but one estate agent was open, and he invited us in to supply some local information. It smelt a bit like cats inside, and I noticed some empty saucers near the door, but didn't see any felines. The chap informed us that prices for the local area were around 10,000 yuan per square metre, which was out of our range. But rental was reasonable, at 2000 per month for a two-bedroom flat.

We caught a number 7 bus back into town, for only 1 yuan each, and got off opposite the port. As we looked around for a supermarket to buy a few snacks, Ling spotted an estate agents', and this proved to be quite a good find. They agreed to put our flat in Rushan on the market, at a price of 2500 yuan per square metre, which was way below what you would have to pay in Weihai, at an average 5000 per square metre. But we were lucky, in a way, that our flat in Rushan was quite big, at 140 square metres, which would yield us about 350,000 yuan – or about £35,000. That would be great, as we only paid about £16,000 four years ago (including interest).

As we were now looking for a smaller flat in Weihai, at about ninety square metres, there shouldn't be too much for us to pay to get a place here in Weihai. So, after having a look at the details, we arranged to look at three different properties tomorrow – as per T.V. programme *Location, Location, Location* – and hopefully be quite busy. The agent did hint that it might be difficult to sell our place, but I was sure that our price was reasonable compared to today's prices.

On our way out we asked for directions to a supermarket, and were told there was a place not far away, within walking distance. We had to cross at a busy crossroads, but I noticed this one had convenient pedestrian waiting areas, which made it a lot easier to cross these busy roads, and I hadn't seen before.

On the way to the shop there were a few street vendors about. One old guy had a couple of very large rabbits in a cage for sale, and another small one, which I was surprised to see in just a small, open cardboard box, from which it made no attempt to escape. On our way out, after buying some black tea, milk and some rather synthetic Madeira cake, we bought a couple of baked sweet potatoes, which were duly weighed on some antique handheld scales, and charged 4 yuan. Then we caught a taxi back to the hotel for 7.5 yuan.

Ling had a shower and, after we sorted out an internet connection, I checked that there were no emails. Then Ling phoned her sister and asked her to fax a copy of the lease of our flat, which we might need tomorrow; that arrived about half an hour later.

We went down at 6.30 for dinner in the hotel, in their Western restaurant. They also had a Korean as well as Chinese restaurant. I ordered tomato soup and spaghetti

Bolognese, which was okay, although with no parmesan cheese, which is understandable, as the Chinese don't tend to eat much cheese. This is rather strange, as they eat about everything else under the sun, such as ducks' lips, chicken feet, cows' intestines, etc. The cheese you buy in the supermarket is either foreign imported – like Brie, which is quite expensive at about 150 yuan for 200 grammes – or the local cheese, which is mainly processed and sold in very thin slices, individually wrapped in plastic envelopes. It is also a bewildering process to buy semi-skimmed milk. We are so used to looking for green plastic bottles in the U.K., but when you find this kind of wrapping in China, it doesn't necessarily mean that the milk is semi-skimmed. It's usually sold in thin plastic sachets of about half a pint, and there are about five different varieties to choose from in the supermarket fridges; it's potluck, so you tend to buy one of each and try it when you get home. I did find one which tasted right, but then forgot which one it was. I showed it to Ling's mum and she was unable to get it from her regular supplier; when I asked Ling about it, she just pointed to stacks of U.V.C. milk, which is processed and doesn't need to be kept in a fridge, so that wasn't right – especially when you're trying to make the perfect cup of tea!

For dinner, Ling had prawns in batter and some stir-fried vegetables.

Went back upstairs to enter these details, while Ling went to bed at 8.30. Had a shower before doing the same.

MONDAY 14TH DECEMBER 2009

Unfortunately, I had a bit of indigestion last night and was unable to get to sleep. Plus, there was a loud disco playing music somewhere close by. I wasn't able to make out if it was a building nearby or upstairs, but was annoyed by the constant drum rhythm, which seemed to be exactly the same for every new tune.

Luckily, it stopped at 10.00 p.m., as most people seem to close down for the night in this cold weather. I eventually dozed off. I awoke shortly to get a drink of water, as it was so warm in bed, compared to the last place we were at. I looked at my watch and couldn't make out if it was 12.35 or 6.05. After Ling woke up, I eventually established that it was 12.35. After that I was unable to get to sleep properly, and had to sit up in bed to stop the stomach pains. I dozed fitfully, until I awoke at 7.40, in time to get up for breakfast.

Breakfast wasn't such a good selection as the Nanjing

Hotel, but I managed to make do with a couple of pieces of toast, some bacon, scrambled egg and a raw tomato, chosen from the fruit section. I poured some coffee from the machine, but it had sugar in it, so I had to make do with weak tea from one of those coffee machines, where coffee is kept warm in a glass container on a hot plate – but in this case it was tea.

Ling seemed to have lost her mobile, and we searched the room several times before coming down. The last chance was that she'd left it on the dining table last night, or at reception, but no one knew anything about it.

We were awaiting a call from an estate agent this morning, so were debating whether to give her a call from the hotel phone. We had tried phoning Ling's mobile, but it seemed it was switched off, which the staff felt probably meant someone had swiped it. However, when we had another search upstairs, I found it in Ling's make-up bag, just as she was on the phone to her mum to report it as stolen, or at least missing. So that was sorted. Then we phoned the agent and she agreed to arrange some visits to various properties.

Two places were near the hotel, so while we waited for a call back, we took a walk up the hill, toward the area where the apartments were situated, in the Heqing area of Weihai.

It was chilly this morning – about two degrees – but sunny, although I was getting warm from the walk and wearing so many clothes. Except my ears were cold.

We got a call and arranged to meet the agent at a crossroads nearby, as she was coming to pick us up by car. I think we waited about fifteen minutes. The road wasn't very busy and we noticed a number 4 bus pass this way, toward the centre. The area was quite well landscaped, overlooking the beach with an almost Mediterranean atmosphere, though not quite so expensive feeling. The agent arrived with a colleague, and I managed to squeeze into the front seat of the rather small Chinese car, with about a 900cc engine. We drove to a building site, over a very bumpy, unfinished entry road, and stopped at a tower block in rather an uninviting area, though apparently completed in 2005. The two flats we were to look at were the last ones still unsold, but it also looked as if the landscaping was never going to be finished, as the builders may have lost interest now that all the flats had been paid for.

The first one was on the sixth floor, with no lift, and was 77 square metres in size, at 7500 yuan per square metre. It wasn't too badly designed, with two bedrooms, a living room, kitchen and bathroom, but was just the bare bones, with concrete floors and no bathroom or kitchen fittings.

The one next door, in another building, was less inviting, as there was a dog lying in the doorway on a blanket, giving off a foul fishy smell, which followed us into another basic flat on the second floor (in U.K. terms the first floor). This was 95 square metres, but with exactly the same design, and it hardly seemed worth paying the extra money just for slightly bigger rooms. We left this place after about fifteen minutes' discussion, and felt we had no interest in it.

The next option was an 81-square-metre flat near the centre of town, but Ling didn't like the area from the outside, so we didn't go in. The agent then took us to their office and we arranged to meet again at 1.00 p.m., after lunch. We ate at a place called Dicos, which was a Chinese version of KFC. I had chicken pieces with a curry sauce and chips. Ling had spicy chicken, which she didn't finish. Plus, we had a bowl of free soup, at a total cost of 48 yuan.

On the way back to the agents', we passed through a Korean supermarket, where Ling bought some compacts and more ear-cleaning torches as gifts.

The agent's colleague met us at 1.00 p.m. and we were given a lift to the flat in Golden Bay, by the flat's owner, driving us in a very nice new car, which smelt very fresh and clean. His flat was in a large complex, which we visited the last time we were here. It was in very good condition, with lifts and secure entry. The flat was again on the sixth floor, but this was second-hand and furnished. It about was 95 square metres, with two bedrooms, a big kitchen, bathroom, utility room and large balcony overlooking the sea, with a great view of the whole bay. There was underfloor heating and the owner said it didn't need air conditioning, as there was always a fresh breeze in the summer.

He then left to go on some business and we remained with the agent, while awaiting another flat owner to show us another place, at the opposite end of the road, nearer the Golden Bay Hotel. I took this opportunity to use the toilet here, in case I couldn't find one later on.

When the agent got the call to go to the other place, we locked up and walked to the other end of the promenade, having some difficulty in finding which flat it was, even after a couple of calls on her mobile. Eventually the owner turned up in her car, as we were waiting outside some flats overlooking the beach. We went up to the third floor flat, which was being rented out, so she knocked on the door a few times, in case the tenants were in.

This place was 56 square metres; a one-bedroom flat the

same as our place in London. It smelt a little of tobacco, and looked its seven years since being built. There was a double bed in the living room, unmade, and another in the bedroom. The flat was still warm, but with no occupants present – like the Marie Celeste. We felt it was a little bit back to front, as the balcony looked out over the back, instead of toward the beach. At 7700 per square metre, it seemed overpriced.

We got a taxi back to the office, where it transpired that we were going to be shown another new complex, not quite finished, at another bay next to Golden Bay. But we had to wait in a boiling hot back office for half an hour, before someone came to fetch us in a car.

We drove through a mountain pass, which cut straight across the town centre and down to the coast, on the other side of the peninsular. We went to another office first, to get hardhats, then were driven to a housing block.

We picked our way through the unfinished building, up open concrete stairs to a large floor area, but I was unable to make out if the area we were being shown was one or two flats. Eventually it turned out that this was the wrong floor, so we went down a flight.

This space seemed better defined, with a doorway and rooms partitioned off. The flat was eighty square metres, at a much better price of 4900 yuan per square metre, and we were even more interested when we were shown a large balcony area reaching from the living room window, which was above a shop. This was actually the roof of the shop, which was only accessed by this flat, so it could be utilized as a sort of rooftop garden, for the sole use of this flat, although no structural changes could be made. It gave open views to the sea, about two-hundred metres away, and would be a great place to sit during the summer, with deck chairs, table, umbrella, plants, etc.

The total cost of this place was 392,000 yuan, which worked out at about £35,000, and we could just about manage, if we used our flat in Rushan to raise a bank loan for half its value – say 180,000. If Ling's mum could lend us 100,000 yuan, we could raise the rest from our savings. Of course, if we could sell our flat for 350,000, we'd be able to pay everything back. But we should still manage to acquire this place, even if we couldn't sell our other property.

Of course, only after this stage was reached did Ling decide to tell me about a news programme she had seen a few days earlier, all about Rushan and how a group of estate agents had been conning buyers into buying property there. It had caused such a scandal, on national T.V., that now nobody wanted to buy property there! One undercover reporter had posed as a prospective buyer, coming from Beijing. It had taken twenty-three hours to drive there, in a special coachload of prospective buyers, rather like the one Ling and I had just completed from Jinan, which took eight hours. People had been promised sea views, but when they got there the agents told them they wouldn't be able to see the sea, as there was too much mist. The following morning, they arranged to take the buyers to several different sights, delaying the actual inspection of the site until as late in the day as possible, hoping it would be misty again, as in fact there were no sea views for these properties. By this time, people were getting fed up.

Due to the long journey back, the T.V. reporter had said that he didn't want to go; he preferred to stay in the area for a few days, then go back with a friend in his car. The agents then turned nasty and said he had to go back with them, as that was the deal. When he insisted, they said they would damage the friend's car, so that he couldn't drive it. When he said that he would call the police, they added that this would result in their smashing up the car. Eventually, all the other buyers sided with the reporter, and he was allowed to leave the group – on payment of an extra 500 yuan!

Of course, all of this went into the T.V. programme, along with other reports of agents using similar tactics, plus the fact that there were no hospitals, schools, police or other services in the area. In fact, property builders had built too many housing blocks, without making provision for any shops, restaurants and other items which make up a new town or city.

We'd noticed a lot of these buildings ourselves last year, but weren't aware of the lack of all the other stuff which goes with all the houses. I pointed out to Ling that we'd seen a hospital in the area when we'd first arrived, but she replied the place had always been empty; no doctors, nurses, equipment or anything!

In spite of all this, we – or, at least, *I* – were hopeful that we could sell the place at 2500 yuan a square metre, which is half the price of property in Weihai.

We went back to the office, where the deal was as follows: tomorrow, if agreed, we could pay a deposit of 50,000 yuan, which is about £4800, which we could just about raise while here from our holiday money. In three months' time, the building should be in a condition for banks to allow mortgages to be arranged, so then we would have to arrange the balance to be paid. Hopefully, Ling could borrow 100,000 yuan from her mum, we could pay

100,000 yuan from our savings account, and the balance of 150,000-odd could be repaid as a mortgage arrangement, over seven years, at about 2000 yuan per month, arranged by the agents. Of course, in the meantime, if we could sell the Rushan place we would settle up early. Phew!

They drove us back to our hotel at 5.00 p.m., and we decided to stay another night, so that we could sort stuff out tomorrow. We went down to the hotel restaurant and had a Chinese meal this time, which turned out very nice. We had fish and vegetable dumplings, with a delicious serving of shredded cabbage, onion, cucumber and garlic in vinegar, with some shredded jellyfish. We ordered a beer, but this never came, so we didn't bother about it, as it wasn't on the bill. We then went upstairs at 7.30, to discuss our property dealings, and the possible advantages and pitfalls.

While reading *The Blackmailers*, by Emile Gaboriau, in the half-hour or so I've been writing this, there's been a Chinese soap on T.V. and the background music is the theme from *Jean de Florette*. It's been playing constantly the whole time, which has been driving me mad. I've noticed that Chinese T.V. producers tend to overdo the special effects or backgrounds to programmes, with all sorts of stupid background sounds, or bubbles drifting across the screen during serious discussions. With the soaps, the background music isn't just at dramatic moments, but constantly throughout the entire show.

WEDNESDAY 16^TH DECEMBER 2009

Well, we did our bit. Ling was up at about 5.30, and I was awake in time to switch off her mobile phone alarm, at 5.50. Looking out the window, I could see it had been snowing again, but it wasn't until we got down to reception to check out, at 6.20, that we saw the snow really was deep and crisp and even.

They were supposed to have a taxi ready for us, but there was only one girl there, and she didn't seem to know anything about it. As she was phoning someone, to check we hadn't broken anything or emptied the minibar, I saw a taxi coming down the hill and thought it might be ours, but it passed by the hotel. Five minutes later it went back up again, with some difficulty, as the roads hadn't been cleared. Later, I watched as a small lorry tried it, but it was unable to climb the hill and had to try and back into a driveway, to get off the road.

Meanwhile, we had finished checking out and another guest offered to drive us up the hill, where it might be easy to get a taxi, while the girl trudged down to the main gate to look for one. But when we got into the chap's car, he was unable to move it, as it was snowed into the car park, so we had to get out. Then the girl came running over, to say that two Korean workers had also volunteered to take us. The guy in the back spoke passable English, and told me they didn't have facilities to clear the roads here, as it doesn't snow very often. First their car couldn't get onto the road then, when it did, it also only managed to get halfway up the hill. We got out to see if that would make it any easier, but he decided to go back down and try again. We continued walking to the top, but realizing he still had our suitcases, I walked back down the hill, in case he was unable to reach us.

By that time it was 6.45, and our train was due to leave at 7.18. When I almost reached the bottom, the driver passed me, going up, and was unable to stop as he would lose his momentum. So, I had to turn around again. I was completely knackered and out of breath as I approached the top, where Ling was calling me to hurry and, I could see, transferring our cases to a waiting taxi.

We got in, but a hundred yards later we reached a traffic jam, with people walking about all over the road, making it dangerous for the cars, some of which started sliding down another hill, while motorcyclists fell in the snow.

By the time we reached the boulevard, it was 7.05 and we had no way of catching our train. But we had to keep going anyway, to book another one. Ling phoned information at 7.20, while we were still on the road, and was told we couldn't get a refund, as the train had left on time and it was up to us to be there. However, when we got to the station at 7.35, she was able to exchange the tickets without paying any more. We now had to leave by the night sleeper, which departed at 10.00 p.m. that night, arriving in Jinan at 7.00 a.m. the next day. So, another "no-sleeper" to look forward to.

In the meantime, we had to have somewhere to stay for the day, and the taxi driver took us to the Hongtai Hotel, which we'd noticed yesterday as being near the station, and where we'd considered staying when we came back next week. The taxi charged us double – about 65 yuan – for danger money, but at least we could start again, from a place where we could always walk to the station. We booked into the hotel for the day, at 80 yuan.

It was cheap, and we were only staying here until about 9.00 p.m., but the hotel was a bit of a story in itself. I'm not complaining, just pointing out the facilities as we found them...

It was a railway hotel, about ten storeys, near the station and bus depot, so it was in a good location. When first built it must have been quite good, but times have moved on, and it now seemed to be fighting a losing battle against being pulled down completely and replaced by another, double the size and at double the price.

The first things we noticed were the girls' uniforms at reception: they were quite a nice colour, but faded and rather badly pressed; they didn't quite present the image of smartness we'd seen at the last place. And, although the reception area was still quite impressive, with a large, marble, carved relief on one wall, as soon as we passed this area things started to go downhill – except for the lift, of course, which took us up to the eighth floor: room 801.

The carpets everywhere looked trampled, and there was no electronic key to the door, only an old-fashioned metal key. The room was warm, although rather shabby. From time to time, someone had made an effort to get things going again, but you could tell that it was all rather too much. Even at reception, the exchange rates for the yuan against the pound were about three years out of date, probably what they were when first put up.

I decided to have a lie-down to pass the time, while Ling watched T.V. The bedding was clean, but twenty years old, faded and rumpled, the stuffing in the duvet all over the place in odd lumps. But one could probably spend a night there, if really tired. The ceiling had been painted white not long ago and there were new curtains, but the carpet made you afraid to walk about; it was covered in various stains of mud, tea and whatever, acquired over a long period. The fitted wardrobe was made of the thinnest wood, which looked like it was just veneer, without being attached to any backing; it was just about falling apart at the seams.

The bathroom had a pool of water in the middle of the floor, just where you might put your feet while on the toilet, so it was a bit of a balancing act if you didn't want to get the hotel slippers wet, causing them to disintegrate. There was a drainage hole nearby, which you usually find in bathrooms here, where you might have a shower with no cubicle; the water just goes straight onto the tiles, on concrete floors, then runs down this hole, which is usually covered by a white plastic cover. In this case there was no cover, so we got a view of rusty piping.

The white enamel bath was also giving up the battle against rust, which was peeping through here and there, although it had taken control of the edges. It wasn't substantial rust, because the metal was so thin that it didn't have much to feed on, but the taps were leaking and starting to fall apart. And the towel rail at the foot of the bath was poised to fall in at any stage, with the Rawlplugs holding the brackets halfway out of the wall. You also had to balance yourself around the pool of water seeping out of the base of the toilet to approach the sink, which made it easier to strip off before starting your ablutions, if you didn't want to get your clothes wet. The wooden door was losing its stained varnish and looked like it was made of matchwood, with a sort of cat-flap at the bottom, which had no glass or covering in it.

However, the hotel did boast a sauna room in the basement, with three or four choices of massage service, so we might go and inspect that later (about 4.00 p.m.), as another way of passing the day until 9.00 p.m.

At 11.00 a.m. we decided to go and look for some food, visiting a KFC we saw opposite. The food package was okay, but expensive at 32 yuan each. However, it satisfied us enough.

After that, we went across the road to a JiaJiaJue Supermarket, to have a general look around. Inside, Ling noticed there was a cinema on the fourth floor, so we went upstairs to have a look, and ended up going to see Yimou's latest movie *A Simple Noodle Story*, which had only just been released, and took him three years to make. Although

I couldn't understand what was being said, the scenery was spectacular, as might be expected. It looked like it was filmed in some part of China's desert regions, with amazing formations of sandstone, in red and yellow colours, possibly caused by iron oxide, unless it was computer-generated.

In the middle of this desert, there was this remote inn which served noodles, owned by a rich, old guy who'd bought a young wife, but only kept her to put her head through holes in pictures of young boys – apparently because he didn't have any sons and wanted to look on this as some sort of compensation. From time to time, his hobby was burning holes in his wife's bottom with his pipe.

The beginning of the film started with an amazing scene, of a wandering Dervish selling guns, who gave displays of sword play. They bargained madly and the lady owner bought one gun for 3 yuan. He showed her how to load it with three bullets. Then this small patrol of soldiers came by, in a rather attractive blue battledress. I'm not sure what they wanted, but it seemed to involve the gun, which the lady concealed.

The sergeant was a great comic character. Ling told me the actor is famous in China, and had once been a farmer with no acting training. He had crossed eyes and a mouth which sloped downward, like a slice of orange.

Anyway, one of the soldiers came back and advised the old husband that his wife was having an affair with the chef, so the old man paid him some copper money for further information. The soldier noticed that he brought the money from a massive safe, which seemed to be full of gold and money. The soldier later came back and reported that he had proof, so the old man offered him money to murder the two lovers; the fee was 5000 yuan. The soldier asked for a 1000 deposit, which the old man reluctantly gave him. Then the soldier went off to find the couple, who were sleeping in a horse and cart, out in the desert. He went through the cart and took away the gun, but didn't kill them, instead taking away some clothing, which he cut with his knife and stained with animal blood. He went back to the old man in his cellar.

But there was then some dispute, so he shot the old man. When he went to get the money, he couldn't open the combination safe. He made his escape out of a window when he heard somebody coming. It was the young man. Finding the old man's body, the young man thought the wife had done it, so he took the body away and buried it in the desert.

Meanwhile, the soldier returned that night, as one of the

other workers – a guy with two buck teeth – went down to rob the safe, as he seemed to know the combination. While he was piling up the money, to run away with the serving maid, the soldier came back and killed the guy, taking his body away to bury and emptying the safe.

There was a bit of coming and going, but when the young man came back to wake the wife, they were discussing their next step when an arrow came through the window, killing him. The soldier started trying to shoot the wife, but she found the gun again, which the young man had found with the dead body of the husband; the soldier had left it there, apparently to make it look like suicide. She hid upstairs, but when the soldier put his hand through a hole in the wall, trying to unlock the door, she impaled his hand to the door with a pair of scissors – rather like a scene in the Coen brothers' film *Blood Simple*. When he broke through the door with his other hand, trying to pull out the scissors, she shot him through the door and he fell back down the stairs. So, the happy ending was that she now became the owner and had all the money.

Ever since watching this film, I've wanted to find a copy with English subtitles, but have been unsuccessful so far in 2020.

This took us up to 2.00 p.m. As we left, we noticed

some Korean buffet dishes at a restaurant next to the cinema, and they looked quite good and at a good price (around 10-15 yuan), so we decided to go back tonight for dinner. We then bought some fruit and went back to the hotel, to check out the sauna/massage place downstairs.

We did check it out, but Ling started having some misgivings, in case I should be led into a separate room and offered "extras". But the masseurs were all men and it all looked a bit seedy. The rooms had beds, in which the sheets didn't look too clean, and a guy behind a desk didn't appear to have any clothes on, although we could only see from the waist upward. Another guy was relaxing in one of about twenty armchairs, in front of a T.V. It was all probably quite harmless but, having changed our shoes in reception, Ling decided they might want to murder us, so we changed our minds and our shoes, and went back upstairs to our room. They even phoned us to ask why we changed our minds, and Ling sort of fobbed them off, saying: "Just looking."

At about 6.00 p.m., we went out in the cold and headed to the cinema area for our Korean meal. I chose beef chow mein for 10 yuan, which I think gave me stomach problems and diarrhoea, while Ling had seafood and rice. I also had a Diet Coke, which only cost 1.5 yuan.

After looking around the shop downstairs, we went back to the hotel, to pass the time until it was time to go for our train. We checked out at about 9.15 and walked to the station.

When we got there, the waiting hall was absolutely chock-a-block, and I couldn't imagine all these people getting on. Although we'd paid for first-class tickets, it seemed that everyone else had, too, as the sleeping compartments made up most of the train. It was a massive train, like the ones you see in American films, and we had to climb up a couple of steps to get on. They'd laid on a couple of extra carriages.

We got bottom bunks – numbers 13 and 14. The train was quite clean and the bunks were in three tiers, with no doors to the compartments.

The train set off on time, at 10.00 p.m., and I lay on my bunk and tucked into the duvet, for another sleepless ride. Ling translated one of the announcements at the beginning of the journey, warning against pickpockets who pretended to be friendly, offering you cigarettes and drinks which were doped, so that they could rob you when you went to sleep, then they would jump off the train somewhere. A ticket collector came round and took our tickets, giving us a plastic card in return. But, before the train stopped, they came back and returned our tickets, so I'm not sure the point of that. Extra security, I suppose.

There was quite a strong smell of smoke, as we were at the front, so I thought it might be a steam train. It also had an annoying habit of sounding the hooter every couple of minutes. However, I was surprised to find that I went to sleep. The next thing I knew, I was awoken at 5.15 a.m. We had an hour left to travel when they switched all the lights back on, half an hour before we reached Jinan.

THURSDAY 17TH DECEMBER 2009

We didn't have long to wait for a taxi back home, but when we reached Ling's mum's we couldn't get her to answer the door or telephone, and the door was double-locked from the inside. After fifteen minutes of ringing, knocking and waking up all the neighbours, Ling went to the concierge, who had an emergency phone, as we thought she might have had a heart attack. After a while I heard her answer the phone, and she came and let us in, having taken a sleeping pill the night before. She was usually up about this time of 6.30 a.m.

I had a shower, shave and change of clothes, but later in

the day I got stomach problems, and was in and out of the loo all day, so I didn't want any lunch or dinner. Plus, I still had some lower back pain which had been bothering me for a while: a muscle strain somehow, I think. Ling gave me some heat treatment in the afternoon, which helped, but I could only drink water all day.

Her sister and Lao came to see us in the afternoon, so I had to get up. They remarked that I always seemed to be getting ill, in one way or another, when I came to China.

When they'd gone, I managed to eat a little rice soup and half an egg, then went back to bed and watched *Lovejoy* on DVD, which I'd brought from the U.K.

So, that was another wasted day – except that Ling managed to get a certificate from the registry office, stating that she wasn't married, to assist with us getting a mortgage on this new flat.


FRIDAY 18$^{TH}$ DECEMBER 2009

It was supposed to be minus-ten degrees today, but it was quite sunny outside. I felt a bit better today, and had a breakfast of porridge and half a dragon fruit, followed by some orange vitamin drink. I also took an antibiotic pill.

Yen Bin came round to visit at lunchtime, to give the

contract for the flat a legal check over, and pointed out a couple of amendments required. He also invited us to attend his school's Christmas party on the 25th, hoping I might sing a carol or some such, or dress up as Santa. I agreed to sing "Twelve Days of Christmas", if Ling agreed to accompany me, and got some lyrics and routine together. It was for about twenty kids and their parents, so I wasn't sure how well it would go down. I had never entertained kids in this way before, especially in a language they wouldn't understand. I spent a couple of hours on the internet, looking for photos to illustrate the song on printed cards.

Yen Bin stayed for lunch, and I managed a couple of bowls of egg and tomato soup, and a few mouthfuls of rice.

Had a doze in bed for a while, then we went to the bank, for Ling to change some of her money from Sterling into yuan, and also transfer some from my account. She was surprised to learn that she only had £1800, when she thought it was £2800, but forgot that she'd changed a thousand last year and since spent it, over the past twelve months. She didn't seem too perturbed, so maybe she was going to ask her mum to top up the balance.

Leaving the bank, we dropped into a clothes shop and bought a pair of thermal underwear each, then got the 36 bus back home.

One goldfish had died while we were away, which wasn't too bad, as we still had eight left. And a guy was fitting a new kitchen sink, which took about three-and-a-half hours, as he kept having to go out and get more washers, or whatever.

Had dinner at 7.30 and I cooked everyone baked potatoes, adding cheese to mine – almost back to normal eating. I was having difficulty consuming some of Xiao Wang's cooking; it looked okay when raw, and I almost preferred to eat it that way, but by the time it arrived on the table, it was usually a soggy-looking mess.

SATURDAY 19TH DECEMBER 2009

Got up earlyish, feeling a bit better on all fronts, although with a few lingering symptoms.

Made a new loaf in the afternoon, which turned out the best yet in appearance, taste and texture – not sure what I did right, as we didn't have any measuring scales.

We went to do a bit of shopping after lunch, with Ling's sister (Zhang Min). Lao came in but went away again – not sure why; sometimes I only get about half of what's going on.

We were looking for cardboard to print some pictures on, to illustrate our proposed performance of "Twelve Days of Christmas". I'd got some nice images from *Google*, but needed to find some sheets of thin card, which we hadn't been able to locate as yet. We took a taxi to the shopping centre opposite the market, which can be reached by walking through the nearby park, called Yin Xu Shang (Heroes Mountain). It is quite a large park, about the size of Hyde Park, with a large statue of Chairman Mao near the entrance, leading up to a large hill, with a military museum at the top. Ling's brother Yan and I went up to it a couple of years ago, but we were the only people visiting it. It contains mainly relics of the civil war, with the Kuomintang and the Japanese occupying army. Tanks, guns and photos, plus a large, revolving stage as a centrepiece, depicted one of the deciding battles to win the city back.

Ling wanted to buy me yet another pair of pyjamas, as she'd got some reasonable ones for 14 yuan before, but whether the shops noticed me lurking around, I don't know; she was unable to get them for less than 50 yuan, which Zhang Min kindly paid. I usually try to hide when bargaining goes on, as they tend to put the prices up if they see a Westerner. Although, when you visit the larger supermarkets or department stores, the prices are generally set, unless there's some small defect which might generate a discount. Zhang Min also bought some sheets to take to her son Gong, in Guangzhou. She chose the material and they took about fifteen minutes to sew the edges.

Then we walked toward another supermarket called Silver Dragon, near the football ground, still looking for cardboard. We couldn't find any, so we bought a Christmas tree, instead, plus some decorations. Then Zhang Min invited us to go for tea and cake, which were being served at the Pizza Hut nearby. I paid for this, as she'd been paying for everything else. The coffee wasn't great but the cake was okay, though expensive, at about 30 yuan for each of us. I noticed the next day that there was a nice little cake and coffee shop near Ling's mum's, charging about half as much.

It was a bit like typical Saturday afternoon shopping in the U.K., and quite relaxing. We took a taxi home at about 4.00 p.m., although the girls dropped me off first, with the shopping, as they were going on somewhere else to get some sausages. Ling's mum let me in, and I think I managed to explain that the others would be along later, as they were shopping for more stuff.

I made up the Christmas tree and put some lights on it, which were quite effective – after all, it was only a token; we weren't going to celebrate in a big way. Apart from anything else, they don't really use ovens in China, so there's no demand for turkeys, etc. You can buy fruit and veg around the corner, which is usually just displayed bare on the pavement. This is okay, I suppose, as it has to be peeled anyway, but I'm a bit averse to buying meat on open display in the street.

When they came home about an hour later, we had some tea and I took Zhang Min's shopping down to the taxi rank for her. She was leaving for Guangzhou by plane tomorrow, at 9.00 a.m. – although, in my ignorance, I thought she said 9.00 p.m.

Back home, we had dinner and I enjoyed a glass of wine with a lamb stew, which has been one of the best dishes I've had at home – or maybe the least worst. I added some lamb Oxo cubes to it, to liven it up, as this is another thing missing from Chinese cooking. If it's not completely disguised by star anise, which I hate, it's usually very bland if not fried, as they don't seem to add salt, either, during the cooking process.

Went to bed at about 9.00, after having a shower and watching a *Lovejoy* DVD. Slept okay.

SUNDAY 20<sup>TH</sup> DECEMBER 2009

Got up at 8.30 and had the usual porridge and banana, followed by half a dragon fruit and some tea, with bread and marmalade.

Worked away at printing my pictures for "Twelve Days, etc...." as Ling found some reasonably thick paper yesterday. It was Xiao Wang's day off, so we cleaned the house, which hardly needed it. Still, we Hoovered and changed the water in the fish tank. A nice, sunny day, but cold.

Had more lamb stew for lunch, at 11.30, which tasted a bit better today. I decided to try and eat just one dish from now on, as I think that was one of the problems with my digestion: the Chinese want to have about ten different kinds of food at mealtimes, which doesn't really agree with me.

After lunch, we went out so that Ling could get some more medicine that she'd prepared, but the shop makes up for her. It was at the place which has more shop assistants than customers; while I was in there I counted twenty shop assistants to about ten customers, and it's not even half as big as a normal Boots store in the U.K. It rather tends to put me off shopping and looking at things, because as soon as you do, someone comes along and tries to press you to buy it. I'm not even confident what is supposed to be the correct price. However, I did manage to buy three custard tarts at the coffee and cake shop next door, on my own, which is almost a first, so perhaps I should start taking a more active role, instead of obeying all of Ling's instructions: "Do your coat up; tighten your scarf; don't open your jacket; wait outside; put your gloves on; wear something warm, etc."

We took a bus back a couple of stops, and bought some more train tickets at a hotel reception area, requiring two sleeper tickets, as we were going to Weihai again on Monday night, to pay the deposit for our new flat, sign documents (with Ling as an unmarried woman) and arrange the mortgage. The train would leave Jinan at midnight, arriving at 7.30 a.m.

Then we walked around the corner, to another large and cheaper supermarket area, where we bought some cards for printing, as they only come in packs of ten, and tried to get some basics for cooking a cake, which I attempted for the first time in my bread machine. Actually, this was the first time anyone has tried to make a cake in this flat, as they didn't have an oven. I managed to get baking soda, but the dictionary translation for baking powder turned out to be dried yeast.

Anyway, when we got back home, with me surreptitiously opening my padded coat – as, although it's cold, I'm always so well wrapped up that I start to sweat if we walk too quickly – I started baking my cake. I made do with sweetener instead of sugar, and walnuts instead of caraway seeds, which nobody seemed to know about.

Had lamb stew again with some fried rice, which Ma made. It was quite nice. But now Ling developed a cold. I hoped she would be better tomorrow, as we were travelling again. It was now my turn to look after her for a bit. She went to bed at 8.00 p.m.

I tried to get her computer connected, so that I could call Uncle Norman in Devon, but it seemed to be dead, so I would have to go and get it checked out tomorrow. Got an email from cousin Janet, to say that Richard's wife Heather died a couple of weeks ago. This wasn't a complete surprise, as we knew she'd been diagnosed with some kind of brain tumour, which meant that she would be bedridden for the rest of her life. I think she must have been about sixty-five.

Also got a nice email from Ricki at M.D.U., my last employer, disclosing a brilliant pay rise of £3500. Just after

I retired, as well!

Anyway, now up to date. Just tried that cake before going to bed at 9.45.


MONDAY 21<sup>ST</sup> DECEMBER 2009

Got up at about 8.00 a.m. and, after breakfast, went to a parade of shops parallel to the main road (Liu Li Shan), to get Trev's jumper. But, after a two-week wait, it was the wrong colour, so we had to ask for the right colour, which they said would take another two days. This is a narrow street, about half a mile long, full of small shop units, like lean-tos, with quite a variety of products: fresh fruit and veg, hairdressers, clothes, live chickens and pigeons, piled on top of each other in cages, goldfish, cakes, sweets, pet food and raw meat, outside on trestle tables. I felt sorry for one as we passed: a lady proudly displaying two joints of meat on a table, and nothing else. There were also fresh fish in washing-up bowls, second-hand bikes and mopeds, nuts, spices and so on.

The shops weren't too bad, even though just one storey, built up against a boundary wall to some flats, with trees growing out of the walls, and bikes and mopeds whizzing up and down. At least the shops had electricity, phones and internet connections, though I wasn't sure where they go for toilet facilities.

With my back still a bit sore, we went back to the main road and Ling took me to a massage place. It was not exactly a parlour, just three beds lined up next to each other, already occupied, as we could see from the glass door as we went in. There was a tiny reception desk between the door and the beds, and a coat hook, which I managed to get all my winter stuff on: hat, coat, scarf and two woolly jumpers. We didn't have long to wait, and I was soon ensconced on a bed, looking out through the glass front door. It was all guys doing the job, but very efficient. He gave a very strong deep-tissue massage (tui na), which lasted about twenty-five minutes, for 30 yuan. I could hardly get off the bed, as if I'd been pushed right into it, but felt a little better. Ling had a neck and back massage, which finished at the same time. They said we should both go back there, as they'd noticed a lot of hardness in the massage tissue, but we said we were going on a train journey that night, and this was just to help with that.

I'd started reading another Emil Gaboriau novel, *Intrigues of a Poisoner*, in which he mentions that, in seventeenth-century France, it was popular for nobility and the wealthy to visit baths and "etuvistes" before undertaking a long journey, or when coming back. Apart from the seedier side of these places, they used to give hot baths and massages for travellers. This book concerns some of the life of the Marquise de Brinvilliers, of which I have more details in another book.

During the afternoon, we managed to book Ling's ticket to the U.S.A. from Melbourne, on the same flight as mine, by Qantas, at 2000 Australian dollars. When I mentioned the price to Ling, she said that she doesn't want to go, though I don't know how she's planning to get out of Australia!

Cleaned the water and filter for the goldfish and had a rest during the afternoon, followed by a light dinner, then a shower and change of clothes.

We set off in the cold at about 11.00 p.m., with Ma seeing us off, and caught a taxi on a fairly deserted road. We reached the station at about 11.20. The waiting hall area was crowded, as usual, but they opened the floodgates to let us on at about 11.35. This train was another three-tier bunk affair, a bit dirtier than the previous one. I had the bottom bunk, because of my back, and Ling climbed onto the one above me. It was near the back of the train and quite cold, so we quickly wrapped ourselves up in the duvet, fully clothed.

## TUESDAY 22ND DECEMBER 2009

As usual, I got the enquiring looks from people passing by our open compartment, so I pulled my cap over my eyes, until the lights were switched off around 12.30 a.m. Didn't get much sleep during the journey, as it was a little cold, mainly with a draught on the back of my neck. But I must have slept a little, as the journey didn't seem too long. I got up for a quick toilet break at about 6.00 a.m., to get there before the last rush, before the train was due to stop at 7.30.

We left the station at Weihai just after 7.35 a.m., avoiding the touts looking to give us taxi rides to wherever. Ling asked one guy the price to Hotel Qiming, just out of curiosity, and he quoted 90 yuan, when we knew the usual taxi fare was about 25, so we told him to get lost. Wouldn't trust these guys, anyway, as there were plenty of taxis waiting in line outside the station. There was no reason to go with one of these probably unlicenced guys, so I don't know why they even bothered.

We made for the KFC nearby, where I had a decent breakfast of egg and bacon with coffee, followed by the use of their clean facilities. We phoned the estate agent, and for some reason she wouldn't come in for a cup of tea, so we had to go outside, and were driven to the office by her husband.

While Ling was going through all the negotiations, I waited outside, and the driver offered to show me a local part of the park, just across the road. It was very pleasant, though cold and icy. He explained that he was a keen fisherman. He didn't look very Chinese, and I would have guessed that he had some Greek blood, but Ling told me later that his grandmother was Russian. Very friendly, though, and he seemed to understand my halting Chinese okay, although I couldn't always understand his replies, except with sign language.

He then got a call on his mobile to say that the business was over, so we went back for Ling, and were then driven to the bank to transfer the fifty per cent deposit and get the mortgage sorted. Ling had produced a company stamp, from her sister, confirming that she was an employee of her sister's company. Even the bank colluded with the myth, and explained how much Ling should show as her earnings, in order to get the mortgage passed.

The driver and I went off again, to another part of the parkland, along the beach, and I took some photos of a snow-covered beach. We went back to wait outside the bank, and witnessed a minor motor collision in the car park, which involved half a dozen people phoning various places with their mobiles. But nobody approached us for statements.

Ling came out, with things apparently settled, so we were now the proud owners of a new flat in the main promenade of Weihai – although the property wouldn't be finished much before 2011.

The couple then drove us to the four-star Hotel Sophia, where we stayed the night for 220 yuan. Had a walk toward the town centre and went to a restaurant serving Western food, though I chose a Chinese-style chicken curry, which was okay, but served by a very sulky waitress.

Feeling a bit tired, we walked back to the hotel and had a rest. We were on the eighth floor, with an excellent view of the town and mountains on one side, and part of the port on the other.

We didn't bother going out again, but Ling got a call from Gong Di in Guangzhou, to say that Zhang Min (his mum-and Ling's sister) had fallen over and broken several bones in her ankle, so her holiday was definitely spoilt. It was to include a few days in Sanya, to the far south of China, which has a warm climate, white sands and luxury hotels. Current temperature there was twenty degrees, and house prices 20k (yuan) per square metre, compared to about 7k or 8k in Weihai.

Ling made enquiries about posting some American painkillers to her sister, but no one was willing to do the job, as it involved drugs not available in China, and might transgress some laws.

We went to the restaurant upstairs, to dine in the hotel, but as we were the only customers, it wasn't worth their while putting on the heating, so the food was sent to our room. I played safe anyway, with a vegetable chow mein.

WEDNESDAY 23RD DECEMBER 2009

Got up around 7.30 and, after a reasonable buffet breakfast of bacon and egg, eaten with chopsticks, plus coffee, we checked out at 9.00 a.m. There was some dispute about whether we'd opened a pack of biscuits from the minibar, but we'd only had a couple of the ones we'd brought with us, and when we asked to see the packet in question, there was just a tear in it and no biscuits taken. Why anyone would bother doing that, I don't know. Anyway, we showed them our own biscuits and didn't get charged, after a call to the manager.

We took a taxi to the bus station, passing the shell of the

building containing our flat on the way, and got straight on a bus to Rushan at 9.45.

It was a rather ramshackle affair, like the ones you see in South American movies, where the passengers are all crowded together, along with chickens and women having babies in the back – well, not exactly. We were fairly crammed in, though, with dirty dust covers over even dirtier seats. Once the bus was nearly full we set off, but the conductor kept the door open and shouted at various people, as we drove by. Ling explained to me that he was trying to cram on more customers, in which case he could keep the money he made for himself. When all the seats were full, he then produced some small camper stools from under the seats and put people on them down the aisle.

One old guy sat next to me, down below in the aisle. I noticed that the ring finger of his left hand was missing and wondered how that could happen. Did somebody cut off his finger to steal his gold ring?

Even though the bus was now full, we still took on more passengers: "Alright, there's room for one more, no problem. Yes, you can bring in your T.V. as well. Move along there, please." Eventually we left town and got on the motorway, but even then we stopped a few times to pick up people waiting along the hard shoulder. Then, just when

I thought we couldn't get anyone else on board, a family of three jammed themselves in, and a guy carrying a baby somehow made his way to the back of the bus, squeezing into the back seat.

When he got off, about fifteen minutes later, the old guy thought he might get a proper seat and tried to take his place, but a big, bully-type Chinese man told him to piss off.

A few people got off here and there, but I was still amazed when a lady brought on a computer desk, with the aid of a friend and the conductor. Then, while the bus was moving, he took over the driving himself, as no doubt there was no more passenger touting to be done, crawling over the driver and taking over the controls.

It took just over an hour to get into Rushan, and we alighted in the bus depot, in Rushan city itself, which is some distance away from the flat. I call it being in Rushan, but it is in fact in the beach area of Yintan (which I call "Ying Tong, Yiddle-Eye Po").

We wanted to book our train tickets back to Jinan first, so took a taxi. We were surprised to learn that the station was miles out in the middle of nowhere, apparently with no bus link, about fifteen minutes' drive away. We asked the driver to wait, while Ling went in to get the tickets. She was out fairly quickly, as there was no queue, and the driver took us back to town, to an excellent four-star hotel: The Oriental Mansion. There was even a firework display as we entered, though this wasn't for us, but a wedding party. We could hardly hear ourselves speak at reception, with the din of rockets going off – and I mean rockets! They were mounted on a sort of rocket-launcher vehicle, like something seen in the Gulf War, and were amazingly loud.

Having settled in a very nice room, with ensuite bathroom, very warm and with no feedback toilet smells, we set off again for Rushan beach, to check out our flat. There was a bus outside the hotel, so we decided to take that, although we had to wait about ten minutes before the driver decided it was time to go. Unfortunately, we seemed to have made a bad choice, as we had to change somewhere near the university, wait for another ten minutes, then the bus took us the back way into Yintan, through the market, before we realized that we were there. The whole journey took over an hour, whereas by taxi it's only about fifteen minutes.

A lady Ling was speaking to on the bus said that she had a flat near us, and was on the same errand, to check out her flat, which she bought seven years ago and was trying to sell. Another younger lady overheard me say something and looked around in surprise, announcing to everyone that she didn't know she'd been travelling with an American!

The market was virtually deserted, except that we noticed there were a lot more estate agent stalls, showing the market price in the area at 2800 yuan per square metre. The outside café, in the middle of the market, was just shutting up, but we managed to order a plate of fish dumplings each, at a total cost of 16 yuan, for lunch, as it was by now about 2.30. The place looked very dirty, and there were a couple of dogs rooting about under the tables, but as the food was cooked in boiling water, we thought it would be okay. It tasted alright, anyway, with some raw garlic, which Ling assured me settles the stomach. The cooker was black with dust, grease and heat, and the lady was doing some washing up in a bowl of cold, soapy water. We sat on stools at a plastic-topped table, under a sort of canvas awning, but we were warm enough.

Across the street I noticed some nice-looking bananas, so after our meal we stepped across to buy some, only to find out they were plastic! However, the real ones weren't too bad, and we also bought some oranges for our train trip the next day.

We stepped around to a more official-looking estate agents', but when we entered the warm office, with three people half-asleep in attendance, we were told they only sold their own property on behalf of the building company, so we made our way to the flat.

The streets were virtually deserted and the main restaurant, which look like a Walt Disney castle, was closed for the winter. Nearly all the flats were unoccupied, except for one or two, revealed by washing hanging out.

When we got to the flat, we were quite surprised by the lack of dust and dirt, and only had to sweep up a few very small dead flies clustered at the windows. We opened a few windows, as it was warmer outside, but things were remarkably fresh. The bedding and towels we'd left behind, seemed in fair condition, as we'd left them all in airy conditions, rather than sealed up in cases, etc., which didn't work last time; the changes in temperature caused condensation which went mouldy, when we'd left things in boxes and a suitcase. I turned the water on to test it, but couldn't get the electricity on. It probably needed to be switched on from a box outside, so I didn't bother.

We stayed for about an hour, then locked up again and went into the estate office, to check anything outstanding. We were told that we had to pay for electricity and water, which came to about 200 yuan – for four years! Then we went down to have a look at the beach area. It was all rather like a ghost town, deserted except for one or two locals, wandering about in a desultory manner.

We decided to go and find a bus or taxi back to the hotel, and were told about buses by a couple of students waiting to get back to the university. Lucky we'd chosen to leave then, as it was the last bus! We had to get off at the university and change to a different bus (also the last one), getting back to the hotel by about 5.30.

After having a wash and general tidy-up, we went downstairs and had a hot-pot dinner. They had these electric hot-plates at the table, with saucepans containing some kind of soup, which you just dipped the finely sliced meat into for a few seconds, which was enough to make it edible, after dipping it in a kind of peanut sauce. I had beef and Ling had lamb, with some cabbage, spinach and rather watery mushrooms.

After dinner we went back upstairs to watch T.V. and read, until going to bed at 9.00. It was too cold to go out exploring.

## THURSDAY 24<sup>TH</sup> DECEMBER 2009

Up at 7.30 and had breakfast of the usual – egg and bacon on toast – although there was a wide selection of Chinese dishes: noodles, fried rice, dumplings, etc. I washed it down with a couple of cups of coffee and some kind of long fried bread called "youtiao" – a little like a long doughnut, but not sweet and quite chewy.

We checked out at 8.15 and got a taxi to the station, arriving at about 8.35, where I was the object of interest for about fifty other people waiting for the train, in the rather cold waiting hall. We were let onto the huge platform at about 8.50, where it was a little warmer, in the early morning sunshine. The train arrived on time at 9.06, and we were the only ones getting into the first-class sleeper carriage, as it was a daytime journey; everyone else chose the seating cars, which were about 30 yuan cheaper. But we didn't mind paying a total of about 180 yuan for the seven-hour trip, to have the carriage virtually to ourselves – although it was an older and dirtier train than the one we'd had a week or so ago. At the end of the journey, one of the attendants ran a wet mop over the floor, after first brushing away the loose paper, orange peel, etc. It was an automatic kind of sweeping, not really removing much grime, but rather leaving the grime to establish itself in inaccessible parts of the carriage.

I took a few video scenes of passing scenery, reminiscent of Greece or southern Spain, with yellow, baked earth and rocks, although there were patches of snow here and there, with frozen ponds. I missed a good shot of a few local women, washing clothes at the edge of a frozen pond, where the ice had been broken up to show clear water. Also, I was trying to get some good views of the long, straight roads leading into the distance, looking as if they were interminable. There was something sad and desolate about these roads, where you might see one or two figures walking, or an occasional motor scooter. I felt that if I ever found myself on one of them, I'd somehow be doomed to stay on it forever, never finding the end, as it receded gradually into the far distance, without a bend, until it reached the misty horizon.

The fields contained very neat rows of apple trees and the remains of sweetcorn, which seemed to be the main crop. They piled the dried husks of sweetcorn onto their roofs in some places, maybe as insulation. Although it seemed to be prepared to make compost on other outbuildings, or in stacks in the fields, I didn't see any livestock along the whole way, except for a solitary cow here and there. There wasn't much greenery, as everything had died off for the winter, after a long, hot summer.

We had a tray of cooked food at 11.30, for 10 yuan, which I didn't really fancy eating. They came round again about two hours later, offering the same dish at half price. One lady attendant kept trying to sell us some souvenir packs of different denominations of Chinese money, which we declined, although she continued trying to sell these to us every time she walked past.

There were facilities on the train for hot drinking water to make tea and, as Ling was having a lie-down, I found the boiler at the end of the coach. It was rather an ancient item, in a cupboard on its own, with a box of coal dust nearby to keep it burning. The boiler was a dark, drab-looking affair, and the water dribbled out of the tap rather slowly.

We reached Jinan at 4.00 p.m. and were home by 4.30. The flat was nice and warm inside, and I made tea.

Ling's laptop had been fixed, and I read a few emails from Trev, Chris and Janet. I was concerned to note in internet banking that there was no pension payment for me this month, so I sent them off an email – although I expected it would be a week or so before I got a reply, it being over Christmas. It didn't really feel like Christmas Eve.

We headed out to Pizza Hut, but because there was a vast crowd waiting outside, we went instead to Barbecue Chicken on the other side of the plaza, which was okay. Everyone was wearing Santa hats and wishing us a merry

Christmas.

After that, we went home to check more emails, write in the diary, shower and to bed.

FRIDAY 25TH DECEMBER 2009

CHRISTMAS DAY

Got up at 7.45 and had a wash, shave and breakfast. Still didn't feel like Christmas, but we had a card each and this afternoon, at 4.30, Yen Bin would be coming to take us to the kids' party. We still hadn't rehearsed our carol singing act. Ling only had to sing the first line, but couldn't quite get into it.

Two more fish dead, so we now had five in the tank, which was about the right number.

Ling went out to get her new ten-year Chinese passport, as all the shops and offices, etc., were open as usual. This took about three hours, but she stopped at a couple of shops on the way back.

Yen Bin's wife came to collect us at 4.20, to take us to the school party. The car was driven by her sister, and their daughter, aged about seven, sat in the back with us – I can't remember their Chinese names.

We found the school with some difficulty, up near the

mountain area, and rather disorganized preparations were still being made. I was introduced to their part-time English teacher, a Chinese student whose major language degree was in German, but he spoke a little English, which I had a little difficulty understanding above the racket the screaming and laughing kids were making. They were running around in a fairly large play area, with marble floors and rather cold, so everyone kept their overcoats on. The teacher was quite a nice guy and we chatted for a while, as the parents set up tables and chairs, for food that each parent had prepared.

One plumpish young boy of about nine, who looked a bit tough but turned out to be very kind, introduced himself in English, and said his name was Andy. He produced a balloon and said: "This is for you." Later he sliced some pizza which was also for me. There were one or two dishes I was able to eat: some veg soup, a chicken wing and some Chinese fried buns.

The kids all sat at a separate table, and I think there were about twenty, aged from about three to nine. There was to be a show after the meal, and I could hardly imagine how they were going to be organized, as they were all running around in different directions. But, eventually some seats were lined up before a sort of stage, and gradually they were persuaded to calm down and do their party pieces. Andy played a couple of reasonable renditions of "Edelweiss" and something else, a couple did some recitations and a group of five kids sang an English song about "five little candles".

At the end, Yen Bin introduced me as an English professor acting as a consultant to the school, and Ling and I stepped up to sing "Twelve Days of Christmas". Ling kept forgetting her line, so I had to do it as well as my part, as we held up cards describing the gifts of each day. By some impromptu arrangement, the kids were also asked to hold up a card with a picture describing each day, which improved things a lot, so we got a good round of applause. I let the kids keep the cards they were holding. I had been kind of dreading the experience, but I didn't want to let Yen Bin down, so I went through with it – and it wasn't too bad.

Then they were to play some party games, so we left at about 7.30 and took a taxi home. It was freezing cold outside: about minus-eight degrees!

Glad to get in the warm again, where we celebrated the rest of the day with tea, toast and marmalade.


SATURDAY 26$^{TH}$ DECEMBER 2009

Got up at about 8.30, as nothing much to do today.

At lunch, Xiao Wang looked a bit fed up. I'm not sure if it was because I was cooking my own food, instead of eating her usual concoction, but mine wasn't much better. Ling had bought a rather scrawny cooked chicken yesterday, and I tried to make a chicken curry, but it didn't taste quite right. I don't know if the chickens here are bred differently, but they certainly aren't as big as the ones you get in U.K. supermarkets, whether battery or not, and I dare say that the food standards are different, although Ling assures me they do have health control authorities.

In the afternoon, we set off to get some electronic wires missing from our camera and DVD player. We took a K93 bus instead of a taxi, but it was about forty-five minutes across town, with a walk at the other end. At first, Ling wasn't sure we were in the right place, but we eventually reached the large electronic superstore.

This was a place over about five floors, full of individual units selling all kinds of electronic stuff: P.C.s, laptops, printers, cameras, printers, MP3, MP4 and even MP5, memory sticks, etc. We managed to get a U.S.B. cable for the camcorder, but when we got home I noticed that it was the wrong one. Ling bought a digital photo display machine with an 8" screen, for 470 yuan, which was quite versatile, playing DVDs as well as music C.D.s.

On the way back, on the bus, I looked out of the window, amazed at the diversity, and also the determination of people to start up some kind of business, even if it's just a load of bananas piled on the pavement, with people queuing up to buy. One lady, wrapped in about three overcoats, had a sort of electric tricycle with a trailer/barbecue on the back, and she was cooking something over the barbecue, pouring on sauce and turning it over while the customer patiently waited. It was on about five wooden skewers and looked like some kind of vegetable – or maybe it was small pieces of chicken; I couldn't quite make out. How they survive all day in the cold amazes me, although I suppose my friends Greg and Jeni do the same, when they work at Covent Garden market through the winter.

We got the bus back, which took nearly an hour, so we were home at about 5.30. We had a light dinner with a glass of wine.

I watched a DVD: *Icon*, by Frederick Forsyth, starring the late Patrick Swayze, who was quite convincing in his role as an ex-C.I.A. man specializing in Russia. It came to an end after about an hour and forty-five minutes, and a message on the screen said: *"To be continued"*. Luckily, part two followed.

At this point, I would mention that I spend a lot of time in the U.K. downloading videos, T.V. programmes and movies, to watch during long periods in China, as there's not much on T.V. here that I can understand. During the evenings, I would usually sit in a spare bedroom, which has been converted for use as a kind of office, with a computer and printer, and watch downloads on my laptop, while Ling and her mum watch Chinese soaps on the large screen in the living room.

## SUNDAY 27<sup>TH</sup> DECEMBER 2009

A sunny day, but about three degrees Celsius outside.

We made fish and chips with onion rings for lunch, which tasted okay, and went out for a walk at about 1.00 p.m. I went up to the bank, to test if my Natwest debit card worked in the A.T.M., and was pleased to find that it was okay, and paid me out in yuan notes without any problem. That would make things a little easier, being able to withdraw cash. I didn't realize this would work before.

Then we walked about a mile down the main road, to try out a nice-looking cake and tea shop we'd seen before. The menu on the wall advertised *"American Coffee, Latté,*

*Cappuccino and Espresso"*, but when I ordered a latté they said they didn't have any coffee at all – which is a bit of a joke. Maybe next time, though I'd have to put an order in two weeks in advance. They didn't even have ordinary Chinese tea. The only hot drink we could get was Chinese date tea. I asked for no sugar, but it was sweet as hell anyway, so I couldn't drink it, though the croissant was okay. But I was disappointed generally.

On the way back, Ling suggested we go for a reflexology massage. I didn't want to go at first, then she said: "Okay, just go home and write your boring diary, then." So, I agreed to go. Not that she's read my diary, anyway.

I was glad we went, however, as a charming young girl submitted my feet to some exquisite agony for about forty-five minutes. We first had our feet soaked in hot water with some herbs in it, then the girl started stroking my feet, which was okay, as I relaxed back on a couch. That was just her putting on some coconut cream, to make it easier to really start digging her fingers into some pretty tender spots on my feet; she knew exactly where to go. I felt a bit of a tinge as she brushed over the underside of my feet, down from the big toe, and thought: *Fine, she didn't notice that bit of pain.* But she soon came back to it and started digging in, causing me to squirm on the couch, while trying to be brave and not cry out; I didn't want her to think that we English are a load of sissies. Anyway, she found all the other spots, and a few in my lower leg. Altogether I think it was worthwhile for 65 yuan, as it was supposed to help with my back pain – we'd have to wait and see. I felt a bit better generally, although the soles of my feet were tender after the mild form of bastinado.

MONDAY 28<sup>TH</sup> DECEMBER 2009

After breakfast, we were invited by Yen Bin to have lunch with him at the Silver Plaza Hotel buffet, which served Western food, and you could eat and drink as much as you want for 120 yuan. I'm not particularly keen on overeating these days, although I knew the food there was quite good.

However, an hour later plans were changed, as Ling decided we should go and visit her sister in Guangzhou, in hospital, so that Ling could generally help out, and also help with getting Zhang Min back to Jinan in a couple of weeks. Her son Gong was a policeman and would be working most of the time.

It was a nice, sunny day, although about three degrees Celsius. At lunchtime, Lao came round with some clothes for Zhang Min, and also gave us some travelling money, probably on Zhang Min's instructions, as I think she had most of the money. Lao was only surviving on his pension, whereas Zhang Min had a business supplying soft furnishings to hotels all over China. She did quite well, although now retired, but I understand one company still owed her about a million yuan in unpaid bills, which she was taking legal action for. The legal system here is not quite so vigorous in private matters, whereas crimes against the State carry the death penalty.

I don't usually look at the newspapers, but there was quite a dramatic picture on the front page of a local paper the other day, which I asked Ling to explain to me. It showed one man on top of another, holding him down, but the man on top had blood all over his head and quite a lot had spilt onto the pavement. There was a bloody piece of pipe nearby, with a crowd looking on. I don't know how the photo was arranged, and nobody seemed to want to help. The man with the bloody head had a bandage on it, and the man underneath had some rope tied around his legs.

What had happened was this criminal had entered a shop, demanding money, and when the owner refused the criminal knocked him unconscious with a thin metal bar, and took money out of the till. While he was making his escape, a customer came into the shop and tried to stop him, but was struck over the head, causing him to bleed profusely. When the customer recovered, he ran out after the criminal, just in time to stop him riding off on a bicycle. The customer, who was about four inches shorter than the other man, then managed to drag him to the ground and hold him until someone called the police. An ambulance came first, though, and bandaged his head, but he refused to let go until the police arrived and arrested the criminal.

Apparently, on the one hand, you have criminals wanting to rob, etc., and on the other hand, private citizens are only too willing to try and stop them, unlike in the U.K. For example, bank staff will refuse to hand over money, even when threatened by criminals with guns.

After lunch, we started packing for a few days' trip and a courier arrived with our air tickets, which cost 600 yuan, one way, for our two-and-a-half-hour flight to Guangzhou. We took a taxi to the airport, which cost 130 yuan including toll charges, and arrived at about 2.45.

The airport building was quite an impressive piece of architecture, built of metal and glass in a sort of bird's wings shape. We quickly checked in and went to the waiting area for gate nine. The flight started at 4.00 p.m. and there was a bit of turbulence along the way, but otherwise okay. We had a nice meal of fish with rice and coffee.

I was reading a small volume of Confucius's sayings, to try and get into the culture a little, and was struck by some similarities with the Christian religion. I wondered if any of his teachings had come out of China to the Middle East, as he lived about five-hundred years before Christ. One of his sayings was particularly familiar in the Christian religion: *"Do unto others as you would be done by."* Maybe various civilizations were just developing independently along similar lines, but maybe ideas as well as trade caused these corresponding values.

We managed to find our way out of the airport with some difficulty, as there were no signs for the bus stop, but we found it by asking an airport employee. We were immediately ambushed by taxi touts, trying to persuade us to go with them. As I mentioned before, I couldn't see why any sensible person would accept their offer, rather than go to the officially licensed taxi ranks, which are safer and cheaper. Plus, there were plenty of coaches to take us to the city centre for 17 yuan, instead of 80 yuan for a taxi.

The coach took us to the five-star Garden Hotel, where we were to wait for one of Gong's friends to pick us up. It was a bit warmer here, at thirteen degrees, as opposed to three degrees in Jinan, but it started to feel a little colder as it got later. We were picked up by the friend, a Mr. Wong, in a brand-new Nissan, and arrived at the flat in fifteen minutes, in an area with quite a few Western food outlets: McDonald's, KFC, Subway, Starbucks and Haagen Das. He let us in with a spare key and left.

It was a modern two-bedroom apartment, but we weren't sure which room would be ours, so we waited for Gong to turn up. Eventually, Ling went out to get a takeaway and I stayed behind to let her back in. We had almost finished our food by the time he came back from work. He made us welcome and put down a large bottle of cognac, which had cost him 1900 yuan. I declined the offer of a drink of spirits, but gladly accepted the gift of a leather jacket, to wear while we were down here.

One new thing I noticed, while we were driving to Gong's place, was a double flyover – by which I mean that we were travelling along a one-way motorway and there was a flyover above us, going in the same direction, and another on top of that, which eventually led to a baffling "spaghetti" junction.

Later on, a guy came down from upstairs – a friend and neighbour of Gong (correct spelling), who could speak a little English. He said he thought I looked like Bruce

Willis, and I replied: "More like his dad." He told us his wife was asleep upstairs, but at about 9.00 p.m. he phoned her anyway and told her to come downstairs, as she could speak good English, having studied this subject at degree level, at Southampton University. She came down about fifteen minutes later, and indeed her English was good; I told her it was better than some you see on Chinese T.V. – or at least some of the announcers you get on the aeroplanes.

They left at about 11.00 and I decided to go to bed, while Gong had a few glasses of cognac. Ling stayed up chatting to him until 2.00 a.m. I couldn't sleep anyway, as it was cold in bed, even though Ling piled on another blanket and some coats.

TUESDAY 29TH DECEMBER 2009

Ling's sister went to visit her son about a week earlier, and fell over and broke her ankle, badly. She would need metal pins put in tomorrow, so we came down yesterday, so that Ling could give her some support in hospital and when she came out. The son, who worked as a policeman, would be at work a lot. He was a bodyguard to George Bush during the Olympics, and the Manchester United football team when they were over here last year. He had a United shirt signed by all the players, which was probably worth a fair bit, though he seemed to have plenty of money. He came home last night, after giving a meal to the surgeon doing the operation, and brought back a bottle of Martell brandy with him, which cost £190.

It was a bit warmer down here in Guangzhou – about 53 Fahrenheit – but cold in the flat, as there was no heating. It was quite cold at night; I had to wear long johns and two jumpers while sitting in the lounge, yet he just sat there in his shirt sleeves. There was even condensation running down the walls.

We had planned to stay here in February, on our way to Hong Kong, as it is only about a hundred miles away, but we could be here for a month at the moment, depending on how the operation goes. Then we would take the sister back to Jinan, which was a two-and-half-hour flight, but would take about twenty hours by train, I believe.

Taxis here are mostly green and silver VW Santanas, with cages to protect the driver, as there is quite a bit of crime here. Guangzhou is China's third-largest city, previously known as Canton, with a population of sixteen million.

We got up at 8.00 a.m., as arranged, but Gong didn't

arise until 9.30, although he didn't have much of a hangover. At 10.00 we went downstairs to have breakfast at a Cantonese restaurant. I had ho fun, a sort of fried egg, with a nice youtiao and coffee, which Gong bought from Starbucks across the road.

After that, Gong drove us in his Nissan to the army hospital, to visit Zhang Min. She shared a room with a young girl, aged about ten, who had fallen off a motorbike. Min's leg looked rather black and blue just above the ankle, which was bandaged. It looked as if the bone had penetrated the skin, but that wasn't the case. I couldn't imagine how they could operate with the skin looking so sore and swollen, and I was proved right later in the day, when they confirmed they would have to postpone the operation scheduled for Thursday, until the skin was in a better condition to heal after an op.

We stayed for about an hour, during which Min turned and changed her position quite a lot, and looked rather uncomfortable. We were shown her x-rays, which were developed in colour, and could clearly see the damage.

Gong drove us back to his flat and showed us where we could have lunch, but didn't stay himself, as he had to go to work at 1.00 p.m.

Ling said he'd been given a promotion, fast-tracked due

to his success as a bodyguard, and for various gold medals he'd received for his shooting ability. He now specialized in the bodyguard department for visiting dignitaries. He said there were a lot of African criminals in Guangzhou, and one was shot by the police last month. But, in spite of this, there were good trade relations with Africa, and we saw a large African trade centre not far from his flat.

Prior to him leaving, we went to a large superstore on several floors, across the road, which catered for Westerners, where I was able to get coffee, tea and Diet Coke, plus bread and butter. We also bought a bathmat for 100 yuan, then later found the same kind in the cheaper place for 55. After a lunch of chicken curry, very like the kind you get in the U.K., and tasting of curry powder, we went to do some more shopping at a cheaper supermarket. There we bought some packs of nuts, two bottles of wine for 29 yuan, another small mat for the bedroom, some glue to repair a panel in Gong's kitchen and some hooks for various doors, as there was nowhere to hang clothes or towels.

I suppose that was to be expected, as Gong was now a bachelor again, having been living with a girl for seven years until they got married; they were now divorced, after less than a year of marriage. Apparently, she was having an affair with one of his colleagues, while he was away at work – which seemed to be a common problem with married policemen here, having to be away from home a lot. We met the girl about six years ago, when they took a train trip to Jinan, which took about twenty hours, just to come and meet me, the first Westerner in the family. The girl could speak good English, but I now found that Gong's English wasn't too bad either. He was showing me how to get B.B.C. on the internet, and said, "Now you can choose whichever channel you want," which wasn't bad for someone who claimed not to speak much English.

We also bought a couple of plastic plates, to make it more convenient for Zhang Min to cut fruit in her hospital bed, plus some extra support cushions. We took the underground, which only opened yesterday, back to the hospital at about 3.45. It was raining a little and we had forgotten to take an umbrella. We stayed until Zhang Min had finished her dinner, and bought some soup for her at a canteen downstairs.

I noticed some rather nice trees nearby, about twenty feet high; they looked a little like flowering pink weigela, but with larger blooms. In a patch of ground in which the trees were growing, there was a mass of greenhouse plants, green with white veins, and leaves like the ace of spades;

there were several hundred of them.

We left about five-thirty and took a taxi, as it was raining quite hard and there was loads of traffic. We went back to get a small rubbish bin we'd bought for the bathroom, which was broken, and took it back to the shop to be replaced, which they did straight away. We spent another 2000 yuan here and carried our load back to the flat, stopping on the way to buy a roast chicken roll at Subway. I never shopped there in the U.K., but now appreciated their food over here.

After eating that, Ling found a small fan heater, which we installed in our bedroom, and I tried to fix the panel, getting glue all over the place. I eventually cleared it up, and think I managed to fix the panel, although the glue perhaps wasn't of the correct kind, being rather thin and more suitable for lighter work; it would probably fall down when Gong came back and went to do something in the kitchen – although, I think he lived more a sort of single person's life, eating out most of the time.

He hadn't come back yet, at 9.30, and we would probably go to bed soon; he'd probably gone out for a meal and/or a drink after work.

Ling then got a call from her sister, confirming the operation had been postponed for a few more days.

WEDNESDAY 30$^{\text{TH}}$ DECEMBER 2009

It was a bit warmer in bed last night, with the heater doing its stuff. Got up at about 8.00 and went to have breakfast in KFC, where you could get bacon and egg in a roll, youtiao and rice soup. There was a rather sad looking Westerner in there, about my age (possibly English, as there was an English school nearby).

After that, we went to the cheaper supermarket next door and did some more shopping, to help us to be more comfortable over the next four weeks or so. We were fitting hooks on the doors in Gong's flat, getting small mats and rubbish bins, plus plates and various other utensils. As he told Ling, she was the first person to cook anything in his kitchen, since he moved in two months ago.

Then Ling went to the hospital, as my presence wasn't required, so I returned to the flat. It was a bit warmer today, but I stayed in most of the time, tidying up and checking emails, etc. Then Ling phoned at about 1.45 to say that she was coming back. After fifteen minutes I went downstairs to wait for her, but she didn't get back for half an hour, as she'd stopped to do some shopping on the way.

We went to the same restaurant as yesterday, where I had

chicken chow mein and Ling had shredded pork and rice. Then we did a bit more shopping at the supermarket, for various groceries, wine, etc., and brought another load of stuff back to the flat.

Gong came back at about four. We were going to have a typical Guangzhou meal, but he wanted to get an extra support pillow for his mum. We drove to another prosperous part of town, where a new sports centre was being prepared for Asian Games 2010. It was an interesting area, and we passed many different restaurants along the way: Turkish, Italian, Spanish, Indonesian and Halal. We parked in a large hotel car park and went into an Ikea next door, where we ate the usual meatballs, having a little difficulty in finding a table.

We didn't buy a cushion which was priced at 299 yuan, but did buy a little folding table for eating in bed. Then we went across the road to another superstore, called Jusco. An amazing place, about the size of Brent Cross, but just one shop selling everything for the home. We found the right kind of full-length pillow for 88 yuan, which Zhang Min had spotted herself the day before her accident. We spent some time looking around, and Gong asked me to write his name on a cup he'd just bought, with a kind of Tippex pen, but it came off later.

We drove back home at about 8.30 and watched one of his DVDs: a disaster movie called *2012*, starring John Cusack and Woody Harrelson. It was in English with Chinese subtitles and, although not my cup of tea, I must say the special effects were very realistic – probably computer-generated. This kept us up late and we didn't get to bed until gone midnight, having had the heater on for a couple of hours.

THURSDAY 31$^{ST}$ DECEMBER 2009
NEW YEAR'S EVE.

Sunny again today, but a bit colder. Got up at 8.00 a.m., still with back pain which started a couple of weeks ago and just won't go away. But nothing compared to Trev's ailments, detailed in his last email: he now had osteoporosis in addition to rheumatoid arthritis, with a lack of bone density, plus a rather worrying red mark on his leg, which might turn cancerous if he was not careful. He had about four sets of scans and tests.

Took a shower and made breakfast of fried egg on toast. Gong didn't get up until 9.30. He and Ling went out to get some breakfast and go to the hospital together, while I stayed at home, catching up on some computer work and cleaning the flat. I went down to the supermarket at about 1.00 p.m. and bought some knives, forks and cups, getting a lunch of chicken and salad.

At 3.00 they came back, Gong having collected Ling's brother Feng from the airport, as an additional family support member. They hadn't had lunch, but just a few leftovers, as we would probably all go out for a meal tonight.

There was a school just down the road, and I could see their playground from the bedroom window. They had this loud music and entertainment going on all day, which was rather annoying.

Trev mentioned in one of his emails that he'd been having a few dreams concerning his fear of heights, which I was beginning to experience now, as we were living on the seventeenth floor. I had to remind myself not to try jumping out of the window. Defenestration, I think it's called.

Gong had to go to work, but we went out to meet him, travelling by underground during the rush hour, at 5.00 p.m. He parked his car around the corner, in a very narrow road, in which other cars sometimes parked, so it was almost impossible to drive out – although there was an attendant there, who would help you do a five-point turn. There didn't seem to be many restrictions, and people parked on pavements and all over the place. In theory, it's okay as long as you don't block other traffic. Bicycles seem to have right of way and go anywhere they want, although sometimes I thought we were going to run them over, as we edged into traffic. Horns are constantly in use, but so far I've only seen two collisions, which I suppose is more than I've seen in the U.K. for the same period.

We went to Gongyuanqian station, and had a devil of a time finding the right exit to meet Gong. The concourse was about three times the size of Piccadilly Circus Underground, and there were about seven exits, so we had to phone him on Feng's mobile, to find him.

The restaurant was located on the eighth floor of the China East Hotel, and we had a private room, designed to accommodate up to six people. There was a goose, plus a roasted chicken, with the head and comb still on, and glass noodles with prawns, which I preferred. We washed it down with a nice bottle of Great Wall red wine. Gong didn't drink too much, as he had to work that evening. The main course was actually a Japanese dish on a large bed of ice, containing raw shellfish and smoked salmon from Scotland. The total came to 786 yuan for four, which is fairly expensive for China, but luckily paid for by Gong.

We left at 9.00 p.m., and went to take some leftovers to Zhang Min in hospital.

Ling adjusted her pillows a few times, before we left at 9.30 to get a taxi home, for which we had to wait about fifteen minutes.

I wasn't sure if I would stay up to see the New Year in, as we were late last night, but we did stay up until midnight and, like Christmas, celebrated the New Year with tea and biscuits.

FRIDAY 1ST JANUARY 2010
NEW YEAR'S DAY

Woke to a new year and cooked breakfast of bacon, eggs and toast, for myself and Zhang Feng.

In the morning, when Gong returned home after his night shift, he then drove us out to a sort of museum. It was built in the Forbidden City style, although smaller, and previously belonged to the Chen clan – a rich family of merchants – in about 1894, although it looks a lot older. I don't suppose it belonged to the family for long; after the Revolution and Cultural Revolution it probably passed into State hands. However, it was completed in an age of traditional craftsmanship, when expense seemed to be no object for people with money and taste. The roof was adorned with numerous colourful figures, depicting various scenes, and just under the gabled roof there were some beautiful carvings in the actual bricks of the wall. Tall pillars, painted black, adorned the massive entrance gate, and there were several courtyards with ornamental trees, colourful shrubs and an atmosphere of quiet opulence. There were cabinets of fantastically carved ornaments in ivory, including the well-known hollow ball, with seven different moving centres. The insides of the stately halls had carved wooden ceilings, and there were fine examples of the furniture of the period. One room was devoted to a celibate woman, who lived her whole life there in elegance, but without male contact.

There was a nice tearoom, but this part of the place didn't seem to interest Gong, who conducted us on a tour around the place, having driven in through crowds of people, with Muslim salespeople selling nuts and raisins from stalls outside. His was one of the only cars in the inner car park; I don't know if he used his official pass to get us all in free.

There was the pleasant sound of someone playing the Chinese gourd-shaped flute, and I went in to watch a Chinese saleslady giving a demonstration of the various instruments. She let me try one, while a small crowd gathered around to watch me play the one tune that I'd managed to learn. I bought it for 58 yuan, as I'd left my other one back in the U.K.

We left the place and Gong took us for a drive around the city, until we stopped for a hot-pot lunch in a very busy place, and had masses of food, as usual, which was mostly fine beef and chicken, cooked at the table in boiling-hot rice soup.

After lunch at about 1.00 p.m., we then drove to a large garden and pet centre, as Gong wanted to get some tropical fish for his large tank at home. It was difficult to get somewhere to park, as the place was packed, so we had to park in a street outside, but not too far away. The place was massive, about twenty times the size of Covent Garden market, with whole streets selling almost everything to do with gardens and ornaments for the home: "You want to buy a couple of boulders? No problem, I'll just wrap them up for you or we can deliver this afternoon."

There were huge bonsai trees, if that's not a paradox: mature trees about six feet high, with twisted trunks, in large ornamental pots; whole streets of them, of all sizes, from teacup to bath size.

Also an array of fantastic flowering plants, which just

made you want to buy them: azaleas of all colours; orchids; exotic plants I didn't know the names of, in bright red, orange and yellow; fly-eating plants of huge dimensions – everything was of the best quality and condition, for just a few yuan.

On the way to the ornamental fish area, I passed some rather untidy boxes of cardboard and polystyrene, and found upon a closer look at the open containers that they held swarms of bees. "You want some bees? Fine, here's a box ready to take away. This one has about fifty thousand, give or take a few hundred."

There were streets of all kinds, with puppies in cages, cats to take away, lizards, toads, frogs, buckets of tadpoles, tortoises with fantastic patterns, and one rather regal looking yellow toad, which I was forbidden to photograph.

Then we came to the fish streets, and shops selling goldfish of all sizes, every kind of carp and tropical fish; whole shoals in aquaria, bubbling away with air pumps. I don't know how they survive in these cramped spaces, when the ones we bought seemed to die off within a few days, after giving them every attention I could think of.

You just couldn't make up your mind which to buy. Just as you thought you were ready to buy a bag of fish somewhere, another even better caught your eye, and you just had to go over to have a look. All these beautiful fish, of every colour in the sea, here just waiting to be taken home in a plastic bag.

After an hour or so, Gong settled on three red and three blue tropical fish, just a bit smaller than the palm of her hand, but roughly the same shape. When I looked at them from the side, they were quite large, with beautiful graded colours, but from the front they were quite narrow, and I kept thinking they must fall over. But no, they just floated around gracefully, with big eyes looking at me as if to say: "You can take me home if you want. I don't mind."

The salesman fished them out expertly and deposited them into a large, clear plastic bag full of water, which he then put into a couple of black plastic bags, then a final clear one, pumping it with enough oxygen to keep the fish alive for twenty-four hours, until we took them home. Gong paid the 350 yuan for six and carried his burden nonchalantly away, pausing at another place to buy about six months' supply of frozen worms.

We had to wait for a while to get out of the car park, as impatient drivers came down the middle of the road, stopping traffic from moving in the opposite direction, until police had to come along and sort out the mess.

Then we went to see Zhang Min in hospital and stayed

for about half an hour. Gong then drove me home, so he could sort out his fish, while Ling and Feng stayed behind. We took the fish home, but had to wait a couple of hours for the water to attain a minimum temperature of twenty-seven degrees. Meanwhile, Ling and Feng came home by underground, and we watched as Gong eventually got all the fish safely into his tank.

At about 6.00 p.m., Ling and I decided it was time for us to get a meal, so the four of us went out to a Spanish restaurant, within a ten-minute walk of Gong's flat. This time I ordered all the food and wine, with the usual: potatoes bravas, squid in batter, mushrooms in garlic, prawns, olives, sardines, paprika sausages, followed by prawns cooked with rice and black squid ink, which made everyone's lips and teeth go black. The meal came to about 600 yuan, which is quite expensive for Chinese standard, although about the same price as you would pay in London.

On the way home, Ling went to look at a clothes sale, and we bought some cheesecake near home, as well as six DVDs, from a guy selling them outside the flat for 50p each.

When we got back inside, we were unable to play one of them, a movie called *Surrogate* starring Bruce Willis (my lookalike). So instead we put one on starring Nicholas

Cage, called *Bad Lieutenant*, which was fine for about an hour, but then kept stopping and starting at crucial moments. I expected Gong to go rushing downstairs to wring the guy's neck, but he seemed quite philosophical, as we'd only paid 5 yuan each, and expected pirate copies not to be perfect. However, I later found that the Bruce Willis one played okay on the P.C. in our room.

SATURDAY 2<sup>ND</sup> JANUARY 2010

We went out for breakfast at KFC, at about 8.00 a.m., then Ling convinced me to go to a Chinese clinic nearby, to see if they could get rid of this back pain I'd been having.

The place was just around the corner, and a bit like the Chinese medicine places you see in the U.K., only this was partly an official government-organized clinic and partly private. We paid 500 yuan for a five-day course, of one-and-a-half hours a time.

The young doctor could speak a bit of English and asked me to lie down on a massage couch. The place was quite informal, with the front door open, so we could see traffic and people passing by. There were about five cubicles in there, mostly open, even though there were curtains available. He asked a few questions and got me to try a few exercises, to get a clue as to where the pain was, then started an exploratory massage. He eventually found a painful spot near my right hip and at the back of my right knee, where he then proceeded to exert extra pressure until it was almost unbearable, telling me to relax.

After about twenty minutes of intensive massage, he then applied a heat machine to my back, and inserted the acupuncture needles to various sore spots. After about half an hour, he removed the needles and I thought it was all over. But then I was moved to another bed, near an electronic impulse machine, and had some pads applied to my back. Then, after the machine was switched on, I could feel electrical prickles surging across my back, which was a little scary at first but felt okay, and that it might be doing some good.

It was time for lunch by the time we left, so we went to a place across the road, where they served a good spaghetti Bolognese for about 20 yuan – except on Mondays, when it was only 6.5 yuan. Then we went back to the flat.

Gong and Feng had already gone to the hospital, as Ling received a call from her sister not to go, as she was looking after me. They came back at about 4.00. At 6.00, Gong took Feng to the airport, as he was due to go back home to Hangzhou. Ling and I went for a cheap meal around the corner, where I had a nice dish of fried beef with tomatoes and rice.

When Gong got back, he had another visit from his friend upstairs, Liu Si Deng. As they were going to have a few beers, I decided to go to bed early, at about 9.30, as I had an early start at the doctors' the next day.

SUNDAY 3RD JANUARY 2010

Left the house at 8.00 a.m. and went to KFC for breakfast, then walked around the corner to the clinic. There wasn't anyone else waiting, so I went straight in to start another round of treatment, only this time he added an embellishment of straightening out my pelvis, with a few painful manoeuvres. While I was having the electric treatment at the end, a young boy came over to watch me. I kept thinking that if I closed my eyes he would turn up the voltage.

Went back to the flat at about 10.15, and Gong took Ling to the hospital again, to see her sister. They stayed there most of the day, so I had the place to myself. I did a bit of flute practice, checked my emails and, as it was a nice day – about eighteen degrees – I went out for a walk in the sunshine, which was almost like spring.

I walked a fair bit past the underground, crossed a bridge over the motorway and walked back, noting a French-Vietnamese restaurant along the way, and also an Italian. On another bridge, back across to where I started from, a guy encouraged me to have a look at some DVDs. As the price was reasonable, at 5 yuan, I bought ten, including *A Simple Noodle Story*, which I'd already seen, but was hoping to get English subtitles this time. There was also a brand-new film, not yet on release – *Avatar* – as well as Michael Caine's latest *Harry Brown, Public Enemy* and *The Men Who Stare at Goats*, which had a good cast, including Ewan McGregor, Kevin Spacey, Jeff Bridges and George Clooney.

Got back home and made myself a cheese and salad sandwich for lunch, then watched *The Men Who Stare at Goats* – not bad; quite funny in places and a good quality pirate copy.

Ling called at 5.30 to say that she was coming back, and we'd been invited to a meal with Gong and his girlfriend. I didn't even know he had one. We went to meet them across the road, at an excellent restaurant called The Greenery Café. I had Australian steak and spaghetti, which was excellent, and Gong had Bolognese. The girlfriend looked about twenty, but was in fact about thirty-five. Her name was Xiao Feng Liu, and she was also a police officer, although she didn't really look like one. She was very giggly and girlish, and spoke good English.

With no alcohol, the meal was over at 7.30, so we went back to the flat for English tea and cake. Ling gave Xiao Feng Liu some acupuncture in her ear, to cure some neck pain, which seemed to work. I'd already got some in my right ear, for the back pain, which hadn't worked yet. Plus, I now had a bit of pain in the back of my knees, where I'd been given acupuncture.

MONDAY 4$^{TH}$ JANUARY 2010

After breakfast of egg and bacon, I went along to the clinic for my third day of treatment, as Ling and Gong had already gone to the hospital to see her sister, whose operation was due at 8.00 a.m. When I arrived at the clinic at about 9.30, it was already quite busy, and the doctor I'd seen before wasn't there. In fact, there only was one doctor, and he was already giving acupuncture to three patients, lying down with needles stuck in them, and had just begun massaging another while writing out a prescription for yet another. I could see there was no point in waiting, so I phoned Ling to tell her I was going back to the flat and would try again in the afternoon.

Ling came back at lunchtime and we went back to the clinic, at 2.00 p.m. which was now virtually empty, though we ascertained that this was because it wasn't due to open again until 2.30, and the doctor was having a sleep in one of the cubicles. Gradually a few locals arrived, so we moved to a desk, where we could be at the front of the queue. He was roused at 2.30.

I was put down on a bed, and he explored the areas where the pain was, which he found after a quick massage. He put in about eight needles, at various painful parts of the lower back, buttock and behind the right knee. He also switched the hot lamp and went off to see other patients. One guy was sitting near the entrance, with a drip in his arm.

After about half an hour, he came back to remove the needles. Ling informed me that he was the main doctor and the guy yesterday was his assistant, although he looked quite young: I'd say about thirty. Anyway, he twisted me about a bit and suddenly jerked my head around. I felt a crunching sound in my throat, which felt like either my teeth or neckbones. He informed Ling that I'd had a joint out of place, which had caused some tension in the muscles of my upper back, but was not related to the lower pains.

He then informed us – correctly, I think – that the strain was caused by coughing, and prescribed some vile medicine to get rid of the cough. He also applied fifteen glass suction cups to my back, to remove water from my lungs. These left big, red blotches on my back, which looked frightening but weren't painful, and were a sign of the cupping doing its work.

Then we went to the dispensary to get some medicine, which was put in brown envelopes, each containing thirteen different kinds of powder, to mix together and drink in hot water. I went back to the flat and Ling went back to the hospital, where her sister was recovering from a successful operation.

Later in the afternoon I watched one of the DVDs I'd bought: *Harry Brown*, starring Michael Caine. It was quite a realistic story, set in a London housing estate run by local thugs and drug dealers, who kill Caine's best mate. So, at the age of about eighty, as an ex-marine fifty years previously, Harry decides he's had enough and sets to seek out the villains, killing most of them in quite tense scenes. Bearing in mind his age, he even has a minor heart attack while chasing one villain.

Gong came back for an hour or so before going to work, then Ling returned home at 6.00 p.m. We went to dinner at

The Greenery Café across the road, where Gong had taken us the night before. We had a cheaper meal this time; I had a good spaghetti Bolognese at 30 yuan.

Ling was feeling tired when we got back, so she went to bed at about 8.30. I followed soon after, having watched some news on CCTV9. I was also lucky to watch Arsenal beat West Ham in a cup tie. England had beaten South Africa in the second test a few days ago, and were currently in their first innings in the third test, on 241 for 7, in reply to South Africa's 295.

In other new records, snowstorms hit Beijing with twelve inches of snow overnight – the worst in fifty years – and Dubai opened the world's tallest building, with 164 floors.

## TUESDAY 5<sup>TH</sup> JANUARY 2010

We got up at about 8.00 a.m. and went to a cheap breakfast place around the corner, which cost 11 yuan for the two of us, except they didn't serve coffee or tea. So Ling kindly got me a coffee from Starbucks across the road, for 25 yuan; next time we'd probably take our own.

Then we went to Bank of China, to transfer 10,000 yuan to her business bank in Weihai, putting it aside to pay the next five instalments for our flat in Weihai. After some arguments, they said they couldn't do it, and charged Ling 50 yuan to give her the money in cash, which she could have got free from the cash machine outside. So, we had to go down the road, to the Guangdong branch of this business bank. But when we got there, they couldn't do it either. Ling had to take out a new account with them before they could transfer the money to Weihai. But, after all the hassle, we got that sorted.

We walked back along the hazardous pavement, which are hardly ever complete or straight. They are either interrupted by square areas holding trees – which would be okay if the pavements were wider, but as they are you have to step into the road – or when you come to driveways, hotel entrances, etc., the kerbstones are double the normal height. Outside the shops where Zhang Min fell over, the pavement slopes down dangerously from the shop to the road, with polished tiles, which become slippery when wet. As I mentioned before, most people feel safer walking on the road itself.

I noticed there were no motorcycles or scooters on the roads. Gong informed us this was because they were banned from the whole city, as too many criminals use them as getaway vehicles.

Just next door to the flat, there was a lot of repair work going on. I noticed that when they put up scaffolding they use long bamboo poles to walk along, when working high up, instead of wooden planks, or battens, as I think they are called. They looked kind of flimsy, but I was assured they are very strong.

News from the U.K. was that temperatures were down to minus-six degrees, and Manchester Airport was closed because of snow. Beijing also had its worst winter in fifty years, with the mercury below minus-ten.

After winning the second test in South Africa, England failed to get South Africa out in their second innings, with a score so far of 312 for 2, so it now looked like a draw was their best hope.

Ling went to the hospital again, after lunch down the road, at the place where the food is cheap but good. I had a chicken curry with rice again, and enjoyed this dish, which cost about 15 yuan.

I went back to the flat and in the afternoon watched the new blockbuster *Avatar*, which I quite enjoyed. It was looking set to be the biggest film in ticket sales since Titanic, also made by James Cameron.

Ling and Gong came home at about 6.00 p.m., but he went off again to meet some friends, and we went out by underground, to venture a bit farther from home for a change. On the way, we managed to avoid a rather insistent young beggar, who kept following us shouting: "Hello." He even tried to grab my arm, but we managed to shake him off. It was a bit disturbing, as he was about seventeen and looked quite smartly dressed, so maybe he had some mental problems. There have been a few beggars on the pavements, displaying where they'd had limbs amputated. A month ago there was a guy with no legs at all, riding around on a sort of platform on wheels, asking for money.

The underground took us to Guangzhou railway station and we had a walk around the large Jusco store. Ling bought some trousers from Uni Qlo, the Japanese store, where prices were about the same as in the U.K. We couldn't find a reasonably priced restaurant in this area, so settled for Pizza Hut, where the food was quite good. Generally, the food in Guangzhou is better than most places I've been to, and Gong did say it was more suited to Westerners. Although I understand that the heat is almost unbearable here in the summer, which makes me wonder how so many Chinese people can survive it, with a population of sixteen million. How do they do it?

Got the train home and went to bed at 9.00, as Ling had a long day, with the early visit to her sister, now recovering well.


WEDNESDAY 6<sup>TH</sup> JANUARY 2010

Got up at 8.00 a.m. and just saw Gong off to work.

I made egg and bacon, which wasn't too good, with the bacon sticking to the wok, as we didn't have a grill here. Then Ling kindly accompanied me to the clinic, where I had another back-healing session, which sometimes seemed more painful than the problem. Two acupuncture points were really painful, but he didn't put so many in today.

After a massage, one of the doctors twisted me about a bit, with me lying on my back, which was particularly painful. He then forced both my knees into my chest and jerked them upward, which sent a pain across my back, causing me to yelp and wake everybody up. I ended with the electric "tingler", with four electrodes on my back, which was quite a relief. I think it was doing me some good, however, as my back didn't feel near so bad – although I was taking it a little more easy.

We went to the cheaper supermarket and bought another fan heater, as the other one packed up. I bought two pairs of trousers, one of which only cost 49 yuan. They altered the lengths free of charge while we waited. Ling bought some slippers for her sister and I bought some veg for tonight's meal, as Ling had bought some chicken pieces, which I would fry with garlic and bacon.

I then stayed in to watch T.V. while Ling went back to the hospital. I prepared some of the food for tonight, which I would start cooking at about 5.00 p.m.

We did two washes of clothes this morning, having some trouble getting the machine to work. The second lot didn't spin very well, so it was now hanging up to drip dry. Also repaired one of Ling's earrings with some glue.

Went off then to see if I could do some animated film work, with the camcorder and a couple of oranges. I used a model of a policeman, a telephone box and a kumquat to make a five-second animation; it was rather limited.

During the rest of the afternoon, I prepared a dinner of fried chicken cooked in bacon grease, with potatoes, broccoli and carrots, and laid the table for three, red wine ready with three glasses. But when Ling phoned at 6.00 p.m., it was to tell me that we would be eating eat out; Gong was waiting downstairs with his girlfriend.

So, we went in the car to a large hotel, about twenty minutes' drive away near a big flyover, in a district which seemed to specialize in car tyres. We must have passed about fifty shops, almost all selling tyres, with just one or two selling windscreens and other motor parts. We went into the restaurant, and upstairs to a largish dining area, with hot pots set up on the tables. This place also had a branch in Beijing, and probably other cities. We had about five plates of thinly cut lamb slices to cook in the hot pot, together with mushrooms, cabbage, etc. and the usual peanut sauce. There was no alcohol, as it must have been a Muslim establishment, so we drank chamomile tea, instead. Ling paid the bill of about 350 yuan.

We left about 7.30-thirty and Ling told me we were going to karaoke. We arrived at a large building, with neon lighting stating that it was a "play centre", and in the foyer we ordered a room. When I say this was a karaoke place, I mean it *really* was. Compared to London, where you can maybe find one or two restaurants or pubs that do it, this was the real thing. It must have had about a hundred rooms, each with facilities for about six people, including their own private toilet. Our room was number 238, and I don't know if that was representative of how many rooms there were; we had to go up two flights of escalators. It was like a large hotel dedicated to karaoke, with several attendants in every corridor, checking you've everything you need. We could have helped ourselves to whatever food we wanted from the buffet, but we were all too full, though there were about a dozen fruit drinks on the table.

Included in the price of 67 yuan per person, for three hours, there was also a free buffet service and as many soft drinks as you wanted. We regretted spending money on a meal earlier on. If we were to go back during lunchtime, we could get three hours for 27 yuan each, including food from the buffet, so it was worth going there just for lunch.

However, we had a great night, and I managed to sing a few Beatles and Stones numbers, plus Chuck Berry and Nat King Cole. The recordings were by Chinese groups, and I was amazed at how well they recreated the guitar work, almost note for note exactly – "Johnny B. Goode", for example. Ling liked "Eleanor Rigby" best, which I managed to sing at the right pitch, as some of the others were in too high or too low a key. I was shocked to see that "Jumpin' Jack Flash" was first recorded in 1968, over forty years ago; it certainly doesn't seem that long. Some of the Chinese songs sung by the others were quite good, mostly Chinese versions of Western music. Gong had a powerful voice, mostly in good tune, while Ling and Xiao Feng Liu also sang nicely.

We left at 11.00, though I could have stayed longer, as I began to remember a few more songs to look up on the index, which was ordered by song titles, rather than artiste or group.

I think we went to bed at 11.45, after I checked the cricket scores on the internet, to see a virtual England collapse against South Africa. They still had to get about 490 runs and the day's score was 132 for 3. Felt a bit nostalgic as I was trying to get to sleep, as so many pieces of music evoked so many different memories.

THURSDAY 7$^{TH}$ JANUARY 2010

Time was passing; we'd now been in China for just over two months.

Was still waiting to hear about this month's rent being paid into my account, and hadn't yet received a reply about my pension not being paid last month – though they did say ten working days after 24$^{th}$ December.

Got up and had a shower. My back was still hurting a bit when we went downstairs for breakfast, costing 10 yuan, then went to the clinic. It was my last day of the course.

I had acupuncture and a hard massage, which lasted for about thirty minutes. The doctor mentioned that I shouldn't drink beer – which I'd had last night – as it was cold and wouldn't get rid of my coughing, but red wine and spirits were okay.

Ling bought some chocolate to take to her sister, then we went home and had a little of the chicken I made last night, washed down with a glass of wine – just for medicinal purposes.

Ling told me that Lao (Zhang Min's husband) would be coming today, as he'd been shamed into visiting by his friends and relatives, saying that he should be at his wife's side – although he wouldn't be able to do anything, and would probably be more of a nuisance. He would also not likely cook or do any housework – just smoke and drink – and we had no idea where he was going to sleep; maybe he would have our room, with its hard bed, and we would have to move into Gong's room. Or maybe he would sleep on the couch. We would await to see what transpires.

At 4.45 p.m. I was looking out of the window, from the seventeenth-floor flat, in a building with twenty-five floors. The view was from the back, and I could see about thirty similar-sized buildings, some even bigger, in a panoramic vista from the large windows. When you're walking in the streets below, the skyscrapers look so high it's almost frightening, and unbelievable that humans can build such massive buildings. In the case of China, most of this has been during the past twenty years. I guess it's like this in

New York, but the residents are used to it by now.

It felt colder today, as it was raining, but some workers across the way were still carrying on working on some renovation, covering themselves with plastic sheets stretched over the scaffolding.

Ling came home at about 6.00 p.m. and we went out in the rain to get dinner. Gong was waiting at the hospital for Lao to arrive by train from Jinan, a twenty-four-hour journey. We went to a place near the clinic, where I'd had spaghetti Bolognese before, so I ordered that again, for about 12 yuan. A free drink was included, so I asked for tea, but they said they only had lemon tea. So I asked: "Can I have lemon tea without the lemon?" But that wasn't possible, so I ordered that and took the lemon out myself. The tea was cold and didn't taste very good anyway, but the spaghetti was fine. Ling had sausage and rice.

We had a walk around in the rain afterward, and Ling bought some woolly leg warmers for her sister. We got back to the flat at about 7.30, and watched CCTV9 until Gong came home with friends Lei and Lao. Lao was Gong's stepfather, as he married Zhang Min after both of them had children from previous marriages. They didn't seem ready to go to bed, so I hit the sack at about 10.45, and Ling followed soon afterward. We had already

watched an episode of *Supernatural*, in English on Pearl
T.V., which I think might have come from Australia. The
others stayed up drinking, smoking and talking until about
3.00 a.m.

I briefly got up to go to the loo, and didn't get up until
9.30, with a sore throat, but my back felt a bit better.


FRIDAY 8TH JANUARY 2010

I don't know how they did it, but Lao and Gong got up at
about 7.30 and went off to the hospital, where Lao stayed
until about 4.00 p.m. Ling had taken him there to show
him the way by underground, but she came back about
11.00 a.m.

After a cup of tea, we decided to go to the Guangzhou
Museum, but it was closed for refurbishment, so we walked
to Beijing Road to have a look around the shops. We had a
nice lunch at the beginning of the shopping area: I had lamb
dumplings and Ling ordered spicy bread with lamb and
pork; we also got free soup. The bill came to about 45
yuan, and we were the last people to leave, at 2.00 p.m.

From the window I had been watching about five
builders, or labourers, loading up wheelbarrows with grey-
coloured breeze blocks, which they seemed to be rather

inefficient at doing. They had a mountain of blocks to move (I guess about ten thousand) and they could move about ten at a time. A couple of times they loaded the blocks the wrong way, the whole lot overbalanced and they had to start again. One guy upset his load and spent the next ten minutes on his mobile, while colleagues reloaded his barrow and took it off. Some of the bricks got broken or split, and I don't know how many were wasted. If that's an example of their work, I don't know how they manage to finish all these tower blocks, which seem to sprout up all over the place.

Beijing Lu is one of the major shopping malls, like Oxford Street, in a pedestrian-only precinct about a mile long with shops. The usual shops were there, and we were approached by several guys trying to sell watches or clothes from a sort of catalogue. We went to a bookstore, where Ling bought a couple of books and I bought some modelling clay, so I might try my hand at making some cartoon-type figures, to make an animated film in my spare time.

We almost went to the cinema to see *Avatar* in 3D, but we felt the tickets a bit pricey at £10, about the same as the U.K. That film must have been making a mint. I'd already watched the DVD, but wouldn't have minded seeing it in

3D. Ling doesn't really enjoy sci fi, being more into romances.

We walked to the end of the mall looking for a tea and cake shop, but couldn't find one with the right combination, so carried on past an interesting park near Guandong Yiu station, where we caught the underground back to the flat.

Ling's sister had just phoned to say that Lao had gone home, but couldn't get in as he didn't have a key, so we had to return to let him in. The marvels of everyone having mobile phones these days; how did we manage without them all those years ago?

We were all invited to a meal with the guy upstairs, Liu Si Deng. He had a shaven head and looked like a Shaolin monk, but was far from being one, judging by his drinking habits.

Gong took Ling and I, together with Lao and Liu Si Deng's four-year-old son and aunt, to the Red Calf Restaurant, about half an hour's drive away, due to heavy traffic. It was a large place on several floors, and we went to the second floor, to a private room, where we were also joined by Liu Si Deng's friend Mr. Chen. Aged about thirty, he worked in the Immigration Department, and assured me I should be okay to get an extension of my visa, which was due to run out on 5th February 2010.

We had hot pot again, with a choice of hot sauce or ordinary rice soup, along with slices of lamb and beef. The other hot pot, set into a black marble table, contained a mass of cooked prawns, frogs, bone marrow and squid, all mixed up with chillies and various spices. It was okay, but Lao started up with his usual obsession of getting me drunk, with the *gambei!* trick, where you have a small cup of Mou Tai, a white spirit, and when someone drinks a toast to you you're expected to empty the glass, even if you're in the middle of eating. I wasn't playing this game, so I just took a small sip each time, to be sociable. Toward the end of the evening, Mr. Chen begged me to have "Just one full cup." But after I agreed to that, they then tried to get me to have more. I probably had about six cups by the end of the evening, at 10.30, while everyone else had finished two litres of the stuff! I don't even like it, but they seem to feel that they are losing face if they can't make me follow their example. It is a particularly annoying custom, which puts me off even going out for a meal with a group, as I don't know how to avoid all the drinking without being disagreeable. If you sit at a table with ten people, they all want to perform *gambei!* ceremony with you, so you end up having ten drinks to their one. It seems a rather cruel way to force you to get drunk, but I suppose they feel it's being hospitable. One day I think I'll try and shock them, by pretending to have a fit and collapsing under the table.

Liu Si Deng drove home, as Gong, being a policeman, didn't want to risk getting caught drunk driving. Lao was pretty far gone, but was probably used to being in this state, which I didn't wish to emulate.

Went to bed at 11.30, but had indigestion through the night, and woke up sweating at 8.30 a.m.

SATURDAY 9TH JANUARY 2010

We went out for a cheap breakfast at about 9.30. Gong had been called to help a friend with something, and Lao went to the hospital. We would go this afternoon, when he came back.

We didn't know what to do, and Ling seemed rather listless and indecisive, so we went to the park we'd seen yesterday: the People's Park, near the Gunghzhoqian subway. There were some fine trees, the proper size of ones you see in bonsai style, and people were practising ballroom dancing in one area, alongside another group who were performing a Guangzhou style of Beijing Opera. We strolled around for a bit and, although there were some pleasant floral displays and statues, the park wasn't very big, so we soon came back to where we started. We watched some people doing a version of ballroom tango, but I couldn't persuade Ling to join in. There were lots of others doing tai qi.

We walked around for a bit, but with no real purpose, so we entered the underground and went for a coffee in McDonald's, before going back to the flat, where Ling went to have a lie-down. I bought some English-speaking papers and checked my emails. No word about my missing pension payment, nor rent for December.

England managed a draw with South Africa, which was unlucky for South Africa, as England were still about 190 behind, with only one wicket left.

Lao was at the hospital after being picked up at the station, so we made our own arrangements for a meal at around 6.00 p.m. We tried the usual place nearby, but as they kept us waiting for a long time, Ling said we should walk out. It was raining, so we took a shortcut to the fork in the road; to the right led to the clinic and to the left headed toward a Hong Kong restaurant and an Indian one, just past it. We decided to go for the Indian, where I ordered a biryani, but Ling burnt her mouth on a very hot chilli dip to go with the naan bread, so she didn't want to eat anything else. I finished most of the biryani, which was okay, plus some mixed vegetables cooked in yoghurt, and the bill came to 127 yuan.

We walked back through a small street, with a lot of brightly-lit shops. Although it felt a little scary down some of the dark side streets, it must have been okay, as there was a kid of about ten skateboarding around on his own, and a large kindergarten for Chinese and Western children. We must have looked like locals, as a Russian guy in a car asked for directions, which we were unable to supply.

We had a look around a shop displaying some exquisite vases and pottery, which was quite expensive at around 5000 yuan, but then Ling learnt there were discounts of eighty per cent being offered, so business couldn't have been great.

We got back about 8.30 p.m. and tried to watch a DVD. Then, just when I got it to work, Ling suggested we go to bed and watch it in the bedroom, as we didn't want to be disturbed when the others got back after drinking, etc. But then we couldn't get the one in the bedroom to play, and would learn from Gong the next day that it wasn't working.

Lao didn't come home, as he must have been offered a room by one of his drinking cronies, so Gong slept in his own bed instead of the couch. I don't know if these guys were alcoholics or not, but they certainly seemed to be set on going that way. I feel I've grown out of the habit of drinking a lot, just to prove how manly you must be. But I guess it's different for me, as I can't enjoy a conversation while drinking, due to the language barrier.

SUNDAY 10<sup>TH</sup> JANUARY 2010

I got up at about 9.15, still with a bit of a cough and lower back pain. I had a shower and shave, then we went around the corner to the left, to breakfast with Gong.

We had to go up about ten steep steps to enter, which seemed pointless to me, as it would be much more convenient to enter from the street, but no one seemed to know why; perhaps there was a surplus of steps going around at the time the buildings were put up. We thought it might be because the area is prone to the streets being flooded, but on the other side of the road you entered shops at street level, and they even had entrances going downward. Anyway, this place was quite cheap. I usually had a sort of ho fun dish, which is layers of congealed rice, with salty vegetables and a fried egg in between, plus youtiao. Ling and Gong each had rice soup with prawns and meat, all for about 15 yuan, which was okay. But they didn't serve tea or coffee, which was a bit of a blow.

As Gong had no real plans, he decided to go on a shopping expedition with his girlfriend, to buy more tropical fish and stuff for the flat, from the garden centre. They took me along, as Ling wanted to go and see her sister in hospital. The centre wasn't as busy as last time, and we found a parking place quite easily. I noticed several units were closed for the day; however, there were still some amazing items to be bought if you had enough money. There was one life-size carving of a rampant horse on a sort of plinth, made of wood, which would have cost about 100,000 yuan, and would need a large hotel foyer to house it – maybe that's where it was destined to end up. There were hundreds of carvings in mahogany, ebony and cherry wood, all beautifully carved out of whole tree trunks; even tree roots had been polished and shaped into items of furniture. There were some lovely porcelain Chinese ladies, in traditional dress, which were beautifully fashioned. I was tempted to buy one for 500 yuan, but managed to restrain myself.

Gong was spending enough for all three of us. He bought two cane chairs and a round table, to put in his covered balcony area, for a place to relax and drink tea. He also bought an ornamental Chinese tea set with a carved wooden tray, into which you pour hot water as part of the cup purifying process. The chairs, etc., cost about 1400 yuan and were delivered within half an hour of us returning home. The tea set was 1300, with a pound of tea thrown in for free. I was offered a seat while he decided which one to buy, and the owner offered me several cups of tea.

He was also looking to buy some ornaments. When I pointed out a reclining Buddha, which looked a bit like his friend Liu Si Deng, he laughed and bought it for 500 yuan. In this shop there were some attractive tables and chairs, made from wrecked wooden ships.

Then Gong bought some more ornamental fish – about twenty tiny ones of pink, purple, blue and orange – to liven up his tank, as the large fish were rather slow-moving.

On the way back, he dropped Liu Xiao Feng off and we returned to his flat, to unpack his treasures.

Later on, Ling came back with Lao and Lao's drinking friend, a rather smartly dressed young chap named Lei, who drove us to the restaurant in his BMW. Gong took his girlfriend when she arrived at the flat.

During this time I started making a model of Billy Bunter, making a framework of soft wire, which I covered with Play-Doh, in order to try making some animations later on.

We went to another large establishment and were served

loads of dishes. I was glad to note that we were only drinking beer instead of spirits. Although Lei always looked immaculate, he had a rather bad habit of spitting on the floor beside him at the table. Lao was looking a bit more subdued than usual and Gong did most of the talking. Three of the dishes, which they all said were delicious, were rather fatty-looking pork which I refused to eat, in spite of their entreaties. The only dish I was able to enjoy were some fried rice pancakes and a large white fish. I noticed the others weren't eating much either, and a whole plate of fried goose, which the waitress cooked before us at a sideboard nearby, was virtually untouched. At the end of the meal, there was loads left over and she looked a bit fed up, but we took most of it away with us in some polystyrene boxes, though I doubted if anyone would bother to eat the stuff.

Lei suggested we all go to the karaoke place, to which everyone agreed. Again it would have food included, so I failed to see the point of driving all the way to this other restaurant in the first place. It seems the Chinese economy has reached a stage where wasting money is now unimportant.

He drove us there in his new BMW, with computerized warning system, which lets you know if you're getting too close to the car in front, or near some obstruction when you're doing a three-point turn. Gong followed with Liu Xiao.

It was 9.30 when we arrived and we booked for three hours. We went up to the second-floor corridor, passing various other groups of people wailing into microphones. We ordered some popcorn, to go with about twenty cans of Heineken, although I tried to stick to tea.

Lei had quite a powerful voice, but was getting gradually more drunk with all the toasts. Ling later told me that he had been drinking with Lao through lunchtime. Ling was only able to sing a couple of songs, as her throat was sore, though Gong belted out a few numbers. Lao attempted a couple of Beijing Opera numbers and I opened with "Autumn Leaves".

During the evening Lei got almost paralytic and kept saying that he liked me, that he wanted Ling to be his auntie and that I was his uncle. When it was time to go, it was obvious he would be unable to drive, so we bustled him into the passenger seat and Gong had to drive him home. I went in a taxi, with Ling and Liu Xiao, in the rain.

We got home at about 1.00 a.m., and Ling phoned Gong to see how he was getting on. He'd delivered the guy home okay, just in time for him to vomit in the bathroom, and

Lao stayed over at his flat. Then Gong had to get a taxi back to the karaoke place, so he could drive his own car home, which he reached at about 2.00 a.m.

MONDAY 11<sup>TH</sup> JANUARY 2010

Gong left for work at about 7.30 a.m. and we didn't leave the flat until about 9.45, to go and have breakfast at a coffee bar we'd seen next to the Indian restaurant, where they served coffee for 15 yuan a cup, as opposed to Starbucks, who charge 25. But by the time we arrived breakfast was over, so we went to KFC and had a chicken roll and coffee, for about 40 yuan.

It was raining a little, so we went back to the flat until lunchtime, then went down the road, where I had beef and tomato with rice again. Ling had fried rice with pork and prawns. They gave a free glass of tea with every meal, but it was rather watery. The place seemed to be quite popular with students and office workers.

We then went into the offices of English First, which was an international language school, to see if I could get any work helping students with English. But after speaking to the principal there, it seemed that they were only interested in people with qualifications, though she did mention a friend running a private school who might be interested.

Later in the afternoon, we went to see Ling's sister in hospital and stayed with her for about an hour, until Lao arrived. We left at about 4.00 and walked down the road to an exhibition of goods from Hong Kong. There were a lot of people outside selling tickets at half price, but we decided to pay at the entrance, in case these tickets weren't acceptable, paying the full price of 10 yuan each.

At first it looked very disorganized, as there were so many people gathered around the booths. We couldn't see what they were displaying, but people seemed to be buying loads of the stuff: mainly dried foods, dried meat, fish and vegetables in plastic shrink-wrap. We were going to leave, but got drawn toward a demonstration of a new electric steam cleaner, which also served as an iron. It looked quite good at ironing shirts, etc., without an ironing board, removing stains and general cleaning – such as steam cleaning mattresses, for example – so we bought one for 200 yuan. It was about the size of a hairdryer.

Then I had about twenty minutes in a free massage chair, which would cost about 12,000 yuan to buy. It was quite good, but a little scary at first, as it felt like you were being gripped by a giant, who used his knuckles to dig into your back. I think it did some good, but I bought a small massage pillow instead for 100 yuan, to use while writing at my computer or travelling by air, etc.

Ling bought a new top, as a gift for the lady who facilitated the renewal of her Chinese passport.

We had coffee and cake at a bar, which was quite expensive, at a total of 100 yuan.

The newspapers reported that China overtook the U.S.A. in the buying of new cars last year, with about fifteen million vehicles being purchased in 2009. London had freezing conditions, with snow lying for about three weeks – its worst since 1981.

After depositing our purchases at the flat, we bade goodbye to Lao, who was catching the 9.00 p.m. train back to Jinan, then went downstairs for a meal of beef and tomatoes again.


TUESDAY 12TH JANUARY 2010

Got up at about 9.15 a.m., which was quite uncomfortable in some ways, as it was so cold in the flat in the mornings, and so warm in bed. We both had sore throats.

It was too late for breakfast, so we went to the cheap place, established in 1978, which served the same food all day and only cost 15 yuan. Then we went back to the flat for a cup of tea, and tidied up for the umpteenth time.

We didn't need to go to the hospital today, so we went for a walk, although it was a bit windy. We lunched at a Hong Kong restaurant called Brother Fat, where I had a Malaysian-style chicken curry. The flavour was okay, but as usual the chicken pieces weren't as good as the U.K. – a lot of gristle and skin. But there were some tasty bits, and the meal was generally satisfying. Ling had mixed rice and prawns. The total came to about 105 yuan.

We went for a walk around the usual area, bought some fruit at the market, and checked we hadn't won anything on the lottery. We had to go back at 2.00 p.m., as a guy had arrived to assemble a chest of drawers Gong had bought from Ikea. When he'd finished, we had a cup of tea and watched T.V. for a bit, then went for another walk. I bought some bread and Anchor butter, from the Friendship Department store across the road.

Gong's flat was quite nice and modern, but it was really built for the long, hot and humid summers, which made it a bit more uncomfortable in winter. In the evening I phoned Pete and mentioned this to him. He said: "If they spend so much money on property, why don't they spend anything on heating to make it more comfortable?" I suppose this was because the heating would be obsolete for nine months of the year, and the heaters would need to be put away somewhere.

The flat had marble floors everywhere, so we bought a few mats for the bathroom and beside the bed. The walls were painted a light green and the windows extended for the whole width of the rooms. There was a large, six-seater leather sofa, facing a large T.V. screen surrounded by dark bookshelves – for DVDs mostly. In one corner was a dining table with four chairs, and at the window another tea table with two cane chairs.

We were now in Gong's room, which had a T.V. and laptop computer. He'd moved into the other room, which was next to the utility room, where all the clothes were washed and hung up to dry. There was no heating, as I mentioned, but we bought a small fan heater which just about heated the space where you were sitting. And there was air conditioning for summer. The usual facilities were in the bathroom and the kitchen was rather small; you could easily bang your head on the extractor fan or fitted units, if not careful.

In the evening we went a bit farther afield, looking for somewhere to eat, but there was nothing which took our fancy, so we walked back toward the flat and had a meal at the Greenery Café opposite, which had several branches in Guangzhou. I had stewed veal with rice and Ling had frogs, which cost about 100 yuan. We enjoyed the comfortable chairs and warm surroundings, before returning home at 8.45 to watch T.V. and prepare for bed.

I forgot to mention that I phoned the Pension Service in the U.K., as they hadn't paid my pension in December. After waiting for fifteen minutes, I was told I'd been given the wrong phone number. I managed to get through on the new one, until I was then told that I had to be transferred to the International Department. They admitted they'd made a mistake and would arrange to pay my pension immediately, plus the payment due in January, which would otherwise have been missed as well.

Went to bed at 9.30 and watched *Fast Forward* – a new sci-fi type series from the U.S.A. – as it was warmer to go to bed early and lie under three duvets.

To sum up the weather, the temperatures in Jinan, which is to the north, are around two degrees Celsius, but most properties have central heating. Here in Guangzhou, quite far south, the temperatures are warmer in the daytime, at about eighteen degrees, but it gets colder at night and there's no heating.

WEDNESDAY 13<sup>TH</sup> JANUARY 2010

Got up at 9.15 and, as we would be late for breakfast outside, with Ling washing her hair, I made us bacon and eggs on toast, with tea, which turned out okay. Then we cleaned the flat again and got rid of a load of takeaway food from the fridge.

Went out to lunch at 12.30 and then to the hospital, where Ling wanted me to see about having a circumcision – which I didn't really want, but we would see. This plan was then abandoned for the time being – thankfully.

We went across the road to a Subway lunch place, where I had a roll with salad and meatballs. Ling left hers, as she didn't like the Dijon mustard.

We started off to go to the hospital but, as it was early, we decided to go to a museum instead, near the Jiuxue Park, which was the underground stop for the hospital, though we came out of a different exit. The underground stations are usually quite large, and sometimes have restaurants and supermarkets near the ticket offices, so if you come out of one exit it's nowhere near the other exits, and you have no idea where you are. The only way to find where you want to go is to head back underground and find the right exit, where there are usually plenty of directions.

The museum was an impressive red sandstone building, in a square shape, except for in the middle, where there were grassy courtyards and a sort of mound surmounted by a glass building, which protected the site of an ancient tomb. You can go right inside the excavations, which have massive blocks of stone covering the burial chambers, dating back to the twelfth century, for Emperor Zhu. The archaeologists found a lot of grave goods, as the tombs do not seem to have been assailed by tomb robbers, and most of these artefacts are on display in the museum – although the museum itself is a lot larger perhaps than the size of the collection warrants.

Entrance was free, and we spent about one-and-a-half hours having a cursory look at the exhibits: mainly gold seals in large glass cases, weapons, the remains of a chariot, pottery and various bronze cooking vessels. Apparently fifteen slaves were sacrificed for the burial, along with four concubines.

When we left, we saw a rather attractive Arabian restaurant nearby, which looked expensive, but they suggested they had a reasonably priced menu for lunch, at 68 yuan for a set meal. However, we decided to leave that for another time. Instead, we went to McDonald's so that Ling could make up for not eating her lunch. She had a chicken burger and I had a coffee.

We reached the hospital at about 3.30 p.m., and it was quite a pleasant afternoon. After paying our respects for about an hour, we went for a walk in Lake Park, across the road. This is quite a lovely lake, surrounded by large trees with long, hanging, fibrous roots, like the ones you see in American films set in the bayou area. On the other side was a large white restaurant, looking as if it was floating on the water: a beautiful building looking like something out of a Walt Disney movie, with a pointed clocktower and a dome on the other side. There was also another restaurant overlooking the lake, on the side where we were walking and, taking a look at their menu, it seemed quite reasonable; most dishes were about 40 yuan.

When we returned to the hospital, we met Gong and his girlfriend Xiao Feng, who said they were taking us for a meal nearer home.

We returned to the flat in Gong's car at 6.30, and met Liu Si Deng and his wife. We all went for dinner together, at a restaurant next to Brother Fat's – a very nicely decorated place, in red and green. We had a private room. I thought we would be sitting on the floor, Japanese style, but there was a deep area under the table where we could put our feet, so we could sit level with the table more comfortably. I was a bit concerned when they produced a bottle of Mou Tai, but Gong realized I wasn't interested, so he did not try convincing me to drink it, and shared the bottle with Liu Si Deng. The meal was okay and I enjoyed the dish of beef fried with cumin, some fried aubergines and potato.

We returned to the flat at 9.30 and Liu Si Deng sent his wife home, so that he could enjoy an evening drinking with Gong. Ling and I went to bed, but I could hear them up until 2.00 a.m., talking quietly. They just about finished the remaining half of a 1.5-litre bottle of cognac between them.

## THURSDAY 14ᵀᴴ JANUARY 2010

Got up first today, at about 8.15, and had a shower, as it seemed a bit warmer today. Gong left for work at 9.25, while Ling and I just made it in time to have a bacon-and-egg breakfast at KFC, which stopped serving this item at 9.30.

After that, we had a stroll down to the Friendship Supermarket, which is State-owned, to have a look at some glass fruit bowls, which we were thinking of buying for Gong as a small token for his hospitality – although we had been making ourselves useful: making his bed, cleaning the flat every day, washing and hanging his clothes. We saw some very nice glass bowls, reasonably priced at about 300 yuan, although China tea sets were being sold at around 2500 yuan.

We returned to the flat so that Ling could wash her hair, and I watched a crime report on T.V. It was quite disturbing CCTV footage of a girl being robbed and murdered at a cash machine, in a late-night cash-dispensing area. Although the criminal thought he was disguising himself cleverly, with a white mask, as worn by many people to avoid catching swine flu, he was wearing a distinctive red anorak and red trousers. You could tell he was acting suspiciously as he moved about in the bank's lobby, while the girl was getting her cash, apparently unaware of the threat. As she was putting the money in her bag, he stepped up and stabbed her in the back, damaging her liver and, grabbing her bag, he ran off. She bravely tried to run after him, but collapsed in the street outside and must have bled to death before the ambulance arrived. The crook was caught thirty-six hours later, having stupidly dropped the knife in the cash area, which he'd bought at a Walmart across the road on the same day. It was a distinctive brand, only sold there, and when the police crossed the road to the shop, they saw the criminal on

CCTV actually buying the knife, minus his mask, wearing the same red clothes. Apparently he'd tried to get a new bank card that day, but was refused as he only had 2 yuan in his account. He had committed this pointless and needless murder just to get 2000 yuan, which he probably didn't have time to enjoy, and would probably receive the death sentence for.

After doing another wash and hanging clothes to dry, and another thorough cleaning of the flat, disposing of rubbish, polishing surfaces, etc., we eventually left for Guangzhou railway station, via the underground, at 12.30.

We were going to take a look at the massive Guangzhou Wholesale Market, to see if we could find any silk pyjamas Greg and Jeni might find useful to sell in their new shop. Apparently the best place for this was Hangzhou, where we were last month, but were unlikely to go again for a while. The market area was a huge, bustling place, similar to Camden Market in London, but on a much larger scale. We saw many African and Indian businesspeople looking for bargains, to buy stuff in bulk, although it was also possible to buy single items at reasonable prices.

On leaving the underground, we came across a large underground complex of small shop units, where Ling bought two pairs of Gucci sunglasses for 100 yuan. They may not have been original, but on the other hand Gucci products were probably made in China anyway; these were just an overflow for local consumption.

Going outside in the warm sun, we asked for directions to somewhere we could look for silk garments, but couldn't find the right place, if it even existed. So we were forced underground again, to inspect interminable lines of clothing factory outlets. We couldn't find any silk pyjamas, except some padded or quilted ones, although there were a few selling nightdresses. One shop selling belts was quite informative; they were selling slim leather belts at about 10 yuan each, and broader ones for about 30 yuan apiece. They wouldn't allow me to photograph some examples, but agreed to send some pictures to my email address. We had a reasonable lunch here, of vegetable chow mein and noodle soup, with a sweetcorn drink, which came to a total of 18 yuan.

We eventually got fed up trailing around the market, so came back to ground level, where we found quite a pleasant walk, in a tree-lined street full of small shops, reminiscent of Chinatown in Paris. This took us to Lake Park near the hospital, which we reached at about 3.30 p.m.

We shared some fruit with Zhang Min and her fellow patient: a lady with a broken arm, who was being comforted by her husband. Zhang Min had also employed one of the hospital assistant nurses to give her some private attention, cleaning the room, running errands and helping her move in bed; this lady would sleep in a small foldaway cot at the foot of Zhang Min's bed. The leg was healing okay, but as her skin was in bad condition, with deep bruising, this was taking a bit longer before the stitches could be removed.

We left a bit earlier today and took the underground home, with the afternoon still quite warm at 5.00 p.m. We had a cup of tea and a biscuit at the flat, then went out to dine at the Honey House Café, next to the Indian restaurant. We had a nice meal, in pleasant surroundings, of Hawaiian pizza. Ling had beef stew on a bed of rice, and I had a good quality café espresso. We left here at about 8.30.

All along the rather uneven pavement, people had their wares displayed on mats resting on the pavement. Ling bought a comb made of cow horn, from a Tibetan street trader.

I forgot to mention one rather unpleasant sight last night. As we left the underground to come home, there was a mentally disturbed youth of about fourteen, writhing about on the pavement wearing only a vest and pants. A man was sitting nearby, stating that this was his disabled son, and asking for financial help, to pay for special care for the boy. However, Ling told me there had been an article on T.V. recently, where these guys go out to the countryside looking for disabled kids, taking them from their parents for a year; the parents are only too pleased to have the kids off their hands. These guys then use them as a tool for begging, and of course keep all the money for themselves, only providing a simple meal and bedding to these kids, to keep them alive until they get too worn out, when they are then returned to the real parents.

The main news of recent days was regarding the earthquake in Haiti, where China sent sixty rescue workers, with funds and equipment. I note that you don't seem to get much voluntary assistance from African or Muslim countries when these disasters happen.

On the way home we stopped at a rather interesting pottery shop, displaying some amazing designs of very high-quality workmanship and design. Ling advised me it belonged to two brothers, who made all the items themselves, showing a great deal of imagination and expertise in different mediums: pottery, metal and wood. When we asked the price of a fruit bowl which took my attention, we were told it was 2500 yuan, so we hastily left.

We stopped at the supermarket to buy a few snacks.

Whereas I might buy crisps and nuts, Ling's taste is more toward dried and salted goods: e.g. crispy duck lips, dried mandarin peel, preserved duckbills in soya sauce, boiled or pickled chicken feet and various other stuff, which we in the U.K. tend to throw away.

Got home at 9.45 and, although Gong's car was outside, he hadn't come home yet. Ling went to bed at 10.00, and myself just after. It was rather cold at first, as the windows, although closed, seemed to let in cold air. I was not quite able to locate the spot, inside the two duvets and one blanket, where it would start to warm up – just this cold air around the neck.

Although we were on the seventeenth floor, there was still quite a bit of noise from the street below, so I presume the windows weren't double glazed, and suppose there was no real need for it. Gong didn't seem to feel the cold, but he weighed about 100 kilos and was six feet tall. When he went to bed, he would wear these huge, padded pyjamas.

FRIDAY 15TH JANUARY 2010

Got up at 9.30 and made breakfast for the three of us, as Gong didn't go to work immediately, having gone to bed at 2.00 a.m. last night.

At 10.15 we went to the police station across the road, to get myself registered as living in the area, which is a legal requirement for all foreigners, and was also a prerequisite step before I could apply to get my visa extended, before leaving from Hong Kong at the end of February. The official was quite friendly and spoke good English, but advised me I needed to provide a passport photo, which we organized from a small shop across the road. The cost was 40 yuan, and for this they gave me six photos, plus a C.D. to get as many as I wanted printed when needed. It was a funny little shop, rather untidy, with mostly Kodak equipment; the girls wore Kodak jackets. They also advertised a floral service for weddings. The equipment was good, but they seemed to have a bit of a problem with the wiring, as their computer kept switching itself off. There were mops and buckets in a sort of foyer, holding empty plant pots and a lot of scaffolding, all the way around the building.

Gong had filled all the forms for me, and handed in proof of ownership of his flat to make it official. The next step was to ask his friend Mr. Chen if he could arrange the visa for me, without me having to go into the office. After all this was sorted, Gong went off to work and we returned to the flat, to tidy up before going out.

Just a bit about the money in China. I think Gong earned about 10,000 yuan a month, which is about £1000, plus he probably received extra bonuses and expenses for travel. His flat was worth about 500,000 and he had no mortgage, having sold his previous flat to buy this one, after his divorce. I think his mum Zhang Min probably helped him a lot with the finances.

The notes mostly in use are red in colour, with a value of 100 yuan or RMB (which means "people's money"), which is about £9, but I count as £10. There are also 50-yuan notes, which are green; 20 yuan, which are brown; 10 yuan, green again; and 5 yuan, which are blue. 1-yuan notes are light green. Then you get 5 mao, which is brown and worth half a yuan – about 5p in U.K. money. Then there are 1-mao notes and even coins of light aluminium worth one-tenth of a mao. As it isn't safe to flash your money around, I keep 100-yuan notes in one pocket and the smaller stuff separately, to pay for buses or underground, which cost about 2 yuan, and taxis at about 10. We can get breakfast for anything between 15 and 40 yuan for both of us, and evening meals start at about 20 – though if you go to Western places or big restaurants, it goes up to about 50 yuan to start. There are loads of KFC, McDonald's and Pizza Hut outlets, plus Subway and Starbucks. Some of the small fast-food Chinese restaurants are better and cheaper than the big ones, in my opinion, as I'm quite happy to have one dish of beef chow mein, as opposed to about twenty dishes on the table, which include only one or two that I like and create a lot of wastage. People here seem to take the stuff home, then throw it away a couple of days later.

We were having to watch the cash at the moment, as we had left Jinan in a bit of a hurry, and hadn't expected to stay here for so long. I had left my debit card there, plus my Bank of China passwords.

Before going to the hospital, we went along to a little shop, to buy some hot chestnuts for Zhang Min. This shop seemed to do a roaring trade, as there was always a queue of people outside. They charged from about 10 yuan upwards for a bag of chestnuts, peanuts or sunflower seeds. While we were waiting there, I counted fifty large sacks at the back of the shop, where they had two large machines for roasting the nuts. The whole front of the shop was open, like a market stall. When they took the cash, they just put it in a cardboard box on the counter, which seemed rather casual.

We took a train to Guangzhou Qian, to go and do some shopping in Beijing Lu, for an ankle support for Ling's sister, We had lunch nearby. I had lamb dumplings, pancake and beansprouts, while Ling had sweetcorn, carrot and rice soup, with a slice of beef in a bread roll and two skewers of lamb kebab. With tea, that came to about 50 yuan.

The shop didn't have what we wanted, although they did try (unsuccessfully) to sell me an electric massage machine. A couple of guys tried to sell me watches, which you could also get in Italy and Spain, but I wondered why anyone would want to buy an expensive watch from a guy in the street, with no guarantee or comeback, etc.

Zhang Min didn't want the peanuts, so I sat eating them, while Ling was chatting to her and the other lady with the broken arm. Zhang Min had a little trip around the hospital in a wheelchair, and had also bought a pair of crutches, so we hoped that was a good sign that she was getting better.

Trev mentioned today that he had signs of breakages in his spine, as shown on a recent x-ray, and had to take some extra pills, with all sorts of procedures involved. Plus, he was getting more pains in his feet and lower leg, which were so cold at night, causing him to take more painkillers.

We left at 5.00 p.m. and took the train home in the rush hour. Gong was playing basketball tonight, so we made our own arrangements for dinner. We didn't seem to do much cooking at night, as it was so cheap to eat out, and avoided having to do washing up. I noticed my pension hadn't been paid in yet, but hoped it would be there next Monday, which was the due date for January.

Ling was handed a flyer by a travel agent today, and we decided we may take a day trip somewhere, like Shenzhen, which was the first city to be created in the new China, around 1992, and now has a population the size of London. Or maybe Zhuhai, which is near Macao.

More news about the relief work in Haiti: about seven-thousand bodies buried so far.

Went to lunch at the usual place, about fifty yards to the right of our building, walking under the scaffolding. Most of the waitresses were young girls of about sixteen, but a couple spoke English and the service was usually quite quick. They always gave a free cup of tea before we ordered, plus chopsticks and spoons in a glass of hot water, for hygiene. I ordered my favourite of fried beef and tomatoes with rice, which I would have almost every day, but Ling always wanted to try something different; she had a Szechuan dish of chillies with pork and peppers. The total cost was 35 yuan.

Went to bed after a shower at 10.00, and watched *Miss Congeniality 2*, starring Sandra Bullock – nothing special –

after Ling had applied some rather painful acupuncture needles to my back.

SATURDAY 16TH JANUARY 2010

Got up at 10.00 this morning and made porridge for the three of us.

Ling went to the hospital with Gong, to help wash her sister's hair, so I spent the time finishing off my Billy Bunter model. Was not very happy with the result, as the Play-Doh was too soft for too much manipulation; I really needed plasticine, but wasn't sure where to get it.

Twenty degrees today. In Jinan it was about five, while Trev advised me it was about thirty-four in Australia. He'd had a long chat with Rob, who was due to retire this year, aged sixty-eight, and planned to move to Dorset.

Had my fave lunch of beef and tomatoes, and Ling had a rice mix with pork. In the afternoon, Gong took us to a sportswear shopping centre, to buy some casual clothes for his mum. He showed us one of the sports centres where they would be holding this year's Asian Games: another massive building with a futuristic design. The shop had everything you could want for sportswear, and even three table-tennis tables where you could practice before you buy, plus a mini putting area for those buying clubs and balls. I saw a lightweight two-person tent for 190 yuan, which I was almost tempted to buy, maybe to use in the U.K. next May for a camping holiday, but decided against it. It was all built in one piece, with a fitted groundsheet and two covers: one to let in air and an outer layer to keep off the rain. I ended up buying a swimming hat, to keep the sun off my head in hot weather, for about 10 yuan. Gong bought a basketful of stuff: trainers, tracksuit bottoms and tops, socks and an ankle support.

It was dark driving back at 9.30 and, as previously, I noted three levels of flyovers in one place. Three levels on top of each other, with another road underneath at ground level, all full of traffic, may give some idea of the volume of traffic in Guangzhou. Twenty years ago it would have been ground level only, with mainly bicycles, and the first road bridge over the Pearl River, which was built in 1932; the second was built in 1967. It got a bit scary driving along these flyovers – which were like a massive spaghetti junction – especially when travelling along the middle section, with traffic flowing above and below us; I had a sensation we would fall off any minute.

When we got home, we decided to go for an evening riverboat trip, while Gong took his girlfriend out for a meal.

We took a taxi to the river, where we were inundated by youths giving us flyers for travel holidays. The river is about the same width as the Thames. The boat trip cost 50 yuan each, for just over an hour and the boat had two decks, with chairs around the sides, and dining tables and chairs down the centre, complete with tablecloths. We were given free tea during the trip, but had chosen the wrong night to get a meal on board, which was only served twice a week. However, it was quite enjoyable, with some excellent views of the high-rise buildings, all lit with various patterns of neon. We passed by the five-star White Swan Hotel and a huge tower, which looked like a giant vase, made of glass and a network of iron. Maybe there would be a building a bit like this when they finished The Shard at London Bridge, destined to be one of Europe's highest buildings.

We got home at about 9.00 and went to the cheaper restaurant. I had chicken chow mein, taking half of it home for the next day.

SUNDAY 17<sup>TH</sup> JANUARY 2010

We decided to take one of the coach trips, from details we'd seen on one of last night's flyers. So we booked seats, at 68 yuan each, for the one-and-a-half-hour drive to the south China coast, at Zhuhai, which is next to Macao, divided by the estuary of the Pearl River. We had to get up at 6.00 a.m., in order to get ready and meet the bus at 6.50, at the entrance to the Garden Hotel around the corner. It was just getting light when the bus arrived.

It was quite a large single decker, blue with about fifty people on board. It was a bit cramped, although the bus was clean. The suspension wasn't great, and I think our seats were just above the rear wheels.

Driving out of Guangzhou, past the Colourful Days Hotel, we crossed the river on one of the bridges we'd seen last night. Along the motorways I could see several banana plantations, as it never gets below zero here. The weather was a bit hazy, but during the day the temperature rose to twenty degrees Celsius.

As we were agreeing that 68 yuan was reasonable for this round trip, returning at 7.30 p.m., we were rudely awakened by a twenty-minute nonstop commentary, after which we had to pay an extra 290 yuan each, to include entry to various scenic spots. It felt like a rip-off, but nobody else seemed to be complaining, so we paid up as we didn't have much choice. Altogether, it was still quite good value at 350 yuan each, for a day trip including sightseeing, lunch and entry fees for the whole day.

On reaching the outskirts of Zhuhai, the first place we stopped at was an agricultural college, where we could see all kinds of plants, fruits and vegetables growing, a bit like Kew Gardens. I took a few photos of huge gourds and strange cucumbers, hanging from a trellis inside hothouses. The whole place looked very well run and organized. That took half an hour.

We were then taken to a famous house nearby, owned by the Chen family, who also had the impressive temple-like building in Guangzhou. The park was well landscaped, with avenues of the palm trees, so perfect they almost looked as if manufactured. The trunks were perfectly straight and unblemished, with about six feet of green leaves waiting to unfurl near the top, and crowned by the well-known palm shape. At the entrance to each avenue was an ornamental stone gate. The house wasn't quite so large as the one in Guangzhou, but this was where Mr. Chen was born. He went to live in America a hundred years ago, and became one of China's first people to earn a million dollars abroad, from his textile business.

We were also given a show on a small stage, with a performance from one of the Beijing Opera face-change scenes, where the dancer performs to recorded music, changing his face mask in the blink of an eye, without seeming to do anything. I think it somehow works having several colourful masks on, which can be released by a shake of the head only – but it's so fast you can't see how they do it.

We spent half an hour in this place, then were driven to a factory making health foods. *A-ha,* we thought, *here comes the sales pitch,* which these tours usually included – like the one in Nanjing, where we listened to a *rat-a-tat-tat* delivery by a nonstop-speaking salesman, using a microphone, for twenty minutes. And indeed, here we were subjected to another twenty-minute tirade, extolling the virtues of their dried fish and Omega 3, 6 and 9 oils to prolong longevity. I almost dozed off, as did Ling, during this patter, of which I didn't understand a word – though I did watch as he set fire to a Styrofoam bowl for some inexplicable reason, and poured various liquids into a glass. At the end, a group of salesgirls streamed in, making noises like seagulls, distributing packets of the product to whom they hoped would be prospective buyers. At the cost of 580 a pack for fish-oil face masks, and packets of thirty pills for 380, we declined, although one or two people bought stuff.

We exited out through another sales area, full of salespeople displaying various packaged goods, like

Woolworths, all containing various dried fish products of precisely no interest to me. But I did buy a hot sweet potato from a street vendor outside, for 2 yuan.

We were then taken to another sales place, this one described as a great opportunity to buy illegal foreign goods, like Gucci, Hugo Boss, etc. at discount prices. This was also a letdown, as I might have bought bootleg DVDs for 5 yuan, but they only had handbags and watches at U.K. prices.

There was a group of hopeful fruit vendors outside this place, and some touts offering a chance to have your photo taken against a backdrop of Macao, which you could see on the opposite side of the estuary. But when we all got back on the bus, I watched them disperse, having sold only a few apples and oranges.

Now it was time for lunch. I heard the words "five-star hotel" and my hopes were raised, but in fact we were being told we would be *driving past* a five-star hotel, to one of the most disreputable streets I've ever seen here; a rundown restaurant in a poverty-stricken back street. We were allocated ten to a table, and were given the most basic meal possible, which must have cost the tour operators about 3 yuan each: we had rice and about six plates of vegetables between the ten of us; the only meat offered was a few bits of chopped up chicken leg, mostly skin and bone.

Next was a boat trip around Macao Harbour, for which they tried to rent us binoculars, for 20 yuan for one hour. As I was feeling angry with them, I decided not to accept this, and instead used the telephoto lens on my camcorder. On the boat, we found people there charging only 10 yuan.

Still, this part of the trip was more enjoyable, as we had quite a good view of Macao, including the Portuguese Catholic Church on a hill, and a massive building called The Lisboa Palace Hotel. We sailed under a massive road bridge, to some distant islands (I'm not sure which), and generally the view was impressive. Macao, of course, had been a foreign concession, owned by the Portuguese for about 300 years, and used by the British in the nineteenth century, to trade opium for tea and silks. It became independent ten years ago and the anniversary had recently been celebrated.

It was quite warm as we left the boat. While Ling used the port's toilets I waited outside, where a young lady tried to sell me Rolex watches for 100 yuan. When I showed her I already had a watch, she said: "Okay, two for one hundred."

When I shook my head again, she said: "Okay, four for one hundred."

"No thanks."

"Okay, four for *two*-hundred!"

I managed to convince her to leave me alone, just as Ling rejoined me and we got back on the bus.

They'd saved the best bit for last. We went to a large park and "Yuen Ming Yen Sin Ming" – a copy of a palace built by the Ming Dynasty, which had been rebuilt in 1992 after being derelict since the 1800s, having been burnt down by European occupiers including the British. It was a fantastic reconstruction, which only the Chinese could afford these days. First there were three gates and palaces, in the Forbidden City style, with grand squares full of statues and incense-burning pagodas. Then there were parks all the way around, where you could take an electric car to get around. We chose to pay 10 yuan each, and were driven around by a young chap giving a rather mechanical commentary, which I didn't understand anyway, stopping occasionally to take photos of a replica part of the Great Wall and some massive rocks, which I'm not sure were real or not.

Past the palace there was a large lake, with a fort at one end. On the opposite side there was a Western-style galleon, complete with cannon. Apparently, every night there was a show depicting the battle between the Chinese fort and the European invaders, with cannon fire on both sides. We would have liked to stay and watch this, but time was restricted. We also missed a show in a lovely theatre, showing scenes of how the emperor chose his concubines.

Up a slight hill behind some trees from the path, we entered a magnificent square, all in white with a huge bronze fountain in the middle, surrounded by waterways and fountains all the way around. On the opposite side to the theatre, there was a flight of steps leading to an ornamental building. Everything was in white stone – some marble, some painted concrete – with more bronze statues, in the shape of the twelve animals of the Chinese zodiac. There were waterfall cascades going down the steps, but nothing was switched on in the time we were there.

The park itself was full of exotic trees. Monkey puzzle and rubber plant trees stood about thirty feet high, and floral displays were everywhere.

When we got off the trolley, we had a pleasant walk around and stopped at a kiosk to eat some hot noodles, as we hadn't really been satisfied with the lunch. All the way around the complex, dotted amongst the plants, there were statues and various tearooms in different styles, plus hot-dog booths and other various refreshments.

It was certainly a place to recommend for a day out. The ticket price for this was 120 yuan, which we'd paid on the bus.

We got back on the bus at about 5.00 p.m., and were told it was time to go back. They refused to stop for Ling, who wanted to find a toilet, but luckily they did stop about forty-five minutes later, at a relief stop for everyone on the coach, once we got back on the motorway. Before that, I enjoyed the beach views, as the bus took the scenic view to leave town. It reminded me a bit of Torquay, but the gardens beside the beach were better.

We got back to Guangzhou at 7.30, and they dropped us off some distance from the station, which was a difficult walk across roads and uneven pavements. The station was a nightmare conglomeration, of thousands of pedestrians pulling suitcases on wheels, and buses and coaches all squeezed up together, trying to stop people walking between them; there didn't seem to be any pathway for people on foot. At last, we spotted the underground entrance and took the two-stop ride back home.

To save money, we ate at the cheap place downstairs. I had an excellent chicken chow mein, and brought some home to eat the next day, which in fact I didn't do. We also spent about 80 yuan replenishing the larder.

We went to bed, quite tired, at 10.00 p.m.


MONDAY 18<sup>TH</sup> JANUARY 2010

Got up at 8.00 and we both had a shower. I made egg and sausage for breakfast, as Gong left for work. We went back to the flat, and spent more time cleaning and checking out the fish, as I had to remove one which didn't look too healthy; it seemed to have grazed the skin off on one side. Then spent some time on the internet checking out hotels in Hong Kong and Sydney, before deciding to leave that until a bit later.

Gong took my passport to try and get my visa extended, but I was told I should wait until we go back to Jinan, where I could get it extended from 1<sup>st</sup> February for an extra month. We weren't going to Hong Kong until 27<sup>th</sup> February, to catch our flight to Sydney on 1<sup>st</sup> March.

Went to the Honey Place Café for lunch, where I had Mexican pizza and Ling had pork and rice. Afterwards, we were planning to take the underground to the hospital, but Gong had come home, so we went with him in his car. Apparently, Zhang Min was feeling a lot better and should be released from hospital this Wednesday. Then we'd go back to Jinan with Gong, who was getting our tickets for a flight on Thursday; he'd be coming with us to help with the luggage.

At the hospital, Zhang Min had a brief practice on the crutches, but would need to do a bit more before she could get about effectively.

It was quite warm this afternoon, at twenty-two degrees; Ling even let me go out without a jumper!

We came back at about 4.30, and Gong changed some of the water in his aquarium, then went out to buy some various medicines for his fish, some of which were looking a bit seedy. The one we separated this morning looked as if it wouldn't survive the night. These fish were supposed to live for about three to four years, and I couldn't really understand what was wrong, as Gong gave them every attention. We consulted the internet several times, trying to understand all the complicated scenarios and advice.

Xiao Feng came round at 6.00 p.m. and asked me to correct her speech for tomorrow, for her competition in English. Then we invited them to dinner at The Greenery Café, across the road, where we had a nice meal. I had spaghetti Bolognese, and Ling ordered rice with various shellfish, for which she had to wait until the rest of us had finished. Xiao had a Japanese soup, with noodles and frogs, while Gong had a steak and finished off everybody else's leftovers.

He took Xiao back home after the meal, then Ling and I went to the Friendship Store, to buy a gift for Gong's hospitality. We bought him a large glass fruit bowl, made in Germany, which cost 318 yuan.

Checked my email when I got home, and found that my pension still hadn't been paid into my account. I'd give them another day before I complained, as it probably takes five working days for banks to transfer money here. I also wrote cancelling my mobile with Vodafone, but they said my contract was until August, so I would have to pay a penalty of four months' payments should I wish to cancel. I wrote back to cancel anyway, as it was still cheaper than continuing to pay rental for the next six months.

Then back to the flat. After checking the fish and writing all this, we went off to bed at 10.00 p.m.

## TUESDAY 19<sup>TH</sup> JANUARY 2010

Got up at 8.30 and Gong already left for work. We had porridge for breakfast and dragon fruit, then did some clothes washing and tried out the steam iron/cleaner. It wasn't very good as an iron, but okay as a cleaner.

I received an email from Sennen (ex-M.D.U. work

colleague from Hong Kong) re. tax advice, and he recommended Stanford Hotel in Hong Kong, where we would be going for two nights from 27th February. There was also an email from Veronique re. change of plans. She was now not going to Spain in June, but maybe Italy, which was nearer.

We went shopping near Tianhe Sports Centre, which we reached by underground. There were a lot of very high buildings when we emerged from the underground and entered the shopping mall, which was so big we didn't know where to start. However, after two hours, all we succeeded in buying was a purple, short-sleeved jumper for me at 49 yuan. Ling had been given 1000 yuan by her sister, to buy some gifts for a friend, but couldn't find anything. We also had difficulty choosing a place to eat at, and settled for a Kung Fu fast-food restaurant, which was pretty crap: twisted pieces of fatty, chewy beef with rice and soggy cabbage. I couldn't understand why the place was so full – mostly of mums with their kids.

We left at about 1.30 and went home for a rest. Ling went to the hospital by herself and I lazed around the flat, reading *Global Times*, hanging up Gong's washing, cleaning the flat and checking emails.

Ling came home at 6.00 p.m. and Gong asked us to

dinner with his friend, Mr. Chen, who was getting married tomorrow. We went to a restaurant nearby and had some decent food. I took a bottle of wine, in case they were in for a heavy drinking session, but this didn't happen, as they settled for a couple of glasses of beer. Ling and I finished the bottle between us, with some good food: fried squid, alligator or crocodile and eel in ice, which was better than the dreaded jellied eels. Mr. Chen's girlfriend arrived near the end and we all left at 9.30.

When we got home, we met a couple of friends of Gong's, who came in for tea, and were later joined by Liu Si Deng in his dressing-gown, as he'd just had shower. He had to go to the hospital tomorrow, having been sent there a couple of days ago, due to excessive drinking.

Another of the Blue Discus died, so I had to remove it from the tank. Then went to bed at about 11.00 p.m.


WEDNESDAY 20TH JANUARY 2010

Zhang Min was due out of hospital this afternoon, at about 2.30, so we got up early to prepare the flat for her coming home. We moved our bedding from Gong's room and put it into the other, stripping his bedding so that he could sleep on the sofa. Then we put clean sheets on the bed Zhang

Min was going to use and commenced cleaning the flat, yet again. I sorted out a few clothes to leave here in Guangzhou, to save bringing them again when we returned on 25<sup>th</sup> February.

We went to the lunch place around the corner and I had my favourite: beef, tomatoes and rice. It was quite a satisfying meal, with lean meat and tasty tomatoes, for the reasonable price of 12 yuan. Ling had some pork with sauce and rice.

Then we went to the hospital on a warm, humid day of about twenty-two degrees, arriving at 2.25. Gong was there with his girlfriend, but then he took her to Guangzhou station, as she was going to Hong Kong for a couple of days, to do with her work.

We waited around for Zhang Min to leave, but she was waiting for Gong to come back with his car. Gong had given us 10,000 yuan to pay hospital fees for his mum, but when Ling went to pay at the office, it only came to 1952 yuan, as Zhang Min had previously worked for this army hospital. Plus, she had already given them a deposit of 20,000, so about 18,000 was given back. By the time we got back to the room Zhang Min was loaded, with 38,000 yuan, which she put in her laptop case.

When Gong got back at about 3.30, he and Ling helped

Zhang Min into a wheelchair, and took her downstairs in the lift. I had been waiting with loads of cases and bags, in the garden below, where it was quite warm outside. Then Liu Si Deng arrived with his Lexus people carrier, and they loaded Zhang Min into it. Ling went with her in the car and I went home with Gong.

It was quite a struggle getting her up the stairs, into the block of flats, although there was a steep ramp to assist with this. She hadn't had much time to practice with the crutches or the wheelchair, and it was very difficult helping her move around. She sat on the sofa for a couple of hours, then went to bed while a few neighbours came to visit.

At 5.30 Ling went out to get a takeaway, and I made myself a cheese and tomato sandwich – not real cheese, like you buy in the U.K., but mostly cheese slices in different flavours.

Zhang Min went to bed at about 7.30, after all the visitors had left, and Gong went out with Liu Si Deng. At 8.00 p.m. Mr. Lei came for a visit, and looked a bit sheepish after his drunken display at the karaoke. When I asked Ling, jokingly at the time, if he was homosexual, she said no, as often Chinese men touch each other with friendly affection, but not in a sexual way. Ling started to tell the others, even though I told her to keep it to herself, and later she mentioned it to Lao, who in turn told Lei. Anyway, there didn't seem to be any hard feelings, because he invited us to tea at his flat the next time we came to Guangzhou.

## THURSDAY 21ST JANUARY 2010

We all got up at about 8.00 a.m., exchanging shifts in the bathroom. Gong had come in at about 2.00 a.m., but was still quite fresh, after having a goodbye drink with Liu Si Deng, as he would be coming back to Jinan with us for a few days. Ling went next door for a takeaway breakfast and I made tea.

The flat looked a mess, with all the cases and bags waiting to be packed. I couldn't imagine how Zhang Min would be able to get so much stuff on the plane, including crutches and a wheelchair. However, somehow Ling managed it, and we were ready to leave at about 10.30. Gong and I took all the cases down first and put them in the car. He didn't pack the boot very well, and we had to put some stuff in the back seat; I couldn't see how he would get us all to the airport. We then went upstairs to help Zhang Min get into the lift, etc., but when we got back into the flat Ling and Zhang Min had already left, going down in the other lift as we were coming up in the other. We had to wait quite a while to get back down again, expecting them to be waiting for us at the bottom, but they'd already got into Liu Si Deng's people carrier. So that's why Gong hadn't worried about the packing, as we were travelling in two vehicles to the airport.

Guangzhou airport is the biggest in Asia, even bigger than Beijing, but I didn't get a chance to see the full extent of the building, as Gong drove us into the police/security compound area. He then took us into the nearby V.I.P. lounge, usually reserved for visiting dignitaries; as there was only us, we were ushered into a lounge, where Gong said the Queen would be ensconced if she ever came to the city. He then went off to get our luggage checked in, taking our passports with him. Meanwhile, we were served a delicious tea, served by a hostess, while I read the free *China Daily* in English. The lounge had eight large, plush leather armchairs and a nice carpet, but I couldn't say that it looked all that luxurious. When I went to the loo, I noticed there were half a dozen more similar lounges nearby. The toilet seat had a cellophane wrapper around it and, when you pressed a button (which I did, to see what would happen), it changed the wrapper for a clean and fresh piece.

When it was time to leave, we passed through the

normal security screen and were then driven to the plane in a minibus. Getting Zhang Min onto the plane's steps presented a problem, but Gong took her on his back, piggyback style, and got her up to the top. We were the first people on the plane and Zhang Min was given a first-class seat; we sat near the front, just behind. When all the other passengers were allowed on, there was a spare seat in first class, so the steward allowed Gong to sit with his mum.

It was quite a good flight, leaving at noon, and took about two hours. Lunch was served at 1.00 p.m., and was quite a good chicken and rice dish. When we arrived at Jinan, we could immediately feel the drop in temperature, down from twenty-two to minus-two degrees.

Lao was there to meet us, with a friend driving a minibus. This was better for Zhang Min, as three guys were able to lift her straight on without leaving her wheelchair.

We went back to her place first, noting quite a bit of snow and ice about. We sat and had tea for a couple of hours, while I sat by myself watching T.V., as everyone was speaking Chinese, of course.

A neighbour came in to cook some dinner for Zhang Min, while the rest of us went to a restaurant with Lao's friend, Mr. Wong. We were going to a place which I remembered we'd been to before, where I hadn't liked the food or filthy toilets. As they had a bottle of Mou Tai with them, I bought a bottle of Chengyu red wine – or rather, Gong put it on the bill. We had a private room, and I was pleased to note that the food was much better this time: fried prawns without the skin, which were delicious, plus duck feet in mustard sauce, which were okay, and some large fried dumplings. I finished the wine off by myself, and noticed the bottle they'd brought was quite small for between the three of them. At least Lao wasn't drunk when he drove us the short distance home. He couldn't get parked right outside the entrance to Ling's mum's flat, so we left him to drive off into the night, while we went upstairs with our cases.

It was good to be back with Ling's mum, who came to greet us. After unpacking, I had a great shower and a haircut, and went to bed at about 11.00 p.m. It was pretty hot with the central heating – a sharp contrast to Guangzhou, where it was quite cold and damp at night. As we'd left, I'd noticed patches of wet on the walls in Gong's flat, just from condensation, as there didn't seem to be adequate ventilation, apart from opening all the windows.

FRIDAY 22<sup>ND</sup> JANUARY 2010

Woke up at about 5.00 a.m., with about three cats wailing outside and someone upstairs chopping vegetables, presumably preparing to cook someone's lunch to take to work. These were just a couple of the annoying things about our room, which I'd noticed before. I was also sweating from the heating, even with a light duvet. We got up shortly after the arrival of Xiao Wang, at 8.00.

I had breakfast of porridge, after the others, who went out to get some local fruit and veg. I took this opportunity to make some bread in my machine, otherwise it would get a bit awkward, with Xiao Wang cleaning and getting lunch ready, usually to be served at 11.30.

I had a bit of lamb with rice for lunch, but the cooked chicken didn't look very inviting: skin, gristle, bones and feet, all mixed up in a rather unhealthy-looking sauce.

Ling and I went out at 12.30 and walked up to the Bank of China, where I withdrew 2500 yuan, to pay Gong back 2000 for our return ticket to Guangzhou on 25<sup>th</sup> February. Then we took a number 4 bus to the Silver Plaza supermarket, to look for trousers for Trev, but they only had winter stuff. We bought a few provisions, including some sugar-free sweets, which Mr. Wong had shown me yesterday. He and Lao both had type-2 diabetes as well. I stocked up on cheese, butter and yoghurt, then we got a taxi back home.

Later on, Ling got a call to take her mum to see her sister, so they went in a taxi while I stayed at home, catching up on my paperwork and checking my rent money had been paid in, which it was. I transferred £1000 to the Jinan branch of Bank of China.

When Ling got back, at about 5.30, she said they'd had to get a taxi, because both Lao and Gong had come home drunk, earlier in the morning at 3.00 a.m. Gong had vomited all over the place and hadn't even bothered to clean it up. He asked Ling to do it, which she refused, so Lao had to do it – which might teach him a lesson, as it seemed to be his hobby getting people drunk for company. While they'd been sleeping it off, there was no one to help Zhang Min get to toilet, so she had to call her neighbour. Her mum had a Zimmer frame, which was easier to use than crutches.

After Ling tidied up the flat a bit, there wasn't much for dinner. So, while Ling and her mum had some rice soup, I was happy to make myself a cheese and tomato sandwich, using the fresh bread I'd made today.

Watched a couple of *Alan Partridge* DVDs and went to

bed at about 9.30. Back feeling better today.

SATURDAY 23<sup>RD</sup> JANUARY 2010

Arose to the sound of Xiao Wang ringing the doorbell, to start her work. She would leave her house at about 7.00 a.m., six days a week, to do the housework here until noon, mostly cleaning the same areas every day. Then she would do some shopping downstairs with Ling's mum, for fruit and vegetables, which were for sale by the roadside. Then came the process of preparing lunch by 11.30 a.m.

I received a long email from Lucy, whose husband now had cancer and Parkinson's disease. She had offered to go back and nurse him, but then found out he was still connected with his girlfriend, who lived not far away, having moved out of his house, probably to avoid having to be a constant nursemaid. As he didn't seem to require any help, Lucy decided not to go there again. She must have been having a hard time of it, as she hadn't heard from Jaspar for a while since he returned to France, and Samantha was busy with her schoolwork on the Isle of Wight, or visits to her boyfriend Paul, who lived in Surrey.

I also had emails from Trev and Veronique, concerning their travel plans to Italy next June. While I was replying to emails, including one from Ricki at M.D.U., Ling came and told me that Gong was coming to pick us up in Lao's car, to take us to visit her dad's grave.

This was something that needed some preparation, so Ling went out to buy flowers, incense, some paper money for burning and a brush, to clean the gravesite. Gong brought a new bottle of Mou Tai and drove us to the cemetery, in the mountains surrounding Jinan, with Ling's mum.

We were quite a while getting there, as it was Saturday shopping traffic, but it cleared when we got outside the city and onto the motorways. As we approached the mountains, we passed by the new Olympic arena, specially built for last year's games in Beijing, as some events were held here. Several blocks of flats had been constructed to house the numerous visitors, but they were now all empty. There was also a large, white government building nearby, so maybe some of those flats had been allocated to staff.

After driving along excellent roads, the final five hundred metres to the cemetery was along a bumpy mud road. In some ways the main building looked a bit run down, and some of the approach steps had crumbling cement. There were a few farm buildings close by, where we could hear and see several dogs and chickens running around.

After parking the car, we walked another couple of hundred yards up a fairly steep mountain slope. The whole mountainside had been converted to terraces for the dead. On each terrace was a slim area for plants, mainly small evergreens, and running parallel to them were the graves, all set on concrete paths, with a granite area of about three square metres. They were all the same, in polished grey granite, each with a wall a metre high, containing small carved lions along the top of the back, with two white marble lions at the front. There must have been several thousand of these plots, yet somehow we found the right spot, where Ling's dad's grave looked toward the mountain on the other side.

The gravestone was carved in polished black marble, with his name and dates at the top: *"1924–2009"*. Ling told me they had even put my name on it, along with others paying their respects; my name in Chinese was written: *"Da Wei"*. There were two black marble stones laid flat, which covered a hole where the remains (ashes) were deposited.

Ling swept the grave area clean, although it was hard to remove some of the debris of withered flowers, as they were covered in a coating of frozen snow and ice. Next, we laid the bouquet of flowers on the grave and Gong poured three cups of alcohol, and the rest all over the headstone. We then placed some bananas, oranges and large strawberries, along with some paper money, for the dead to be well provided for – rather like the Egyptian tombs. Then Gong lit the incense sticks and we each offered a prayer for the spirit of Ling's dad. Finally, Zheo Di lit three cigarettes, which he put down on one of the grey granite stones, as the dad had been a heavy smoker. These are traditional Chinese methods of dealing with bereavement, which don't seem to have been affected by the Cultural Revolution.

We went back down the mountain, to another area where there was a small pagoda. There we burnt some special paper money, as another burnt offering, making sure the spirit would have enough in the afterlife.

It was a fine, sunny day, although about zero degrees as we left. Gong drove us home and, for a change, we had a decent lunch prepared by Xiao Wang, who'd made a very nice dish of fried chicken in batter, with no bones. Although, yesterday's unfinished item was also served up again. Gong tried some of my bread and then went home.

Ling and I decided to have one last attempt at keeping fish, so I cleaned all the equipment and placed the pump in a better position, also adding de-chlorination crystals, leaving the water to reach room temperature before buying more fish tomorrow.

Then we walked through Hero's Park to the large market, where I bought some aquarium sand and a thermometer, for 6 yuan. It was quite busy, but we decided to go shopping in the underground mall: a large underground area, originally built as protection against Japanese bombing raids in WW2, but now miles of small shops and cafés, where you could go shopping or just walk from one exit to another, if it was raining. I was feeling a bit tired, so Ling went off to get some clothes for a niece, but after she'd gone I had urgent need of a toilet, so had to go in search of one, hoping I wouldn't miss her while I was there. I asked directions and had to walk quite a long way, but when I got back I'd only been away for ten minutes, so I could rely on Ling's thorough shopping methods; sure enough, she didn't get back to where she'd left me for another twenty minutes. My blood sugar was a bit high today, at 7.2, so I didn't pass the time going for a coffee and cake.

We then went to the Silver Plaza shopping centre, to buy English teabags, Lipton's being the only brand available in China; Brooke Bond are missing out on an opportunity!

Also, there seemed to be a general lack of postcards around here, which might be another business to get into. We found some delicious nuts, like mini chestnuts, which usually come from Hangzhou and are already shelled, and I was unable to find in Guangzhou. So I bought a packet, at the rather expensive price of 30 yuan, but thought it was worth it, as I'd been unable to find any like this, other than the variety still in their shells, from which it was very difficult to extract the kernels.

It was still sunny when we went outside at 3.45, although cold, and we caught the first bus which came along: a number 5 at 2 yuan, instead of 1 yuan, as it had air conditioning and a lower risk of pickpockets. We then arrived home in time for me to make tea.

I then cleaned the sand for the fish tank and fitted the thermometer, which showed a water temperature of twenty degrees. Apparently, tropical fish require at least twenty-six degrees, but goldfish would be more hardy, I hoped. Ling's mum thought that we shouldn't put in water plants, as they clog up the filter, but it had to be changed every week anyway, and plants add oxygen to the water.

I did some typing during the afternoon, while Ling was knitting. It appeared she'd caught a cold, as I could hear her coughing, which wasn't that surprising, as I'd already had my usual cold for about a month. Although, the effects had reduced in the last couple of days, and the back pain was slowly going.

We had dinner, similar to lunch, rice, chicken, tomatoes and a slice of bread. Then I watched a DVD about *The Great War*, which was filmed by the BBC in 1974, while Ling watched a soap in the living room, and her mum watched another programme on T.V. in her bedroom – all catering to our own tastes. I could only usually watch CCTV9, which was in English. Ling went to bed early, with some pills for her cold and a hot drink, while I went to check the internet in the spare bedroom, now acting as cloakroom and computer room.

Tomorrow we would go and have lunch with Gong over at his mum's, before he was flying back to Guangzhou, and on Monday I would go to the bank, to change my money from GBP to RMB.

SUNDAY 24ᵀᴴ JANUARY 2010

Ling had a cold, so we didn't follow the plans made yesterday. She stayed in bed all day, and by 5.00 p.m. seemed a lot better. It was sunny outside, with blue skies, but probably cold. Ling's mum phoned her sister, saying we wouldn't be going to their place for lunch, so Gong came over to take Ling's mum and pay a visit to the patient. He brought some fruit with him; being Gong, he brought a crate of apples, oranges and milk, rather than just a bag full. He took Ling's mum for lunch at about 11.30, while I made omelette and potatoes.

We stayed in all day watching a DVD, starring Daniel Craig: *The Defiance*, about Jews surviving in the Belarus forests, during German occupation in WW2.

I tidied up a bit, as is my wont, and relaxed after that. Pretty uneventful Sunday, but so far so good.

Watched another DVD, downloaded from BitTorrent before I left the U.K., called *Lady in the Lake*, starring and directed by Robert Montgomery, with attractive leading lady Audrey Totter. Despite what I advised Trev in my email, I was able to find quite a bit of info about her on *Google China*, but not all websites would download. They mention she was born in 1918, but nothing about her death, so she must be ninety-one by now. She had some amazing facial expressions in this film, but looked quite dishy in some poses. Pity her kind of role died out in the 1950s.

Ling seemed to be getting better, but then went back to sleep again at 8.00 p.m.

MONDAY 25<sup>TH</sup> JANUARY 2010

Got up at 8.00 a.m. and had porridge for breakfast. Ling's cold was a little worse, after seeming to improve last night, so I went out to get medicine. Her mum joked that she hoped I wouldn't get lost, but I replied that if I did, I would come back and start again. It was only on the main road anyway, and I'd been there a few times before; it was the place with more staff than customers.

It took me fifteen minutes to walk there, on a crisp but sunny morning, passing Hero Mountain Park on the other side of the road. I still had to be careful where I walked, avoiding cyclists and mopeds travelling along the pavement in both directions; crossing the main road at a trot, as the lights seem to change when you're halfway across; avoiding broken pavements, crumbling cement, trees and spittle.

I wasn't in the shop for long. They laughed when I came in – not sure why; maybe it was because my nose was red from the cold. But I was served straight away and bought four boxes of pills, after handing them a note Ling had written in Chinese.

Then I walked back and decided to make a detour, to buy some goldfish. I found the small shop in the side-road market and bought three goldfish – I hoped they would be able to endure water which wasn't heated, but just room temperature – and a couple of plants, at a total cost of 10 yuan; I was probably overcharged. I took them home in a thin plastic bag.

Ling was impressed with my solo sortie, and we had tea.

We had lunch at 11.30. Xiao Wang made the same chicken dish as the day before, as I'd eaten all of it. Then we watched a T.V. film about the end of the Qing Dynasty, ruled by the empress dowager Cixi, which stuck to a similar story I'd already read, called *White Orchid*.

I paid some money, by online banking, from the U.K. to Jinan on Friday, which should have been processed on Saturday, and last night we received a telephone call from the bank here at nearly 7.00 p.m., to tell us they'd received it! Apparently, if I didn't go into the bank within two days to sign for it, they would send it back!

TUESDAY 26<sup>TH</sup> JANUARY 2010

Got up to the sound of Xiao Wang ringing the doorbell at 8.00 a.m. Luckily Ling's cold was a little better, so after breakfast we took a 36 bus to the Bank of China, East Central Branch, to sign for the money I'd sent and convert it into Chinese money, at a rate of 11.04 yuan to the pound. This involved the usual vast amount of paperwork. Plus they'd made an error, the inkjet printer putting information into the wrong boxes, so we had to do it all again.

Took the same number bus back, after a ten-minute walk, and arrived home in time for lunch at 11.45. Didn't bother going out again.

Ling went to have a nap and I continued reading my omnibus book of *Dr. Thorndyke* short stories. Made some bread during the late afternoon, which I would send to Bai Min via Ling's mum, who was going over to see her tomorrow. Bai Min phoned yesterday to complain about Lao Zhang, who became exhausted having to do the washing up. When he goes out to eat in a restaurant, there's no one to cook Bai Min any meals.

Trev sent me a photo of a twelve-storey building falling over in Beijing. Then I booked our hotels for two nights in Hong Kong, at the Stanford Hotel, plus four nights at the Aaron Hotel in Sydney, all costing about fifty quid a night.

WEDNESDAY 27TH JANUARY 2010

Got up before 8.00 a.m., as we were going to the immigration office to apply for my visa to be extended by a month, until 28<sup>th</sup> February 2010. At 7.50, Ling's mum was accompanied by Xiao Wang on the free minibus ride to Zhang Min's, to visit and take some stuff, including a loaf I'd made last night.

I had bacon and eggs for breakfast, then Ling and I went to the Immigration Office, in a side street not far from the central station. I couldn't find the spare passport photos, which I probably left in Guangzhou, and had to get another set done. Then we filled in an application, but the guy wasn't sure about our wedding certificate being genuine, so he sent us upstairs to his boss. Ling explained the English words to him, having to explain that Westminster is in London. Then we went back downstairs and paid to get some documents photocopied. We had to wait about twenty minutes while some Russian people were being attended to, before the same guy checked the papers again and took my photo with a webcam, to save on his P.C. They kept my passport and we paid a 160-yuan fee. We would have to go back on 2<sup>nd</sup> February.

After that, at about 11.30, we took a taxi to Liu Lingsheng's – an ex-colleague of Ling's, whom we had seen quite a bit of in Rochester and London, when he tried to set up a parcel delivery office with his son Liu Pei. Liu Pei got fed up with it a couple of years ago, and decided to move back to China, where he now had quite a good job at another international delivery office, because he speaks good English. He got married last year. I think I gave some detail about him earlier, when we went to see him in Beijing, in November.

Liu Lingsheng lived on the twenty-fourth floor of a block of flats near Jinan football ground. He and his wife Zhang Mei had a nice, clean three-bedroom flat, mostly devoted to their only son Liu Pei. Liu Lingsheng explained that he would retire this year, and they were going on an eight-day holiday to Taiwan.

After a few cups of tea, we went down in the lift and took the fifteen-minute walk past the football ground, taking them to lunch at Pizza Hut. We had to wait about fifteen minutes for a table and had a reasonable meal, at 240 yuan for the four of us.

Then we parted company, as we went to check out the local department store for Trev's trousers (I don't know why or how he may have left them there). But they only had winter stuff. We'd probably have to wait until we got back to Guangzhou, where I'd seen some summer clothes in the shops.

There was heavy snow up north, about forty-five degrees below zero, and helicopters had to deliver food to remote farms. Plus, the sea was frozen oven over for about forty kilometres, near Yantai, which is next to Wehai, where our new flat was being built. Veronique sent an email with a photo of their villa in Toulon, and it looked great, with the balcony and proposed wrought ironwork on the top.

On the way home, we stopped at another indoor market, and bought two coat stands for 80 yuan, and a tea set for Liu Lingsheng, as it would be his birthday next Monday, and we were invited for dinner. Got back in time for tea, at 4.00 p.m., and put up a few pictures we'd brought from the U.K.: three done by Mum in 1992 and one I did in 1990, after Gaugin! About a hundred years after!

Had dumplings for dinner, read a bit more of *Dr. Thorndyke*'s short stories, and watched the Billy Bunter DVD given to me as a leaving present, from colleagues at M.D.U., as part of a leaving souvenir. It contained the last two episodes from the B.B.C. series in the 1950s, starring Gerald Campion, aged twenty-nine when he started; I think the series ran for about eight years. It was televised at 4.45 p.m. for kids, and repeated at 8.00 p.m. for parents. It also starred Kynaston Reeves as Mr. Quelch, and Anthony Valentine as Harry Wharton, who had a series of his own when he grew up, called *Raffles*, about a master crook. He also appeared in *Lovejoy* and various other T.V. series, in minor roles. As to be expected, the film work was very grainy, in a sort of green colour at the beginning, until it settled into black and white. It wasn't exactly a top-notch production, but for its time was pretty good, and was still funny in places. The series ran for a long time, although it appeared to be recorded live. Kynaston Reeves would forget his lines occasionally, but recovered like a trooper. The episodes I watched were "Backing Up Bunter" and "Bunter Won't Go", which I also have in book form.

Had a shower and went to bed at 10.30. Ling's cold was better.


THURSDAY 28$^{TH}$ JANUARY 2010

The plan today was to go and visit Ling's "second mum" – not really a relative, but a lady who looked after her and her brothers and sisters, while her mum was away from home working with the Red Air Force. As we were waiting for a bus, I suggested Ling ring her first, which was just as well as she was just going out, and asked us to go tomorrow, instead.

We passed by the guy on the corner who had set up a bicycle repair business. In all weathers, you could see him crouched down in a squatting position, used by a lot of

Chinese when there are no seats available – and also when using the hole-in-the-ground toilets. He had the basic equipment of a box of tools, spare inner tubes and a bowl of water for tracing punctures, and there were about three customers waiting to have their bikes fixed. What sometimes amazed me was how some of these people expected to go into business, just plonking down somewhere in the street, on no official basis, with no rent, rates or planning permission. What's more, they seemed to get enough customers to make it worthwhile.

We went to the bank and I withdrew some money, to give to Ling's mum toward our expenses. Then we went to a newly opened branch of the Silver Plaza supermarket. This turned out to be a store selling off the rest of the stores' products at sale prices, except for the food department. We wasted a couple of hours here, as Ling couldn't decide what to get. We also started looking for her mum's New Year gift, which was also unsuccessful. She ended up buying a scarf for herself. We went down to the food department and bought some non-sugar sweetener and toothpaste, all the while carrying some sausages we'd also brought with us from Ling's mum, as a gift for the second mum.

We arrived back home in time for lunch, and I just

heated some dumplings from last night, as I couldn't see anything I fancied eating from Xiao Wang's cuisine, apart from a bowl of rice she thrust in front of me.

Checked my emails after lunch and browsed the net for a bit. Then Ling said we should go and visit her sister. We caught a bus halfway, so that we could buy some roasted chestnuts from a small shop, similar to the one we used to go to in Guangzhou. This place was a bit cheaper, but the nuts, although small, were well cooked and delicious, at a cost of 5 yuan for half a kilo – so I bought a bag for myself. They seemed to cook these chestnuts in a special machine, which looked like a huge cigar cut in half, with some smouldering newspapers at one end. I'm not sure if this was some kind of plug or gimmick, or if it provided the smoke to add flavour. Whatever, it was a rusty old thing which revolved as the nuts were being heated, so they got an even temperature. The purveyor would check if they were ready by hurling them onto the floor; if they break into pieces, this is apparently a good sign. Anyway, it seems to work, as all the nuts were equally well cooked, the skins came off easily, and there was no mixture of burnt and raw bits, like when you try to do it yourself on a fire at home.

We got a taxi to Zhang Min's, after we waited about

fifteen minutes for a number 15 bus then gave up. I noticed a pile of empty Mou Tai bottles piled up outside the door, so her husband Lao had obviously been keeping up his celebrations. She had only just got out of the shower and was pleased to see us. She answered the door while propping herself up with the Zimmer frame, which now seemed to be her favoured mode of transport.

Ling went to change her bandages and fitted a sling to the frame, so that she could put her injured foot into it for extra support. I made some tea and listened to a talking book on my MP3, as most of their conversation was in Chinese, so I left them to it. Lao came home about half an hour later, with some new shoes he'd just bought. There was also a lady cleaning the house, so we didn't stay for long, as it seemed that everything was organized.

Before we left, however, Zhang Min sent her husband out to buy us some dumplings. He trotted off and returned half an hour later, with two kilos of dumplings costing 100 yuan. We went home by taxi – just as a number 15 bus went by – and cooked some of the dumplings for dinner; Ling just managed to stuff the rest in the fridge.

Was having some trouble getting into Hotmail lately, on the main computer, although it was okay on Ling's laptop. Not sure what the problem was, although there seemed to be some antivirus icon in the address field, which may be blocking it.

Watched another DVD I'd bought for 50p in Guangzhou: Russell Crowe and Ben Affleck in *State of Play*, a political conspiracy-type thriller. which I'd only bought as I wanted to get a few English-speaking DVDs for a low price, while I had the chance.

FRIDAY 29ᵀᴴ JANUARY 2010

Days were now passing; we'd less than a month before the next stage of our travels.

The weather felt warmer today, although still only about eight degrees. Had breakfast and went to one of the cheaper supermarkets near Ling's mum's flat: turn left onto the main road and then right, and it was about a fifteen-minute walk away. A sign outside said *"K Mart"*, but everyone knew it as "Da Yun Fa". We'd been to this supermarket a few times. It was quite big, although only on one floor, about double the size of Selfridges' ground-floor area. A few people had set up their own business outside in the parking lot. The last time we were here, on a freezing cold day, there was a lady sat on a folding stool, wrapped up in half a dozen overcoats, repairing shoes. She had some ancient contraption – like an old homemade sewing machine – and rolls of leather and rubber, with an assortment of tools and other shoemaking stuff on the ground. It still amazes me how they could survive working like this, outside in the freezing cold, but they seemed to get enough customers, and at least they were not begging. There were a few more established open-air stalls selling buns, fried tofu (which has a vile smell, to my taste), sticks of satay chicken, cakes, soup and nuts. There was also a stand selling electric mopeds, which were quite cheap at less than 2000 yuan (two-hundred quid) for a two-seater.

We went in, brushing aside the heavy padded curtains which kept out the cold air, and went into the supermarket. Before we entered, we had to show a security guard some sausages we'd brought from home. Ling bought three packs of some mysterious stuff in fancy wrapping: some kind of mushroom medicine, to help her aunt sleep.

Then we walked another ten minutes to her second mum's flat, around the corner. It was quite a big estate, with a security entrance, although I daresay burglars could scale the surrounding railings. I think Second Mum lived on the tenth floor.

The door was answered by her 83-year-old husband in his underwear. Not a pretty sight! Well, they were long johns, anyway, covering his spindly legs. Otherwise he was in quite good health – apart from being a bit deaf.

It was quite a nice, new flat, about three years old, and very bright and airy. They also had a lady cleaning for them, and she brought us some fruit she'd just washed. Second Mum came in later, as she'd been out shopping, and the old guy made us tea. Ling and Second Mum caught up on the gossip, while the old guy and myself nearly dropped off to sleep; him not taking part because he couldn't hear what was being said, and me not understanding the lightning speed of the conversation.

After several cups of tea and some fruit, we all went out at about 12.30 to have lunch. We went to a place about a five-minute walk along the road, and the food was quite nice. I asked, as usual, for Kung Po chicken, and was surprised to learn that it was on their menu. Ling was always going on at me about wanting the same thing, but this was the first time since I'd been here that Kung Po chicken was on the menu. It was quite good, and the others seemed to enjoy theirs as well. There was also a nice, jelly-like brown-mushroom dish, which I ate, as it was supposed to reduce cholesterol, and a delicious fish without bones, which came last and I was too full to enjoy. I paid the bill of 160 yuan for the four of us, although Second Mum tried to give the money back to Ling. We went our separate ways outside the restaurant.

We dropped into the supermarket again to buy some groceries: bananas, tomatoes, crisps, some bread (which looked like the real thing, in the shape of a French baguette) and some American butter – at least, I think it was American, as it had a picture of a Red Indian on the wrapper; the sales assistant didn't seem to know where it came from. We also bought some minced beef, as Ling informed me that I was making spaghetti Bolognese tonight, plus a bottle of red wine for 13 yuan. We walked home carrying our provisions, as the sun felt warmer.

Ling also bought a new coat for her mum, as a New Year gift, and one for another aunt. As might be expected, when Ling showed the coat to her mum, they found something wrong and took it back, while I played around on the internet. Ling has a habit, when shopping, of investigating every single item in the shop before she decides to buy something, then takes it back the next day to change it.

I made tea when they got back at 5.00 p.m. Then I began the dinner, which took quite a lot of preparation: skinning the tomatoes, marinating the meat, boiling the spaghetti, etc. I sliced some of the new bread, which proved to be okay, unlike the sweet, cake-like stuff they usually sell – and it was only 3 yuan. The meal went down well at 7.00 p.m., washed down with a glass of red wine, and Ling did the washing up.

Nothing much happened during the evening, so we went to bed at 9.30, after a shower.

We were roused by a call at about 11.30 p.m., from Ling's younger brother's wife Betty (Zhang Feng). They'd had an argument about where he should spend his Chinese New Year celebrations; he wanted to come here, after some obscure call from Lao about him coming home a year after his father's death, to try and raise the spirit of his dead father. Not sure what it was all about, but that was the gist. The wife wanted him to stay and visit her family, so they had a big row. She locked herself in her bedroom and he broke down the door, so she phoned here to get Ling's mum to tell him off. Anyway, he was now coming here for the Chinese New Year.

SATURDAY 30<sup>TH</sup> JANUARY 2010

Got up at about 8.30, after not a very good sleep, and sweating with the central heating and slightly higher temperature outside. The central heating system here was provided by the local government and controlled by them.

They usually switched it on in November, then off in March. You could see the large pipes, covered in some kind of insulated wrapping, all over the city. The problem with this system is that you can't switch it off if it gets too hot, and you waste a lot of heat by having to open windows. Then again, if it gets cold occasionally, after they switch it off, you can't switch it back on again.

I was going to the bank to withdraw some cash, but Ling insisted we both go for a massage down the road. I didn't really want to go, as my back was getting better, but she wanted one, so I went to keep her company. After the guy pummelled and pulled me about for twenty minutes or so, I was then given some cupping treatment to get rid of dampness, whatever that means. Then we paid 80 yuan and left.

This cupping system involved them lighting a match inside a small glass bowl, which creates a vacuum, then they apply it to your skin, where it sticks, the vacuum sucking in a layer of skin. If it goes red and looks uncomfortable, that means it's working; the marks usually stay on your back for a couple of weeks. They wanted 300 yuan for a twelve-week course, but luckily I didn't have enough on me.

As we reached home, Ling went back to her mum's flat

and I carried on to the bank, withdrawing 1500 yuan to keep us going through the week. It was lunch when I got back. I was going to have last night's leftovers, but there seemed to be enough edible stuff for me to eat, so I saved it for dinner and had a bit of fish, some rice and potatoes. We both felt a bit lethargic after lunch, so we went to lie down for a couple of hours.

I wanted to go and try to find an art shop, to get some drawing paper and see if I could find anywhere that sold oil paint, but nobody knew of anywhere like that. While we were debating what to do, Yen Bin came over (Ling's former colleague, from working in the countryside during the Cultural Revolution; he who ran the small private school where I sang a carol at Christmas). He was going to take us to see Ling's sister, but we felt too tired, so he just took Ling's mum.

I stayed in looking at U.K. properties on the internet, and found a rather nice Victorian-style house in Webb Street, Lincoln. It was pleasantly situated next to a river, with three bedrooms, two receptions, an enclosed garden, and the living room had a view of the river, as did the back garden. The price of £99,000 was just about within our price range, if we sold our flat in London. Not a real prospect at the moment, as we were committed to our flat until at least next October, and I expected this place would be sold by then – not sure why it hadn't gone already. We had visited Lincoln with Ling's mum in the summer, and quite liked the area.

Ling and her mum were now watching an Indian soap, dubbed in Chinese, which would go on until 7.00 p.m., so I went to watch a DVD in the other room. Had an email from Veronique, saying the builders doing their balcony asked for an extra 6000 euros to finish it – which is out of order, to say the least. Not sure what the extra was for.

The temperature today was about ten degrees and sunny, and the three fish I bought last Sunday still seemed to be okay.

I watched an episode of *Blake's Seven*, from a DVD I'd compiled in the U.K., starring Paul Darrow as Avon. I wished I'd brought more, as I quite enjoyed this one. It was a bit wooden, but convincing enough. I wondered where they managed to find such strange scenery, having filmed somewhere in the U.K.

After that, Ling went to bed at 8.30, and I sat in the living room reading an excellent Billy Bunter book, *Just Like Bunter*, though mainly concerning the shady exploits of the school "bounder" Herbert Vernon Smith. It was quite a good, old-fashioned story, but tense in places; a morality tale about the errors of gambling. I finished it at 9.45 and wished I'd brought more with me; would have to raid our storage place, when we got back to the U.K. in May.

We've been coming to Jinan every year since 2002, usually during my three-week holiday allowance from work and have built up a fair collection of English books brought from home, plus a load of clothes. This means that we had a duplicate set of clothes in the U.K., along with the ones here, and even a few at our flat in Yintan. Since I retired last year, we would probably be spending longer periods in China.

## SUNDAY 31ST JANUARY 2010

Ling told me we were going to see her cousin today and, as it was Xiao Wang's day off, we would be lunching out with Ling's mum. I'm not sure of the exact relationship, but it was through Ling's grandfather, on her father's side, and this girl's uncle. We had already bought a dress for her three-year-old daughter, plus a large tin of mixed biscuits and a pack of something that all the shops were selling at the moment, ready for the Chinese New Year on 14th February, St. Valentine's Day and also Ling's mum's birthday. I'm not sure of the logic of this visit. Ling explained that it was to do with the Chinese New Year, in two weeks' time; if we went today we wouldn't need to go on the 14th.

We caught a taxi at about 11.15, and arrived at the cousin's place at about 11.40, as the taxi driver wasn't exactly sure how to get there; it was a little past the bus station – that's all I can remember. We approached the narrow street, between a row of shops, into a rather rundown street covered in a fine, grey cement dust and dried leaves. It looked like a poor area, which in London you might be afraid of entering because of gang problems, but in China it was just the home of hardworking people who haven't yet benefitted from the new prosperity.

As we left the taxi I attracted a few curious stares, as usual, as probably not many Westerners venture here, but there was no hostility. It was a bright morning and people were going about their business. Huge piles of cardboard were being wheeled along on bicycles, scheduled for recycling. I don't know how much they can earn from all this waste packaging, but it must be enough for them to do it. Others were collecting old bits of scrap metal, wood, etc., on trailers drawn by three-wheel bikes.

Ling found the flat and her cousin came out to greet us.

They had a small, untidy courtyard, with an old shed in one corner and a cracked concrete surface. We went through a thick blanket draped across the doorway, straight into the living room, where a large double bed was the first item of furniture. Farther inside were some sofas and a marble-topped coffee table, covered in apples and oranges, Brazil nuts and macadamia nuts, still in their shells. Also dark brown hazelnuts, almost perfectly round, a huge pile of sunflower seeds and a dish of almonds. Although rather a poor looking flat, with only one additional room, plus a kitchen and bathroom which I didn't venture into, apparently the husband had a successful factory business. They had a large, 40-inch, flat-screen T.V. and offered generous hospitality.

The husband was about sixty and the cousin about thirty, and they had a cute three-year-old daughter who could count up to her age. Although a little shy, she was happy looking.

We sat there drinking some excellent coffee and feeding on the nuts. Ling's mum hadn't seen Brazil nuts before and I opened a couple for her. There were no nutcrackers, but all the shells had already been split, possibly with a hammer, and we prised them open with a small metal tool, rather like a flattened radiator key.

They had a couple of rather bedraggled houseplants, which looked as if they were growing in mud, in clay pots. The cousin put them outside in the sun, where they would probably grow into beautiful exotic blooms in the spring, though at the moment they looked on their last legs.

Then it appeared that we were invited to go out to lunch, and the husband, Mr. Zhang, drove us in his white Volkswagen Santana, in two trips, as there were also his sister and her husband in the party. He dropped us off at the restaurant at the corner of the road, opposite another Silver Plaza supermarket, and went off to get the rest. Ling, her mum and I went upstairs with the cousin and her daughter.

The floor upstairs was empty of customers, so the waiter had to switch on the lights and turn on the heating. He took us into a private room, where the table was already laid, and we sat around it, waiting for tea and the others to arrive. About twenty minutes later, Mr. Zhang returned with his sister, husband, daughter and the daughter's boyfriend.

Although the restaurant hadn't looked that auspicious, after I'd visited the toilets – which were of the hole-in-the-floor variety, with no locks – the food was excellent and I was able to enjoy quite a few dishes. There was a sort of scrambled egg and diced vegetable dish, which you folded up into a sort of pancake, and I had a couple of. There was also some jelly-like mushroom in a sort of brown vinegar, which I can't remember the name of— oh yes, balsamic vinegar – which was apparently good for cholesterol. There was a large fish steamed with soy sauce, chicken soup, crispy fried tofu stuffed with minced lamb and carrot (which was excellent) and, when everyone was full, a huge plate of dumplings.

The host had ascertained that I didn't like the Chinese spirit drink, so he ordered two bottles of red wine for my benefit, although most people joined me in a glass. There were about ten of us at the meal and about fifteen different items on the menu, though only one pork dish, as Ling had informed them that I don't like pork, so altogether it was an excellent do.

We finished at about 2.00 p.m. and Mr. Zhang drove us to Ling's sister's house, which was close by, then went back to drive the rest of the party home. Ling's sister's house was in a new block of flats, built by the army hospital she used to work at, and entered via a barrier controlled by a security guard.

Zhang Min had a couple of friends visiting her, but was glad to see us, and we stopped for an hour or so for tea, and a foot massage in their massage machine. She gave us a bag of fruit to take away with us and we got a taxi home.

On the way back, I asked Ling if we could find an artists' shop, so we all got off near the Jinan Large Building Area, as Ling's mum wanted to go shopping somewhere else. We went to a large bookshop on several floors and I bought some artist's paper and a brush, as I wanted to do some watercolours, to pass the time. They didn't have everything I needed, but we were told about a specialist shop not far away, so we made our way there. It was about a twenty-minute walk. It was feeling a bit colder by now, and we had several roads to cross. One had been closed off, and people were watching the demolition of a large building, which was finely balanced on a couple of pillars, and looked likely to fall down at any minute.

Up a flight of stairs, the art shop was excellent and seemed to have everything. I bought some brown masking tape, to prepare my paper, a small block of soapstone and a carving tool. They had a large selection of oil paints, at 4 yuan a tube, which in the U.K. would probably cost about five pounds each. There were easels, a canvas, frames, brushes, coloured paper and pretty much everything, so I might return here if I managed to get down to some serious work.

We found a stop for a 52 bus nearby, but missed a couple, as we were diverted to a shop selling hot chestnuts, and kept waiting to buy a bag. We got back home about 4.00 p.m., in time for tea, but didn't have dinner as we were still full up.

Downloaded a load of talking books and short stories from *Audiobooksforfree.com*, for my MP3.

MONDAY 1ST FEBRUARY 2010

Woke up this morning thinking it was still Sunday, for some reason – I suppose that's being retired with no work to go to. Saw Arsenal get thrashed 3-1 by Manchester United.

Had breakfast at about 10.00, then Ling insisted that we go out for a massage. I went along just to keep her company, as she had a bit of back pain, but I was talked into having one as well. After getting pummelled and pulled for half an hour, the guy said to me, in English: "Welcome to Jinan."

On the way back, I bought a small metal file, to help with my soapstone carving project, after some difficulty explaining what I wanted, as Ling was next door. But I got the right one eventually, for 4 yuan.

Went back then for a light lunch. I finished off Saturday's spaghetti with some bread and a glass of Chengyu red wine.

The paper I'd prepared for painting yesterday had come unstuck, so I had to do it again, wetting it first then sticking it on a board to stretch, so it wouldn't "pockle" when I applied watercolour – at least, that was the theory. Trying to carve the soapstone, I found it a bit harder than anticipated, as the stuff comes off like talcum powder during the scraping and filing process. But at least I knew it was the right stuff, as it fitted the description I found on the internet.

I kept saying that I was going on a diet, but every day we seemed to be getting invited out for a massive meal; today it was Liu Lingsheng's birthday bash. We decided to walk to the restaurant, which was near the Silver Plaza branch at the end of Liu Lin Shang Road. We left a bit early, as we wanted to have a look around the shops. I wanted to buy some butter to go with the bread I'd made, as a gift to go with the tea set we'd also bought a few days ago.

At the plaza we went to the fourth floor, as Ling wanted to buy me a new polo-neck sweater, fed up with seeing me in the navy-blue one I would always wear, but we couldn't find a single one. The crew-neck tops on sale were quite expensive anyway, at about 800 yuan, which was even more expensive than the U.K. I went back downstairs again and bought the butter, while Ling bought a decoration to hang up in the house somewhere, to celebrate the Chinese New Year of the tiger. She managed this after the usual deliberation and checking every item in stock, finally selecting the one I'd suggested in the first place.

From the heat of the store, we walked around the corner in the cold, to find the restaurant. It was on the adjoining road, near a huge exhibition building belonging to the army, which has quite a high profile in Jinan, due to the conflict with the Japanese occupiers during WW2. We found the place at last: a large red building, with two ladies greeting us in costumes at the door. We were a little early, but they showed us to the reserved room upstairs, and I was able to inspect the loos before anyone else used them: clean, but another hole in the floor.

When I got back, everyone else had arrived, including Liu Lingsheng's old mother, still smoking at eighty-odd years old; she had apparently started when she was seven. We'd met her once before, when she came over to the U.K. about five years earlier. There was also Zhang Mei's (Liu Lingsheng's wife) sister, her husband and their twenty-year-old son Yen Dong – he could speak English, and we had a few conversations during the meal. This was another good meal, of the hotpot kind, where you cook your own thin slices of meat in a choice of chicken and duck soup, or chilli hot soup/gravy, which can sometimes make you cough and sweat if it's too hot, but this one was reasonable. Yen Dong was curious to know if I'd had it before. I was able to get some of the others to understand some of my Chinese, and they said it was quite good – but unfortunately, while I can make up a sentence in my head before saying something, I can't always understand the response.

Liu showed us a nice photo album, which his son Liu Pei had given him, made up of family photos going back sixty years, all imprinted on a specially produced book. The pictures were compiled over the cover and inside, with descriptions for each picture – rather like a published book, but a photo shop could make it up for you. The old mother looked quite beautiful when she was first married, with luxurious, long, plaited hair, and you wouldn't tell that it was the same person after a lifetime of smoking, which otherwise didn't seem to have impaired her health.

Of course, when everyone was full up, we then had to have a few dumplings, and forced them down. They were served by a pleasant girl who tried out her English on me, saying that she was a student, working her way through college.

After the meal, Yen Dong and I walked back to Liu Lingsheng's flat for some more tea. We made a date to have a day out, so that he could practice his English, which his parents had seemed keen on during the meal. I said I would like to go to the main museum, to which he agreed, although he still hadn't got round to seeing it himself yet. He was studying to be a civil electrical engineer, and sitting his master's this year. He wanted to go and work in Beijing – along with several thousand others. I hoped he would also show me how to download free movies; he suggested I buy a 100-gigabyte hard drive for about 400 yuan – "Ask for a discount," he added.

We stayed at the flat until about 10.30 p.m., although Ling's mum had already taken a taxi home. Liu Lingsheng tried out one part of the tea set we'd bought: a clay dish with a lid, into which you poured excess tea. Part of the ceremony is to put boiling water in the teapot, then pour it all away to clean it, and also pour it all over the cups for hygiene reasons; the next pot full has a better and cleaner flavour, getting rid of any tea dust. It is then served, rather annoyingly, in cups little bigger than thimbles.

During the tea drinking, we were served with sliced oranges, almonds and dried sunflower seeds, off of which you have to take the skins, cracking them first in your teeth to obtain a minute kernel. It is quite tasty, but in my mind not worth all the hassle. Ling and the others amassed a large pile of empty shells during the evening, while those still in the serving dish never seemed to go down.

I was gradually getting fed up, and was relieved when we left at 10.30, to get a taxi home. It was quite cold outside, so I guessed we were in for another spell of cold weather.


TUESDAY 2^(ND) FEBRUARY 2010

We had planned to go to the passport office this morning, to get my visa, but Ling explained that she was going shopping early with her mum, to a local supermarket which provided a free bus service; they left at 9.00 a.m., while I was still washing and shaving. They were back an hour later, while I was attempting my first watercolour painting in several years. Ling had managed to find some of my now-favourite mini-chestnuts, peeled in sealed packets, which we thought were only available in Hangzhou. She had also bought a decent-looking chicken breast, so I would be able to make a chicken curry – maybe tomorrow, as there was already enough food for lunch.

At about 1.00 p.m. we went out to the passport office, via the 36 bus, and walked down a rather elegant looking road, called Culture Street. Ling explained that this used to be the main thoroughfare in Jinan, back in the 1960s, which was apparent from some of the European-looking architecture. But since then the city has developed in another direction, which resulted in this area losing some of its former glory. The plain trees remained, however, and were well matured, similar to London Plain – although Ling told me the Chinese call them French Plain.

The passport office had dealt with my application favourably, and we were only in there for about two minutes, just showing a receipt at the desk and picking up my passport, with the new visa stamped on it.

It was quite a crisp day and we were wearing long overcoats and gloves. Ling wanted to buy me a new polo-neck jumper for New Year, but we couldn't find any. We decided to continue shopping in the area, which seemed almost devoid of pedestrians. Ling pointed out the first department store in Jinan, built in the 1920s, but it had been subsequently used as a cinema and was now empty. Instead of pulling down all these old buildings and building new ones, it might be a better idea to renovate some of these elegant streets and shops, to preserve at least one or two examples of life from the past.

Ling wanted to go to a cheap marketplace, which was four stops away, so we took a bus. When we alighted, there were huge crowds of people about, at a thriving outdoor sales area. We entered the large store across the road, which turned out to be a large building containing lots of market stalls and individual shop units on six floors, rather like Camden Market. This place was called New World Market. Ling bought some artificial flowers, which only cost a couple of yuan each, as opposed to about 20 yuan elsewhere, and also another New Year decoration at 4 yuan, compared to the 15 yuan she'd paid at Silver Plaza.

While she was looking in another artificial flower shop, I looked around a shop across the passage, selling cigar equipment, pipes, lighters and penknives, one of which I bought for 15 yuan. The salesman looked like a young punk rocker, and followed me about the shop while I was looking at the penknives. I thought I might need one to peel fruit, etc., while we were travelling, although I doubted if I'd be able to carry it on a plane in my hand luggage.

Even inside this building we could feel the cold, so we went across to KFC for a coffee, cake and a general warm-up. Then we got a taxi home, in time for tea at 4.00 p.m.

We watched a crap DVD starring Tom Hanks called *Angels and Demons* by Dan Brown – pretty much a copy of the formula for *The Da Vinci Code*. Then, to round the evening off, I watched *Name of the Rose*, an historic detective story by Umberto Eco, starring Sean Connery, but I hadn't copied it from the T.V. correctly and missed the beginning, which would have explained what he was investigating. I also missed the last five minutes, so I didn't see the final summing up.

WEDNESDAY 3<sup>RD</sup> FEBRUARY 2010

Ling went out early on her own again this morning, to go to the dentist at last, as she'd been putting it off for about a year while we were in the U.K. She was back at about 11.30, returning with her mum, who'd been visiting Zhang Min.

Xiao Wang had made prawns for lunch, which looked good, but somehow we only ate a couple each. I get a bit fed up eating prawns while they've still got their skins on, instead of the peeled variety we get in the U.K. The Chinese seem to prefer leaving the skin and bones on everything, which is supposed to add to the flavour. I ate some lotus roots, which were quite tasty, and had soup made of tomatoes and egg.

After lunch at 1.00 p.m., Ling said we were going out to look at a food exhibition being held nearby, so off we went, taking Ma along as well. It looked like it might snow during the afternoon, but we were all wrapped up well with long johns – or, as Ling calls it, "wearing two trousers." The bus was quite full and a young girl got up and offered me her seat, so I guess old age is creeping up.

Entrance was free to the exhibition, but it was the usual collection of dried and bottled indescribables. There were huge piles of various spices in powdered form, but I didn't buy any, not knowing what they were; even if Ling knew, she didn't know the English translation. They bought some legs of cured and smoked bacon, sausage, plus some shrink-wraps of salted and pickled vegetables, ducks' heads and feet, etc. I bought – as a bit of fun, really – some polishing cloths that you could wear on your feet, for polishing the floor. Ling's mum also bought some packets of tea, which the house is already full of, and I finally bought a couple of red peppers, as I was planning to make my chicken curry.

We left at about 4.00 p.m. and came home, where I made tea and, after a rest, I prepared and made the chicken curry, with some bottles of spices I'd brought from the U.K. It turned out quite well this time, especially as we had a decent cut of chicken.

While Ling and her mum watched some Indian soap, I watched a Sherlock Holmes DVD I'd got free with *The Daily Telegraph*: *The Last Vampyre*, starring Jeremy Brett and Edward Hardwicke, with a good supporting cast including Roy Marsden, Maurice Denham, Elizabeth Spriggs and Freddie Jones in rather a small cameo part, of a completely unnecessary character.


THURSDAY 4TH FEBRUARY 2010

Ling went out early with her mum again, to go to the bank at 8.30 a.m., so I had a leisurely breakfast.

They didn't get back until 11.30, by which time Xiao Wang was getting anxious about when to prepare lunch, as she had to leave at about noon. The reason for the delay was that they'd bought a new kettle for 140 yuan and walked back from the shop. Ling was quite cold when she got back, but after lunch I walked down to Silver Plaza supermarket by myself, and got quite hot and sweaty. The sun felt quite warm and I was well wrapped up, as if going to the North Pole. According to the weather report last night, winter was now starting to change to spring, although some cold spells were still expected.

Maybe because I was on my own, I seemed to get more stares in the shop and a couple of girls tried to sell me stuff. But I didn't see the point, as I couldn't understand what they were selling, nor identify the product in its fancy wrapping. Things which look like sweets or chocolate, in pink and silver wrapping, turn out to be dried fish or pork fat, so I tend not to buy this stuff. I did get some fresh fruit, including a luxury of blueberries at four quid for about 75 grammes, which were imported from Italy. I was looking for a Pyrex dish to use in the microwave, as I planned to make a pear crumble, but had to settle for a plastic dish, which I hoped was microwave proof.

I decided to walk back, and the whole round trip took an hour. When I got home, Ling's mum protested that she already had a microwave dish, but as it was at the back of a cupboard, under the cooker, I don't know how I was supposed to know. During the search, we did find a lid which was the right size, so I used that to make a crumble with sliced pears, from a recipe book I'd brought with me. It was rather strange, because we already had all this stuff in the U.K., and were gradually duplicating most of our possessions so we wouldn't have to keep bringing suitcases back and forth, full of stuff we might need. Plus, with our flat in Yintan, we had a third set of stuff, although not quite so much: beds and bedding, cooker and washing machine, etc. It was becoming like having three homes instead of one big one, which might have been more permanent. Ling had always wanted a big house with a garden, from watching all these property shows on T.V., but it didn't look as if we would ever realize that dream, even though I did enjoy the fruits of my parents' house while I was growing up.

The crumble turned out okay, and as I had some flour left over I made an apple crumble, as well. But, as Ling and her mum were not really interested in pudding, I'd probably end up eating it all, like Billy Bunter (note: they were made with sweetener, not sugar).

It seemed a bit colder in the flat during the afternoon, and transpired that the whole area was without heating. Luckily, due to insulation, the temperature didn't drop that much, but I was sent downstairs to get a small heater for the living room, from the outside storage place. The heating gradually started to come back on at around 8.00 p.m., while I was watching a rather ridiculous, gung-ho American movie, about a marine on holiday on a tropical island. I'd never even seen the lead man before, and only bought it as it was going cheap in Guangzhou, so I would have something to watch in English, because my store was gradually running out. Did a bit more of my painting then started reading *Mysteries of Paris*, by Eugene Sue, which I'd read before, but couldn't remember much about the plot. I think a film was made about it in France, with Mel Ferrer, but not a very good version if I recall, as it didn't have Gerard Depardieu in it. Just noted on the internet that this book was reviewed briefly by Karl Marx. I wished I'd brought some talking books by Anthony Trollope with me; maybe I could find some in an Australian library, in a couple of weeks. I enjoyed listening to the collection read by Timothy West, but had probably already heard most of the main ones, even though I understand he wrote more than fifty novels. Just checked on the internet: it was forty-seven, plus some other works of non-fiction. In addition, he was the inventor of the red pillar box.

FRIDAY 5TH FEBRUARY 2010

I was due to spend the day with Yan Dong, the nephew of Liu Lingsheng, a friend of Ling's. This boy would be sitting his master's degree in Electrical Engineering in June, but his parents were anxious for him to take the opportunity of practising his English with a native English speaker. We were supposed to meet at the Qianfoushang Museum at 10.00 a.m., but I decided to leave in plenty of time to allow for waiting for a bus, getting lost, traffic jams, etc. Ling was convinced I would get lost sometime during the day, so had given me the boy's telephone number, a map of the bus route (which I think I already knew), how many bus stops I should count on the way, plus our home address, written in Chinese, and also the destination. I knew I had to catch the 64 bus, and it was supposed to be four stops to the Exhibition Centre, to which I'd already been twice; then I would just stay on the bus for another four stops. We'd seen the place before, in passing, so I knew what to look out for.

From the gates to our compound I turned left, walked about a hundred yards to the Chinese Lottery sub-office, turned right into rather a rundown area of flats, with black-and-white Chinese paintings on the off-white walls – like authorized graffiti – then down a lane to the bus stop. Like the previous time we'd taken this bus to the exhibition, it was already at the stop, so I had to run across the road for it.

I started counting the stops, but it was eight to my destination, not seven, as Ling had advised; the seventh stop was for the Jinan Museum, which was at the bottom of a hill, but I knew the place I wanted was at the top, so I stayed on for another stop, until I saw the entrance gate to the Shandong Central Area Museum. I got off the bus at 9.30 and prepared for a half-hour wait, but Yan Dong had also arrived early, so we set off for the museum.

The security guard told us we would need to get a ticket, although it was free for Yen Dong. They asked to see my passport, which I hadn't brought with me, but they gave me a free ticket anyway when I showed them my Chinese debit card. We entered the museum, surrounded by security arrangements, and I had to leave my camera bag in reception. It seemed rather a palaver if the tickets were free, and you had to press them on an entry sensor. Ling phoned me on my borrowed mobile about this time, and I assured her I'd arrived safely, etc.

It was a very large museum, as might be expected for the Province, but seemed to consist mainly of stairs and corridors. It took us a while to find the first room or any exhibits. Apart from the staff, we were the only people in the museum.

Yan Dong asked me about museums in London, and I advised that the British Museum was usually packed. He admitted that he'd never been to this museum before, but when we found the Natural History section he seemed quite interested. A lot of the items were similar to the ones you see in the U.K., apart from some large, white cranes which are protected in China, as they're a symbol of good luck and longevity. One display behind a glass wall was quite impressive, containing trees with birds – like hawks and peacocks – perched in them and, below, stuffed leopards, tigers and even foxes. I explained to Yan Dong about fox-hunting traditions in the U.K., which he thought was cruel, especially if the fox wasn't eaten. It reminded me of the Oscar Wilde epigram: *"The unspeakable in pursuit of the uneatable."*

It was freezing cold in the museum, and obviously electricity was being saved, as the exhibits only lit up when you approached them. There was no heating, nor even a tearoom. There were very clean toilets on all four floors, although, of course, there were no people to use them – apart from the staff, who walked up and down, flapping their arms to keep warm.

The next room contained some beautiful porcelain vases, going back to Ming Dynasty, and a large collection from the late Qing Dynasty – still preserved in spite of predations by British, American and French armies during the nineteenth century.

We found another gallery going back to the bronze age, which made the collection of British pots from that era look pretty pathetic. As writing had long since been invented by the Chinese, they were able to identify a lot of items from around 500BC onward, and there were some amazing designs on well-preserved pots, bells and weaponry; pots for cooking or pouring wine had animal heads sculpted on the handles and lids, in all shapes and sizes. They seemed to be very artistic in their designs for basic utensils.

We tried to go upstairs to the fourth floor, but were told that it was closed for redecoration. Anyway, what we had really come to see was back down on the ground floor, which we'd somehow passed by: Yan asked for directions to the dinosaur section.

The entrance to this was through a sort of cave or grotto, containing manmade stalactites, which Yan Dong considered quite scary. We passed by the fossil section, with a few large ammonites as can be seen in the U.K., past larger animal bones like horse, deer and tiger, until we came to the reconstructed carcass of a mammoth. It was much larger than an elephant and was obviously a mammoth skeleton, although all the pictures nearby depicted elephants.

We saw some petrified trees and then, just near the exit,

we spotted another room, with something big inside. We hurried across and were rewarded with an amazing specimen of some genus of dinosaur; I can't remember the first part of its name, but the last part was "giganticus". Apparently, this was the largest skeleton in the world, standing at eight metres high and fourteen metres long, including the tail; a man would only come up to the knee bone of its rear legs. It really was an awesome sight. Contrary to previous illustrations, the forelegs were quite large as well, at about two metres long, with large claws at the end, about six times the size of a man's hand. We stayed here enjoying this exhibit for a while.

Then, as it was past 11.00, and our hands and feet were freezing, we decided to leave, as it was warmer outside. We passed two more people coming in as we left, and Yan Dong had to remind me to go back and reclaim my bag and camera.

We decided to walk to the restaurant, where I was standing him lunch. It was down a straight road, but took us about twenty minutes to reach the corner where the restaurant was situated. I could see a large McDonald's on one corner, and thought that was where we were going, as he'd recommended a place used by a lot of Westerners, but instead we stopped at a place called Jenny's Café, with blue doors and window shutters, and seating outside for summer. Once inside, we felt the warm and welcome comfort of a very nice restaurant, giving an atmosphere of the Mediterranean, with red tablecloths and square tables of four seats each – and some with two – in contrast to most of the Chinese restaurants, which have round tables. This place was run by Chinese owners, but had an extensive menu including pizzas, spaghetti, Mexican, Thai, Indian, Chinese and Australian steaks, which were priced at about 500 yuan, or nearly fifty quid! As I was paying, I prayed Yan Dong didn't choose this!

He settled for fish and chips, which he'd never had before, and even this was quite expensive at 130 yuan. I explained that this wasn't the only food we eat in the U.K., but it used to be the most popular kind of fast food before KFC, etc., when fish and chips were served up in newspaper. I also explained that in the U.K. we usually remove the bones from fish before cooking – immediately after my having said that he removed three or four large bones from his mouth. But he confirmed that he enjoyed the food. When he'd nearly finished, my twelve-inch pizza arrived, which looked the size of a dustbin lid, so I had to share it with Yan Dong, and even took away a couple of pieces for dinner.

The toilet was very clean, with a sit-down loo and plenty of hot water, soap and paper towels. The whole feeling in the restaurant was warm and comfortable, although some of the items on the menu were quite expensive – except for spaghetti at 35 yuan and the large pizza, which was 89 yuan, this time with plenty of cheese and an authentic taste. On the way out, I was given a free stuffed-toy tiger.

We caught a taxi with a rather disgruntled driver, probably because we stopped him as the lights were changing to green, and motorists behind started sounding their horns as we got in. He took us to a large electrical store, on five floors, which was the second biggest in China, selling all kinds of computers, cameras, mobile phones, memory sticks, spare parts, etc., on lots of individual, independent sales counters. The place was like PC World on five floors, but more crowded.

Just before we entered, I suddenly remembered I'd left my bag at the restaurant, so we had to catch another disgruntled taxi back to the restaurant. Yan Dong explained that they paid approximately 70,000 yuan for a VW Santana and, as the minimum fare was only 7.5 yuan, it could take several years of hard work to get the money back, especially with all the other costs involved: petrol – which was about 6 yuan a litre – repairs, taxes and insurance, etc.

The café had my bag ready for me, but now, as it had started to snow, taxis were in great demand, so we walked back about halfway to the store, until we found a bus which would take us the rest of the way.

With Yan Dong's help, I bought a 160GB hard drive for 300 yuan (under thirty quid), a spare internet U.S.B. cable and a new U.S.B. cable for my six-year-old Canon camcorder. He bought a 4GB memory stick for 70 yuan. When we'd finished our purchases, I asked Yan Dong to come home for tea and help me install the hard drive; he also offered to show me some free movie download sites.

We couldn't get a taxi again, so I thought I knew where we could get a K52 home, but must have made a wrong turn, and could only find a number 55. He seemed to know the way back, so I left it to him, but there was so much traffic it took us nearly an hour and a half to get back. When we reached familiar territory, I realized we'd gone a long way round, and saw a number K52 pass by.

We got inside at 4.00 p.m., Ling answering the door for us. I made tea while Yan Dong had a go at the computer. After a few difficulties, he got everything sorted and saved some software on my desktop, then showed me how to get the movies, which he said should only take about fifteen minutes each. This proved incorrect, probably because he had been choosing popular ones, which had input from a lot of other people, who somehow share the uploading system around the internet; if you choose a film that's not very well known it takes a lot longer, as there's no one else using that channel. The two he chose would take about ten hours to download, but he said that you could do about ten at the same time. I chose *Kiss Me Deadly*, which I'd tried unsuccessfully to download from BitTorrent, plus *Mystic River*, mainly because it was highlighted.

Lao had come round to the house, after bringing Ling's mum home from a visit to her eldest daughter Zhang Min, but he soon left.

Yan Dong left at 5.30 and I took him down to the bus stop, where he caught a 36 bus to go and visit friends. When I got back both my computers had crashed, one from a previously recurring problem with the electric plug, and the main one stating that the disk was unclean, and it needed to shut down and be restored. When I got it working again, I was unable to recommence the downloading, as all the instructions were in Chinese, and I hadn't followed the various buttons Yan Dong had been pressing.

After that, I got fed up with computers and just checked

my emails. I was glad to see that our rent for the flat in London had been paid into my account.

Watched a DVD of E M. Forster's *Where Angels Fear to Tread*, which I'd got free with *The Sunday Times* in the U.K., before going to bed.


SATURDAY 6TH FEBRUARY 2010

After breakfast, we went out to buy vegetables from the local market, just outside our compound. I hadn't wanted to go there previously, as it all looked a bit primitive and dirty, but once I was in amongst it, it wasn't so bad. The vegetables looked as if they'd been brought straight from the farm, with most of the earth still on them, and they were laid out neatly on sacking instead of the pavement, as I'd first thought. We would have to clean and peel them anyway, so it didn't really matter if we bought them in their natural state, instead of all cleaned and wrapped in the supermarkets. They were also remarkably cheap: one pound of tomatoes, onions, carrots, a whole cauliflower or a large broccoli, all about 1 yuan each. We spent more than we'd spent on vegetables altogether when we added a pound of strawberries for 10 yuan. Ling was pleased with my introduction to this shopping experience, as I could now be sent out on my own!

After lunch, we went to the sales discount section of Silver Plaza, up the road to the left, opposite Unicon telephones and taking a 36 bus. I knew that Ling would spend ages shopping, so I found a place to sit and wait, listening to a talking book on my MP3: *The Big Bow Mystery* – a load of crap by Israel Zangwill, a writer I'd never heard of. It was about a locked-room murder in Bow. Very over-flowery and pretentious writing, but I had to read it all, to see how the murder was done. I was disappointed to find out it was the investigating detective who'd murdered the man, immediately after breaking down the door in front of a witness, who was too hysterical to notice him quickly slit the throat of the sleeping man. I'd read the same scenario before in *The Yellow Room*, by Gaston Leroux. Anyway, it passed the time.

Ling showed me her choice of two tops and a pair of trousers, which cost a total of 570 yuan; gifts for the New Year. The trousers had been reduced to 370 from 1500 yuan, although I couldn't imagine why anyone would pay that for them.

Back home, I tried to download some movies with my new software, but was unsuccessful after several hours, during which I caught another cold in the computer room, which was a bit colder than the rest of the house.

I went to bed early, at about 7.30, after some leftover pizza and pills for the cold.

SUNDAY 7TH FEBRUARY 2010

Stayed in bed most of the day, as I felt I had a touch of flu, and there was no point in getting up, as I had nothing special to do. Ling went to see her sister in the morning and came back about lunchtime, having been given a lift by Lao, who was lunching with friends.

I watched a couple of my recorded DVDs in the afternoon: Richard Widmark in a rather standard U.S. Army training film, with Karl Malden, and *Where the Sidewalk Ends*, with Dana Andrews and the lovely Gene Tierney. Felt better during the evening, but decided to stay in bed, to get over this cold (or flu).

MONDAY 8TH FEBRUARY 2010

Got up at 8.30 feeling a bit better, but sweated a lot during the night, so had to change the bedclothes.

Ling went out shopping with her cousin and I managed to download two films successfully: *A Serious Man* (or at least the first 54 minutes), released by the Coen brothers and *The Hangover*, which I didn't know anything about, but reviews said it was the funniest film of the year. Tried also to download *Double Indemnity* but that failed, so tried again to get *Kiss Me Deadly*.

I think my cold got worse during the day, due to spending so much time in the computer room, trying to download more films; these things always seem to take longer than people let on. Anyway, I also downloaded a couple of new releases, including *Law Abiding Citizen*, a rather gruesome revenge film and *The Box*, which again I didn't know anything about. I chose these films as they downloaded more quickly.

Ling had been to her sister's, and by the time she got back with her mum I was feeling worse, so I went to bed about 4.30 p.m.

Didn't get a wink of sleep all night, with a blocked nose and constant sweating. Ling wanted me to go to the hospital, thinking I had swine flu, but I put it off until the next day.

TUESDAY 9TH FEBRUARY 2010

I got up at about 10.00 a.m., after sleeping a little from 8.00

a.m., but still felt rough. Managed a normal breakfast, but after a cocktail of antibiotics and other medicines, I had no appetite for Xiao Wang's lunch concoction of vegetables swimming in grease, salted fish full of bones and various pork fat dishes.

There still seemed to be a few ants around the flat. I don't know where they were coming from, but they were even on my computer in the bedroom. They must have been somewhere in the fabric of the building, behind walls and along pipes, etc.

Ling and her mum went back to her sister's again, as the wound from the broken bone operation had started to swell, and was maybe infected somehow. Like me, though, she didn't want to go to the hospital, instead taking her own supply of antibiotics. She used to be a nurse, so I hoped she was going to be okay. As usual, her husband Lao was spending most of the day at restaurants and bars with his mates.

The P.C. had now developed an annoying habit of failing to register the letter "b" during typing, so I constantly had to go back and check. Plus, it was prone to switching itself off, so I was having to save constantly. Maybe it was all these ants, living inside the machine; another had just appeared on the keyboard, like the beginning of some horror film.

I watched *Law Abiding Citizen*. A bit ridiculous and gruesome; the acting was okay, although no famous names – I suppose new stars have to start somewhere.

Another ant appeared from inside the laptop and the system crashed again – not sure if it was full of ants eating all the circuits! – so it was back to the dreaded computer room, wrapped up well in a scarf and hat.

Started reading *Caesar's Commentaries* and found it quite fascinating; hard to believe it was written over 2000 years ago. I wished I'd paid more attention in Latin lessons at school, as we covered most of the same events, but the teacher was so dry and boring (Miss Marjeson, who also taught my dad) that there was no interest in the subject. What I found amazing was that Caesar refers to all the place names in France (or Gaul, as it was known then) which still exist today, like Aix-En-Provence, Montigny, Boulogne, etc., so all these places had names that far back which are still used today. Of course, that might be due to the translator having updated the names. There were quite large populations in these cities and regions, judging by the sizes of the armies they were able to raise; e.g. around Brittany there were several examples of standing armies, with cavalry etc. over 30,000 strong. He also refers to two campaigns in Britain, where there don't seem to be so many place names mentioned, as he didn't really know much about the country before his invasion, apart from the names of some tribes and local leaders. After his first invasion, he decided to go back the following year and had about eighty ships specially built, although they did have difficulties in navigation, and problems with rough seas and tides, having previously been used to sail in the Mediterranean.

As there don't seem to be any cases of writing in Britain before that, little is known about the people or country, other than news gathered during trade by sea, but it seems they had lots of warring counties and small kingdoms, which all had their own armies and troops of chariots. Still, although efficient among themselves, they were no match for the disciplined troops and more worldly experience of the Roman army under Caesar. He does, however, mention the River Thames, so that name has remained over the centuries. Funny to think of him coming ashore at Hastings beach, two thousand years ago; I wonder if he tried the local fish and chips. I suppose they wouldn't have had potatoes in those days.

WEDNESDAY 10<sup>TH</sup> FEBRUARY 2010

A general improvement in health, but still a lot of cold, with muscle pains in my side and back from coughing. No appetite, apart from eating a generous supply of cold remedies.

After a couple of mouthfuls of lunch, I watched a DVD I'd recorded in the U.K., *A Simple Plan*, with Bill Paxton and Billy Bob Thornton, about three guys who find about four-million dollars in a crashed plane and decide to keep it, before everything goes wrong. Unfortunately, the last ten minutes didn't get recorded, due to a mistake in timing the end of the programme, but I gathered the gist.

It was getting colder outside – about minus-seven degrees – but snow had not yet arrived, in spite of the forecast. In world news, Toyota was recalling up to eight million cars worldwide, due to design faults in braking and accelerator systems. A massive new deal was announced, with China buying coal from Australia worth about fifty-billion dollars or thereabouts. The Haiti news seemed to have died down, apart from one survivor being saved after twenty-eight days.

In the evening, Ling was showing signs of being fed up, worrying about me with my cold and her sister's leg, but brightened up after we played cards with her mum during the evening; we played Bu Ker, as we had done during our holiday to Scotland and back. At least it kept me up until 10.00 p.m., so as not to go to bed too early, hoping that this would encourage a longer night's sleep.

## THURSDAY 11$^{TH}$ FEBRUARY 2010

Awoke at 5.00 a.m., to the first signs of the arrival of the long-predicted snowfall, along with the sound of workers outside clearing the pathways. Went back to sleep until 8.00 p.m., when it appeared that Xiao Wang wasn't coming, as she was unable to get a bus, due to the roads being laden with snow outside the city. Within the city there always appeared enough workers to clear the roads, even with temporary workers using shovels and brushes.

Ling made a boiled egg for breakfast, so I didn't bother with porridge. Managed to get the internet working during the morning and transferred some funds from the U.K. to my account here in Jinan.

Healthwise, the cold was improving, but I still didn't have much of an appetite and no energy. Took the usual dose of pills, but was getting fed up being laid low like this. Hopefully I would get rid of it by the time we went to Guangzhou, on the 25$^{th}$. Ling made lunch, but I was only able to manage a bowl of rice and some vegetables, though

I seemed able to eat as much fruit as I wanted to.

Continued reading *Caesar's Commentaries*, in between listening to talking books, and went to bed at about 10.00 p.m.

Just to mention, before I forget, while looking out of the kitchen window at the army hotel opposite, I noticed rather an attractive light-blue bird flying onto a sort of ledge. About twenty feet from the ground, just below a row of windows, there was a sort of covered ledge with waterpipes running along it, partially covered in some insulation material; following the flight of this bird, I saw that there was a small colony of about twelve of them there, apparently settling in to build nests. They were like magpies in shape, with long tails and the same sort of hopping movement, but they were grey in colour, with very light blue wings. I suppose that to them these large buildings are like mountains or cliffs. This ledge was roomy and sheltered, and just high enough for a man to crawl along – I suppose in case there was ever any need to work on the pipes.

We were in the compound of the Chinese Air Force, and there was a ten-foot wall separating us from the army hotel. I could see into some of their workshop, kitchen areas and a couple of dining rooms, but never saw many people in them.


FRIDAY 12<sup>TH</sup> FEBRUARY 2010

Got up at about 8.00 a.m. and had the usual porridge.

Afterwards, at about 9.15, we took a 36 bus to the Central Bank of China, to confirm my transfer of cash. It was pretty cold and icy out, although sunny, and I was well wrapped up. We walked a little way after getting off, and the pavements were a bit more tricky than usual, with patches of ice and snow.

There was only one girl on duty in the bank, and she seemed to be dealing with three or four people at once, as people kept pushing in. Although I transferred money online, from Bank of China in London to Bank of China in Jinan, I still had to physically go in to sign for it, otherwise it would be sent back. Plus, there was a lot of other paperwork involved to convert the money into Chinese yuan, otherwise it would remain in Sterling, and couldn't be used to pay bills or withdrawn from the machines. The paperwork required another photocopy of my passport, which they already had half a dozen of, as well as filling in a form with my name, address, telephone number and passport number, then three sets of triplicate forms, all of which necessitated different rubber stamps to be applied.

After all that, I had to transfer 11,500 yuan to our mortgage account in Ling's name, so the mortgage in our flat could be paid up to August 2010, while we were away travelling. This took another load of paperwork and another copy of my passport. Eventually we were out at about 11.30.

I felt a bit tired then, as it was my first day outside for three days, so we went home for lunch. Xiao Wang was just leaving as we were crossing the road back, and we went in for egg and tomato soup with rice.

Ling and her mum went out to do some shopping for food, preparing for a few days when the shops would be closed for the New Year (of the tiger), and I made some bread. Later, Ling made a nice dinner of king prawns in a chilli and tomato sauce, and I felt my appetite returning.

Her younger brother Zhang Feng was due back from Hangzhou at around 11.00 p.m., so we waited up for him. I felt a bit sorry that there was no one to meet him at the airport, as Ling's mum was reluctant to request the service car, which was available with a driver for various occasions; but she could only request it about six times a year. Anyway, Feng arrived safely and didn't seem bothered; it was just a matter of him coming back to his hometown, anyway.

The news was reporting this year that in China 200-million people would be travelling to their various homes for the week-long holiday. These were mostly migrant workers, who had to work on the other side of the country, and only got to see their wife and kids at this time of the year. Most travelled by train, a few by plane and the rest by bus – except for a group of 100,000 travelling en masse by motorcycle; they had to have police escorts during the twenty-two-hour trip, with rest and food stops along the way, so it was quite a big concern.

The favourite firecrackers used seemed to be a string of bangers, about four times the size of ones in the U.K., all strung together, about fifty to a string. Then, they were hung over a tree branch or whatever. After lighting, the connection is burnt through and they go off with a bang when they hit the floor. Some of the army people next door would have more heavy-duty stuff, with engineers making all the noise.

SATURDAY 13TH FEBRUARY 2010

## CHINESE NEW YEAR

We all got up around 8.00 a.m., and for a change someone else (Feng) was up later than me.

The fish were still surviving, although one of them kept bullying and chasing the other two, so I don't know if that meant they were weakening. Anyway, it was now three weeks, which is the longest we'd ever been able to keep this kind of pet.

We went out at about 10.30, to go and buy a present for Ling's mum, but Ling changed her mind, so we bought some flowers – stocks and carnations – and went to visit her sister instead. We waited outside the shop for Ling's son, Qiang Qi, recently arrived from Beijing, to come and pick us up in his dad's car (his dad being Ling's ex-husband).

We had lunch at Zhang Min's, cooked by Lao, and sat around a small, round tea table. There were lotus roots stuffed with sausage meat and cooked in batter, which I ate most of, declining various parts of duck head, leg and skin in a black sauce. The prawns were quite tasty, with some vegetables soaked in vinegar, sliced cucumber, mushrooms and carrots. They tried to get me drinking Mou Tai or white wine, but I said I would rather have red wine, and Lao produced an expensive bottle, which was rather sweet.

After lunch, Zhang Feng and Qiang Qi went downstairs to let off some very loud fireworks (or "fireworkers", as Ling calls them), leaving a lot of red paper debris all over the place. Zhang Min's leg was still strapped up and she hadn't been able to walk on it yet.

We left at about 3.30 and saw a couple of interesting crested birds, pecking away in an area of exposed grass. They had long, curved, spiky beaks and black-and-white striped wings, and seemed quite happy until they noticed we had stopped to look at them, when they became uneasy and flew off. Qiang Qi had already gone home, but we were lucky to catch a number 15 bus most of the way. There weren't many people about, but still few taxis and fewer buses.

We had a rest during the rest of the afternoon, and a late dinner with wine.

The fireworks had begun in earnest, and I went to bed during a lull, at about 8.00 p.m., but it got louder by 11.00 and we could hardly sleep with all the thunderclaps; it felt like the Blitz. As we were surrounded within a military compound, there were heavy-duty explosions everywhere, booming in the distance and right outside the window.

SUNDAY 14<sup>TH</sup> FEBRUARY 2010

After not much sleep I got up, and everyone had a shower before breakfast. Fireworks continued again, but not so loud as last night.

We went out at about 9.30, to walk down to Suning Electricity Store, to buy Ling's mum a birthday present of a C.D. player, as her original one was broken. Most shops were shuttered up and closed, although a few hopefuls were open here and there, including the electrical store. They tried to sell us an expensive set of C.D. player/DVD speakers, etc., but we settled for a Philips portable, which looked quite well made for 490 yuan, ans also had a socket to attach MP3. We carried it to Silver Plaza supermarket, which was also open, and bought some fruit and vegetables. Then we walked to an Aili cake shop on the way home, to collect a birthday cake ordered by Zhang Min: a mix of coconut, walnuts and chocolate.

We caught a bus the last two stops home, opposite Hero's Park, as we were carrying quite a lot by then. I was beginning to sweat with all the warm clothes I was wearing, and still with cold symptoms, but otherwise not too bad.

We had lunch when we got back, and at 4.00 p.m. I made tea to go with a slice of cake each, having had a doze during the afternoon. We watched some of the Winter Olympics in Vancouver, although there was not much U.K. interest. Zhang Feng then showed me a new website for downloading free movies, but I found it a bit difficult to negotiate.

I can't remember much of the sequence of events over the previous few days, as I didn't have much of a chance to get to the computer. Both our laptops weren't working very well, and Zhang Feng was using the one in the computer room. We went over to see Zhang Min at some stage, and had tea, then they came over to Ling's mum's flat on Tuesday. We had a few visitors, including Yen Bin and his wife, and Ling's son Qiang Qi. I had been dozing in the bedroom, under Ling's orders, but joined the rest of the party – although I usually just sat around trying to look interested most of the time.

Lao insisted that we go out for a hot pot at 6.00 p.m., and drove us quite a long way to find a place we'd been to once before. It was quite a large place, with several rooms, run by people wearing army uniform. It was cold inside, but soon heated up with the charcoal burners on the tables. We had four massive plates of thinly sliced lamb, with the usual peanut paste to dip it into, and various other mixing pastes. When the water was boiling around the charcoal burner, we dipped a piece of meat into it with a chopstick and held it there for about ten seconds; it was then ready to eat. We had two half-litre bottles of Mou Tai (a white wine spirit about thirty per cent proof, which tasted a bit like vodka). For some reason, Qiang Qi got quite drunk very quickly, which made Lao Zhang happy, but the rest of us paced ourselves.

Qiang Qi was talking about his new girlfriend, whose father owned a large construction firm. If they married, they would go and live with her parents and enjoy a nice lifestyle – but he still seemed to be regretting splitting up with a previous girlfriend. He was hoping to start over with her again, now that he was running his own business of home delivery meals, busy enough to warrant employing an extra worker.

I thought we were going home at 8.00 p.m., but Qiang Qi, insisted that we go to a karaoke place nearby, complaining that he had never heard his mother sing. This was a bit more expensive, at 400 yuan, but Zhang Feng paid, as it was part of his hobby to go to these places. He also paid for the meal, which was quite cheap at 180 yuan for five people, including the two bottles of alcohol. Qiang Qi sang a couple of songs enthusiastically, but Ling persuaded him to go home early, as he was staggering about all over the place. We stayed behind, but I was a bit disappointed about the limited choice of Western music. I sang: "Pinball Wizard", "When I Fall in Love", "Help", "Long and Winding Road", "Return to Sender" and "Put Your Head on My Shoulder".

We got a call from Ling's mum at 10.00 p.m. to go home, as Zhang Min was waiting for Lao to go and pick her up. But it was decided that she would stay the night instead, and Lao went home by himself. Ling, Zhang Feng and I caught a taxi home at about 11.00.

Zhang Feng was a little drunk as well, but they stayed up talking until about midnight, in Zhang Min's room. I went to bed, where I sweated until I changed into lighter clothes, making sure that Ling didn't add an extra blanket when she came to bed.


TUESDAY 16ᵀᴴ FEBRUARY 2010

Got up at 8.30 a.m.

Xiao Wang was back at work, after three days' holiday. I washed my pyjamas and Ling went out to do some shopping for her sister, while Zhang Feng got up at about 11.30.

I had been reading *The Golden Pool* by R. Austin

Freeman, in between watching the figure skating. The U.K. couple came in at about 12th place, and most people had falls. Then read an email from Trevor, attached with a photo of him and cousin Chris.

Managed a bit of lunch: some chicken barbecued on sticks, with rice. Lao came round for lunch. Then we played a few tunes on my erhu, which wasn't of a very high quality, plus I seemed to have forgotten most of my lessons.

It was another cold but sunny day, with snow on the ground, at about minus-two degrees. We would soon have to start getting ready for our return to Guangzhou, where it was about twenty-one degrees, prior to going to Hong Kong, then Australia on 1st March. I wasn't sure what clothes to pack, as we would need to wear warm clothes when we leave Jinan, but two-and-a-half hours later would then arrive in a warmer climate.

After lunch, Qiang Qi came round, and Ling chatted with him about his girlfriend, whose father owned a construction company. If he married the daughter (Vicki, whom we met in Beijing) he was wanted to go and work for the company, but would first have to take a three-year study course in construction work. At the same time, he was still pining for his previous girlfriend, who studied Russian with him in Moscow and Volgograd; she had just returned to China after finishing her studies. Then Lao took Zhang Min home, with Zhang Feng helping her down the stairs.

At about 5.30 p.m., Yen Bin – Ling's friend who ran the school – came to take Zhang Feng to the airport. His school wasn't doing that well, as there weren't enough students. He paid 50,000 yuan to buy a teaching method, with materials, etc., which was supposed to help pupils develop the left or right side of their brains – I can't remember which. It was something to do with using pictures to identify words, Chinese characters, etc. At the moment he was losing money, but I guessed it would take him a couple of years to get on a proper footing.

## WEDNESDAY 17<sup>TH</sup> FEBRUARY 2010

I went through most of today thinking it was Thursday, and it wasn't until the evening that I realized my mistake. Not that it mattered much, as we wouldn't start our travels for another week.

During the morning, I watched a Tommy Lee Jones film, *In the Valley of Elah*, made in 2008, which I'd downloaded the day before. It was about two hours long, and I quite enjoyed the detective element of a father trying to find out who murdered his son, when back from fighting in Iraq. The day before I'd watched *Burn After Reading*, which I also enjoyed, although it was only one-and-a-half-hours long. About errors of identity and motives, it starred George Clooney, John Malkovich, Brad Pitt and David Rasche, and was quite funny. I was now currently trying to download an Ed Harris film called *Appaloosa*, but it had taken two days so far.

After a lunch of some leftover dumplings, we went out and took a K52 bus to Baotu Park, to view a lantern festival, for which Yen Bin had given us two free tickets. Jinan has about seventy-two natural hot springs around the city, most of them at Baotu Park and gardens; pools and traditional-style buildings have been built around the springs. There are also lots of pools, ponds, little canals and lakes here, with loads of ornamental fish, including goldfish, carp, etc., living in the warm water. It has been used for bathing, drinking and relaxation for about 3500 years, and in the thirteenth century a famous lady poet lived within the gardens. There were a lot of people there, in the cold but sunny air, enjoying the displays of scenes from history, floating lotus models, shows, food stalls, music and small shops. We had tea and a plate of pistachio nuts for 90 yuan, in a tearoom we'd visited a couple of times before, including once with Ling's elder brother Zhang Yan.

We left here at 4.00 p.m. and walked across the main square, watching the fountains, which were moving in time to some music playing over loudspeakers. Then we went to a large supermarket behind the main Silver Plaza store, near the Crown Plaza Hotel. This was quite a modern shopping area, a little like Oxford Street.

I bought a couple of videotapes for my camcorder, for 50 yuan each. We also had a look at some electric ovens, which I thought I might buy when we returned next year; they were about the size of a microwave and cost around 400 yuan. You could cook bread, cakes and meat in them, so I might then be able to find more food I'm used to, as I have never really adapted to Xiao Wang's cooking. Ling bought some face creams in an American store called Watsons, which has branches in most cities.

We caught a taxi home at about 5.00 p.m., after a few hours' exercise, as my blood sugar was up to 7.8 this morning, possibly due to my cold medicines (which seem to have a lot of sugar in them), lots of food during New Year celebrations and a lack of exercise, as I hadn't been out much – not even for a walk in Hero's Park, down the road.

I finished reading *The Golden Pool* by R. Austin

Freeman. It was quite a good treasure adventure story, set in Africa during the nineteenth century. I know he worked as an army doctor in the Ashanti territory during that time, before returning to the U.K. and settling in Gravesend, so he probably used a lot of his experiences. He also worked as a medic at Holloway Prison, where I guess he gained material for his *Dr. Thorndyke* detective stories.

Later on in the evening, I transferred six-hundred quid online, from my Bank of China account to Natwest, as this would be easier to withdraw from while travelling. I also renewed my car tax for six months online, which was due to run out at the end of February. We later booked two nights at a four-star hotel in Guangzhou, on 25th February, for 346 yuan per night.

THURSDAY 18TH FEBRUARY 2010

Got up at 8.30, feeling a bit better today, but still with a slight cough. One thing about all these antibiotics is that they cleared my skin of spots, etc. The weather was still cold outside, but sunny – although I could see a bit of snow still lying around. Fireworks were still going off spasmodically.

After lunch at about 12.30, we decided to go out, mainly

for some exercise. It was quite sunny, but cold as usual. We caught a K52 bus, then changed onto a 41, which took us past the main Silver Plaza superstore, just past the main square again, until we came to a large park, which was built around a lake, rather like West Lake in Hangzhou. The entrance was through some Chinese-style wooden gates, like the entrance to a temple; lots of bright colours – red, blue, gold, etc. – with curved roofs. We paid 30 yuan each for entrance and the place was pretty packed.

It was quite a large lake, which I think is called Daming Lake; I'm not sure how to describe it, but it is about the size of Hyde Park. We decided to walk most of the way around. There were pleasure boats at 10 yuan each, but we decided it was a bit cold to go out onto the water, and the walk would be better exercise for us.

There were booths, kiosks, bookstalls and fairground attractions pretty much all the way round. They were selling thousands of books in the open air – so many that I could hardly imagine how they'd pack them all away at night. Then there were stalls selling all kinds of good-luck trinkets, and guys making models with modelling clay, surrounded by crowds watching with interest. Another group were dressed in brightly-coloured clothes, taking people for rides in sedan chairs, while others were playing music or doing acrobatics and dragon dances. There was a great atmosphere everywhere.

We bought some kebabs outside, which were delicious, at only 1.5 yuan a stick. Ling bought some sugarcane drink, which they were making on the spot, and we passed an area of about a hundred yards worth of food stalls. We bought some Muslim bread, which was delicious, cooked in a clay oven, with the dough stretched over a kind of cushion, which was then thrust into the oven and whisked out again. When the bread was cooked, it was covered in a thin coating of salty sauce. The guys were singing and dancing while they were making it, and all the vendors seemed to be having a great time, doing a roaring trade. There were tearooms, drinks stalls and people making and selling toffee apples. It was certainly an interesting walk, which probably took us about three hours.

We caught a 41 bus all the way home, on which I nearly fell asleep; it dropped us off not too far away from home. We passed through the street market and bought a half-kilo of strawberries for 10 yuan, before arriving home for tea at about 5.00 p.m.

Watched a rather weird movie I'd downloaded called *The Box*, starring Cameron Diaz, then a short film starring Ralph Fiennes and Kate Winslet, called *The Reader*. I had to watch them on the computer, as they wouldn't seem to play on any other medium. Then went to bed at about 10.00 p.m.

## FRIDAY 19<sup>TH</sup> FEBRUARY 2010

Got up at about 9.00, after a long sleep, feeling a bit drowsy but the cold was improving. Just in case, I continued with the antibiotics and cough pills.

During the morning, I watched an excellent movie which Zhang Feng had downloaded, called *The Secret in the Eyes* – an Argentinian murder mystery, which at first I thought was in Spanish, but luckily it had subtitles.

After lunch we packed our suitcases – or at least got ready the clothes we intended taking with us, in one large case and one small one. Then we went out again, this time just to the nearby Yin Zone, which was a twenty-minute walk down the road, for some dry cleaning to take on our continued holiday. It was busy at the counter, but Ling had a small argument with the shop girl, who said something about how Ling's jacket wouldn't clean up as white, which was a bit ridiculous, as it was a grey coat anyway. Plus, they didn't think my pink jacket would get much cleaner. Ling answered: "Well, I don't expect it to get much dirtier."

We walked to the pharmacy on the way home. The doctor there took my pulse, to diagnose my cold, while a couple of girls watched with amusement. They then mixed a load of dried leaves, roots and various other concoctions, which they were going to boil up for me, but we had to go back for them at 6.00 p.m.

When we got home, I made tea and finished my painting of a scene near Weihai.

I was still trying to download *Appaloosa* which, after three days, was only at seventy per cent. But at least now the only issue seemed to be which film to choose, though some downloaded a little bit quicker than others.

Had a couple of chicken croquettes and a baked potato for dinner, which tasted okay, then after that we went to the pharmacy to collect the medicine. Ling had another argument with the staff, as she wanted a copy of the fourteen ingredients, which they didn't want to give, as it was against the rules; they changed the rules when Ling asked for our money back. She wanted to know what was in the medicine, in case I had any aftereffects. Of course, they didn't want to give it in case we somehow copied the medicine ourselves, when it was finished.

There were still a few fireworks going off as we walked home.

## SATURDAY 20<sup>TH</sup> FEBRUARY 2010

Weather was feeling warmer and the cold was improving, with the occasional cough. I was still taking the liquid medicine; I had a three-day supply for about 20 yuan. Also started taking some Royal Jelly pills, which were supposed to reduce blood sugar; in fact, it went down from the danger level of 7.8 to 6.2.

Watched another download: *Raising Arizona*, starring a young Nicholas Cage, made in 1987 by the Coen brothers. Ling was starting to get fed up with me watching movies in the computer room, but my only other option was sitting through Chinese T.V. in the lounge.

Had to bury a fish today, but the other two seemed okay after four weeks. Then had a small lunch of rice, with egg and tomato soup – no salt and not much flavour.

We'd been invited for a going-away meal by Ling's friend from her hospital days: Liu Lingsheng and his wife (the parents of Liu Pei), whom we'd known in the U.K. They were running a delivery business from China to the U.K. We left at about 3.00 p.m., intending to walk through the Hero's Park and down to the market area. It was a nice day for a walk; the temperature was up to about fourteen degrees, which felt like spring. We passed by several caged birds hanging from trees, as owners would bring them down here to get fresh air and be near other birds.

We noticed the Weihai Bank was open, so Ling had her passbook updated, which was done very quickly for a change. It now showed a balance to pay the mortgage on the new flat, up to next August, by which time we should be back in China.

Ling phoned Liu Lingsheng to check that they were in, as we'd bought them some lilies, but they were at his wife's (Zhang Mei's) mum's. So, we walked around there and had some tea, having to sign a visitors' book at the entrance gate to the flats, which backed onto the open market area, where you could buy antiques, pottery items, bonsai and ornamental stones, etc. The old lady had a three-bedroom flat, which was rather sparse, with a stone floor, to cater for the hot, humid summers.

We had tea and nuts for a couple of hours, then went to have dinner in the next road, which housed a whole street of restaurants. This place was famous for its rice soup and fried bread, with various kinds of fillings. The soup was good, with salt for a change, and quite tasty. The fried bread stuffed with spring onions and beef was also okay, but a bit greasy. Another dish which got served up was even more greasy, so I only ate one. But it was all quite cheap, at about 12 yuan a plate; I think we had about six plates between the six of us, including Zhang Mei's sister, the mother of Yan Dong, the young guy I spent a day with about a week ago. We had a reasonable meal, then Liu Lingsheng took us home in his car.

We went to bed at about 10.00 p.m., still trying to download *Appaloosa*.


SUNDAY 21ST FEBRUARY 2010

Woke up to a fine day. Ling got up at 6.00 a.m., as she couldn't sleep, and I got up at 8.30. Had the usual breakfast and felt free in the kitchen, as it was Xiao Wang's day off, so she wasn't there preparing food, which always looked okay before it was cooked.

We went out at 10.30 for a walk, and we took a bus to the mountain area of Qian Fou: "One thousand Buddhas". Strange, this was the third time I'd been on this bus, and it was always there at the stop as we arrived, meaning that we had to run across the road to catch it.

We got off at the park gate and paid 30 yuan each to get in. There was a huge set of steps leading to the top of the mountain, though at first a very gradual gradient. The granite stone paths and steps looked centuries old, as they were almost metal smooth, and the first part, to the foot of the mountain, was an incline for about one mile. We passed several terraces containing temples, a set of toilets almost every hundred metres, tea places and kiosks, etc., with a fairground halfway up.

We could see a huge statue of the goddess Guiying, with what looked like water geysers, but when we paid a further 5 yuan to go and have a look, the geysers turned out to be fountains from piped water; I think there used to be a waterspout here, as there were about twenty in Jinan, but lately they had dried up through lack of water. This feature was probably just to maintain the tradition. Then we saw a huge statue of reclining Buddha, which was carved out of a single piece of granite weighing fifty tonnes, in 1996.

When we reached the foot of the mountain, we could see steps continuing up, albeit rather more steeply, with a view of a temple painted yellow halfway up, then another at the top, in the shape of a pavilion, with the curved roof. However, we decided we'd had enough exercise for the day, not having been out much recently, while I'd been trying to recover from this cold, so we just went up one more flight of steps, to look at a thousand-year-old tree, then walked back down again – though this must have been over a mile. With all these steps and terraces, made of carved granite, it must have been a huge undertaking to build, along the lines of the Great Wall.

Near the bottom, we stopped to buy some books at a stall. Ling bought three, about antiques and medicine, for 50 yuan, which was pretty good; the retail prices, if bought in a shop, would have been over 300.

Just next to this I noticed that we could have taken a cable car to the top, at 30 yuan return, but we needed the exercise anyway.

I then saw one of the light-blue magpies I'd seen near our house. I couldn't tell if it was the same one, of course, but the ledge opposite our home was now deserted of the dozen or so I'd seen, and the flat did back onto the other side of the same mountain.

We had another long walk then, to have lunch at Jenny's Café, which served Western food. I ordered a pizza and garlic bread, while Ling had a Spanish paella. We added lemonade and a tomato juice, and the total came to 170 yuan, which wasn't bad for a place serving Western food.

We walked around the corner to a large supermarket, withdrew some cash from an A.T.M. and bought some fruit. Then we walked a bit farther to a bus stop, which turned out to be near the Bank of China, where I had to go to sign for my online cash transfers. We were able to catch a 36 bus all the way home, on a fine, sunny day.

When we got back, I had some bread which I'd just bought, then watched the end of *Appaloosa* – not a bad Western, but not great, with Jeremy Irons as the baddie and Timothy Spall playing a local businessman.

Then Ling got a call from a girlfriend, who wanted to meet for a chat. Ling arranged to go and meet her at about 6.00, while I stayed in to download some more movies, and finish some of the pizza I'd brought home.

MONDAY 22ND FEBRUARY 2010

Got up at 7.30 and had a shower.

Yen Bin was coming to fetch us at 9.30 a.m., as we had agreed that I would go to his school and give a quasi-English lesson to some of the kids there. I prepared a sort of "lesson plan" just before we left, based on teaching them to sing "Old MacDonald Had a Farm", printing some pictures to illustrate the idea, and also "Three Blind Mice", in case I had any extra time.

When we arrived at the school, it turned out that there were nine children waiting for my lesson, aged between seven and ten years. Most had English names, but I had to christen one boy with the name of William, as he didn't have an English name; no doubt this would now stay with him. I explained that it was the name of a future king from the English Royal Family. Others were called Cindy, Susie, Calista, Alice, Michael, Kevin, Sunny and another girl, whose name I can't remember (nor can Ling). I got them to write their names in English – which only one could do already – plus their ages.

After about forty minutes, I taught them to sing "Old MacDonald…" Then we had a tea break, before I went back to teach them "Heads, Shoulders, Knees and Toes". I think this also helped the two Chinese English teachers, as I gave them my material when I'd finished, and heard them all singing the routine by themselves.

I think Yen Bin was well satisfied with the morning's work, and he took us to a buffet at a very posh restaurant/hotel called Shungeng Hillview Hotel, near the mountains, which was owned by the government. It was an immaculate place with brilliant decorations, and the large dining hall had small trees to decorate it, with ornamental stone blocks representing mountains and a stream full of goldfish, running underneath a meandering glass floor.

We were joined by Yen Bin's son. During the meal, he explained that he was making a loss during his first year, as might be expected, as he only had twenty students enrolled; he needed thirty to go into profit.

We had an excellent selection of food, at a cost of 110 yuan each, including crab, sushi, steaks, a choice of fruits and vegetables, cakes, yoghurt and fruit drinks. The waitresses were very friendly and smartly dressed, and we could watch a curling competition between Canada and China on T.V.; they were 5-5 by the time we had left, at around 1.30 p.m., when Yen Bin gave us a lift home.

Later in the afternoon we walked down to the medicine shop, to buy some plasters for back pain, to take to the U.S.A. with us for Ling's brother. Then we walked to New World Market to buy batteries for a clock and a watch, which cost 25 yuan. We also bought some silk material for Ling's brother's wife Ang Li, before catching a number 88 bus home.

It was about sixteen degrees and sunny today, and as my cold was better I was able to wear my sports jacket for the first time, instead of a quilted coat.

During the rest of the afternoon, I repaired a coffee machine for Liu Lingsheng, as he had been unable to read the instructions in English; I needed to unblock the coffee-grain hopper.

## TUESDAY 23<sup>RD</sup> FEBRUARY 2010

Got up at 8.30, had a shower and washed all our clothes.

Then Ling advised me that we were going to return the coffee machine to Liu Lingsheng, so we went there after breakfast. But when we got there the machine wouldn't work.

We invited them for lunch at Jenny's place, and were joined by Ling's son Qiang Qi, who only drank water; he must have had a hangover. I had spaghetti Bolognese, but Ling didn't enjoy her fish with pasta. The meal came to 330 yuan for the five of us.

Qiang Qi drove us home, then we all went with Ling's mum to Ling's sister, for a last farewell before we would leave. She had a new lady to help with the housework, but Lao was out, and we noticed the usual empty alcohol bottles piled up outside.

We left at about 4.00 p.m. and came home to relax, after a warm day of about nineteen degrees. We shortly went out again to collect some dry cleaning, as the shop was open until 9.00 p.m.

## THURSDAY 25TH FEBRUARY 2010

I left out yesterday's entry, as there was nothing to report.

Ling got up at 5.30 and I arose at 6.00, to get ready, as a car was coming to pick us up at 7.00 a.m. This was a free service provided by the Chinese Air Force, requested by Ling's mum.

Yen Bin came to help, and while I was having breakfast he carried our cases down to the car. He was going to come to the airport with us, but we said it wasn't necessary, as there were two of us, and the driver would also help.

We arrived at the airport at 7.40. The weather was a bit chilly, but we were wearing jackets and light raincoats. However, after checking in (my case was 21.9 kilos and Ling's was 18 kilos), we found out that the plane was delayed, due to bad weather the previous night. As compensation, we were all given tickets for a free breakfast, which was served in a special restaurant called The Delayed Flight Restaurant. The food was prepacked, like aeroplane food, but it was quite nice, and certainly better than Xiao Wang's cooking.

Ling told me that Xiao Wang had asked for a pay increase, although Ling's mum was already paying her over the standard rate – 600 yuan per month instead of 500 – plus free lunch. In fact, Ling's mum decided she was going to ask her to leave on 8<sup>th</sup> March, as she didn't need someone every day, and saw no reason why she should pay more. So Xiao Wang would be disappointed! We weren't sure how she would take it, as she showed a bit of a temper when Ling's mum tried to get rid of her before.

After the meal, we were told the flight time was changed from 9.00 a.m. to 11.40 a.m., so we sat reading while we waited. I was reading *Dark Hollow* by John Connelly, which I eventually finished during the flight and left on the plane, to reduce our luggage weight a little bit.

We arrived in Guangzhou at 2.40 p.m., where it was a humid twenty-seven degrees, so we had to remove coats and jumpers.

We caught a bus at the number 2 stand, which took us near the hotel, although it stopped in rather an awkward place, along a dual carriageway, where there was a fence, and we all had to walk about a hundred yards along the road with our cases. Fortunately we caught a taxi here, and were taken to the four-star Fortune Hotel. We checked in for two nights, at 348 yuan per night, but I couldn't remember my credit card pin number, and they wouldn't accept my Natwest debit card, so I had to pay with a mixture of cash and my Bank of China card. We were shown to room number 1026, on the tenth floor. It was a very nice place, with air conditioning, clean carpets, bedding and ensuite.

After washing and changing into summer clothes, we went out to the train station, to order our tickets to Hong Kong, but we had forgotten to bring our passports. So, we walked to an Ikea nearby and had meatballs for dinner, as usual. It took us ages to find our way out, then we walked over to the Jusco store to look for Trev's trousers, but I'd forgotten the sizes and they were a bit expensive. I bought myself a summer hat, though, as it was so hot.

We returned to the hotel and tried another store, where they had some nice trousers, but we still weren't sure of the leg size, so would go back tomorrow. I checked when we got back to the hotel: waist 97cm and leg 75cm.

We went to bed around 10.00 p.m., quite warm.


FRIDAY 26<sup>TH</sup> FEBRUARY 2010

Ling got up at about 5.30 a.m., but I didn't get up until 8.00. We went down to breakfast, which was included. It was a good choice buffet, with many selections. I had orange juice, cornflakes, and a fried egg on toast with youtiao, followed by coffee and a croissant.

Then, armed with Trev's trouser size, we went to

Mopark Supermarket next door, and bought a pair we'd selected last night. We waited for about fifteen minutes, while they altered the length to fit. We then went to another supermarket, to buy padlocks for our cases at 5 yuan each, and some flip-flops for use in the shower.

We took a taxi to East Guangzhou train station, to buy tickets and assess how long it would take to get us there. We bought two first-class tickets to Hong Kong for 380 yuan, when we found out they didn't want to see our passports after all, so we could have got them last night.

The hotel menu looked quite good, with a Szechuan menu. I had fried beef, which was excellent and Ling had frog; we shared some green vegetables. The total cost, with tea, was 86 yuan.

After lunch I had a snooze, while Ling went back to Mopark and bought two pairs of shoes.

At around about 4.00 p.m., we took the underground to Gong Di's area to buy more trousers, by which time Ling began to think this was our only reason to come to Guangzhou. After making the purchase, we went to Gong Di's flat, as he was back from work. I was pleased to see most of his fish were still alive, but his flat had a lot of condensation on the ceiling and walls, which also seemed to be affecting all the common areas of the block, as well.

We left at 6.00 p.m., as he was taking us to dinner, after we met his friend Liu Si Deng and his wife. They took us by car to an excellent place, where they served Kung Po chicken, having chosen this place in my honour, as it was a sort of standing joke that this was the only dish I would eat. He also bought two bottles of red wine to go with the meal, but we only drank one bottle, as Liu Si Deng had given up drinking because his wife was pregnant. The food was excellent.

Liu Si Deng then drove us back to the hotel, as Gong Di was a little tipsy – even though he'd said that he didn't really like red wine, as it wasn't strong enough.

## SATURDAY 27<sup>TH</sup> FEBRUARY 2010

We got up at 8.00 a.m. and went downstairs, to the same breakfast as yesterday.

Gong Di was supposed to come and pick us up at 10.30, to take us to the station, but after he'd left us last night he went somewhere to have some drinks for a friend's birthday, and had woken up with a hangover. We therefore checked out at 10.20 and the page got a taxi for us, which cost 30 yuan, to get to the station. We arrived early for the 12.12 train, and sat in the waiting area for about an hour.

To go to Hong Kong, we had to put our luggage through a security check, plus complete a boarding pass.

It was a comfortable journey, although I had a bit of a problem getting all four of our cases up on the overhead luggage rack. We had a packed meal during the trip, at 85 yuan: I had chicken and rice, while Ling had scrambled eggs.

At Hong Kong station, we had to hand in our boarding cards and show our passports. We had a small problem directing the taxi driver to the Stanford Hotel, but found out later that there were two hotels with the same name; the one we wanted was in Mongkok Area. Although the meter said 30 yuan, we had to pay an extra 15 yuan for our cases, which were put in the boot, which didn't close properly and had to be tied down.

The hotel was okay, but our room was tiny and we could hardly move around at the same time. At least there was a shower and air conditioning, but no breakfast included. After freshening up, we went out for a walk.

As we were looking a bit bemused, an English guy who had lived here for ten years stopped to give us directions to the nearest underground. We had planned to go to the harbour, but when we encountered the crowds, we felt quite shocked; there were so many people, everywhere we looked, thousands of small restaurants, with tables for about ten people, and small shops all piled on top of each other. It looked as if every inch of the place had something going on.

Ling saw a sign saying that a two-bedroom flat cost two million HK dollars. She told me there was a saying in China, that every inch of land in Hong Kong was worth its weight or measurement in gold.

We could hardly stand it for more than twenty minutes. Although amazing, it was daunting being among so many people; you could hardly move. And, anyway, we had no idea where we wanted to go! So, after a while we returned to the hotel, to make some plans about what to do tomorrow. We decided to go on a conducted tour of HK, including Victoria Park, which cost a total of sixty-two pounds for five hours.

As money seemed to be going fast here, I wasn't sure if I needed to draw more cash out, but it looked as if it might hold out for another day. Prices were much higher here than China, certainly.

On the way back to the hotel, we bought some cakes and fruit, then went back to watch Pearl T.V. for a while.

Then, at 7.00 p.m. we ventured out, to look for somewhere to have dinner, but everywhere we chose seemed to have queues of people waiting outside. However, we found a Vietnamese restaurant which looked good. Ling ordered pineapple and prawn mixed rice, which came in a hollowed-out pineapple, and I had beef and fried noodles, washed down with a bottle of beer, which came to a pricey 130 dollars (or yuan, as HK dollars are about the same as Chinese yuan).

We had another walk around in the madding crowds and bought some bread, as we would be out early tomorrow, at 8.15, so probably wouldn't have time for breakfast.

There was no internet in the room, but there was a business room somewhere here, which I might try tomorrow. Had a shower then an early night, at 9.45 p.m.

## Sunday, 28 February 2010

Got up at 7.00 a.m and went down to reception, although the lift from 18<sup>th</sup> floor seemed to stop at every floor on the way down. Just reached reception in time to meet the tour guide 'Teri' at 8.15. We stopped at 4 more hotels to collect everybody, giving 26 people in our group. We had quite a good chat with a middle-aged Jewish couple, sitting behind us, Mr and Mrs Cooper, from Canada.

The tour guide was excellent and made some good jokes, likening the shape of Hong Kong to her face- with her mouth representing Hong Kong, her nose, eyes and mouth and forehead as Kowloon, and one ear as Lantau Island and the top of her head to The New Territories. Hong Kong island has a population of 2 million and Kowloon which is a bit bigger has 1.7 million and the rest 3.3 million.

The coach took us from Kowloon, through a tunnel under the bay, to Hong Kong. I thought our hotel was situated in Hong Kong, but it turned out the Chinese guy at MDU, Sennen Chiu had recommended a place in Kowloon, not that it really matters as we seem to be in quite a convenient area for shops, markets and restaurants.

The first place we were taken to was Victoria Heights, up a winding mountain road, which is apparently the best area for private properties owned by the wealthy, as it's a bit cooler in summer, with better views and warm in winter. It was an amazing view of the city, which we hadn't realised was so big. There were sky scrapers built on top of hills or small mountains, which doubled their height and huge buildings all round the bay. At the view point there was a huge cable car building with restaurant and various shops around the square. We were allowed half an hour here and the coach photographer took our picture-the first of the ploys to extract money from us!

Then we were taken to a jewellery factory and were supposed to have a lecture an demonstration of how the pieces were designed and made, but there was only one worker there, being Sunday and this lot only lasted 5 minutes, before we were taken into the sales room. We were shown some amazing stuff but mostly too expensive of course, but we learned Ling's birthstone was Topaz, so I managed to buy her some Topaz and silver earrings for about 60 quid.

Then we were taken to the Aberdeen fishing boat area and took a Sampan ride round the bay, for an extra 55 HK dollars. The tour itself had cost 350 dollars already, so it was an expensive day, in some ways but good value for the tour. There were some huge luxury motor cruisers in the marina, plus a lot of houseboats, sampans, junks and fishing boats and it was quite a hive of activity, although the fishing personnel is gradually decreasing, as younger generation don't want to do this work. We saw the floating Jumbo restaurant, which can seat 2700 people and the sea water in the bay, which leads to the South China sea, was remarkably clean, a rich green colour and looked a bit like the water in Venice, which I think is actually rather more blue.

Next stop was a drive around Repulse Bay, with its sandy beach, golf course with a 20 year waiting list and luxury hotels, on to Stanley Market. We had an option to stay here 45 minutes and catch the coach back, or stay longer and go back by public bus. There wasn't that much of interest in the market and we just bought a HK T shirt and a small gift for my Aunt Peggy and a photo of HK in 1939 for Uncle Norman, as he served here during the war.

The bus took as back to the hotel at 1.15, so it wasn't too bad. We went in to freshen up and then went along the road and had a simple lunch nearby, of beef curry and beef with noodle soup. We then had a little walk round, with not so many people around on a Sunday.

Had a rest until 5.00 and then attempted to get a 1A bus from the main street, Nathan Road to Starr Ferry, but unfortunately, by the time we reached the bus terminal, I found we'd gone in the wrong direction, which didn't please Ling at all. We then had to get the bus all the way back and by the time we reached Starr Ferry, it was gone 7.00. This was the harbour area and there was a great view of HK skyline all lit up on the other side of the bay and we went for a coffee at Haagen Daas, where I was conned by the staff giving me a 20 Thai dollar note as change, which is only worth 4 HK dollars, which I didn't find out until I tried to spend it later.

At 8.00 we returned to the harbour side and watched a light display with music, which went on for 10 minutes and then got the bus back to Soy Street, along Nathan Road, mostly, which is pretty much the same length and width as Oxford Street, mostly jewellers' shops, Cartier, Tiffany, Loo Foon Kwik.

It was a bit late for dinner, so I bought an excellent youtiao for 5 dollars, where I found out about the dud note and Ling bought 2 boiled eggs, which we had back at the hotel.

**Monday 01/03/2010**

Our last day in China, but as we had to check out at
noon and our flight wasn't due till 8.10 pm, we had to
find some way of passing the time. First thing, we
went along to a small cafe along the road for breakfast
and had youtiao fried inside some congealed rice
stuff, which was OK and Ling had rice soup, after
some difficulty with the waiter, who seemed a bit
mentally impaired, although maybe it was because he
only spoke Cantonese and we only spoke Mandarin
and English between us. Went back to the hotel and
had some fruit and at 11.30 we took our cases to leave
in reception for most of the day and then checked out.
It was very misty today and it was rather eerie to see
high buildings emerging from the mist, as if floating,
as they were shrouded in mist from the bottom up to
about a quarter of their height and then they soared
above the clouds.
We took a bus to Starr Ferry and caught a ferry across
to Hong Kong, which only cost 3 HK dollars, for the 5
minute crossing.

It was rather bewildering on the other side, as we didn't know where we wanted to go. We planned to go and see some shops in Causeway Cove, but after entering the underground, were met with such a huge choice of directions we had some difficulty in locating the right line and had to walk what seemed like miles, along long passageways, with shops and various exits to different lines. At last, we got the right train and took about 4 stops, but then couldn't seem to find a way outside, there were several floors (underground) with shopping malls and other train lines. We decided to shop for lunch in Times Square, which turned out to be another shopping mall, with a choice of several restaurants, with tables in the centre. So, you chose which cuisine you wanted and then found a table for the customers of all the outlets. I had Thai crabmeat with rice and Ling had a Japanese vegetable noodle dish, which neither of us finished.

Then we managed to find our way to the surface and were going to take a tram ride, for fun, but couldn't work out where they were going or which direction you were supposed to choose. They were quite narrow but had two levels. In the end we decided to go to HK International Exhibition Centre at Wan Chai Ferry. We had to walk a long way to find the right bus stop and the one we took only took 2 stops to reach the terminal.

We saw the centre which was a massive building, in the shape of a kind of bird with spread wings, but there was no exhibition going on so no point in going inside, so we walked along the river for a bit. You could just see Kowloon on the other side, through the mist. Some Indian guy approached me and said I had a lucky face, but Ling warned me against speaking any further as it some kind of con to do with offering Feng shui or fortune telling. There was also a Bhuddist monk begging, but again, Ling said he was probably someone just dressed up.

We then took a ferry back and had a walk around in Harbour City in Kowloon, which was about the size of Brent Cross shopping mall and with loads of top names-Gucci, Cartier, Louis Vuiton etc, but eventually stopped at a Starbucks as we were getting quite tired. Then we walked to the bus terminal and caught a 1A bus back, but got off the wrong stop and had difficulty in finding our hotel, located in Soy Street, first walking in the wrong direction. It seems best to ask for directions in English here and we just managed to get back to the hotel in time to use the toilet and catch our taxi, which had been booked for 5.00 pm. We reached the airport about 5.45 and paid 230 HK dollars which had been negotiated by the hotel.
We checked in, but Ling had some problem as her visa for Australia, was on her Chinese passport, which had been cancelled a month ago, as she had applied for a new 10 year one, which of course didn't have the visa on it. So, they had to telex ahead to advise the Australian authorities, she would be showing 2 passports.

We didn't have anything to eat, although we weren't sure what the arrangements would be for a meal on board the plane, which was due to fly at 8.10 pm. Hong Kong airport is very modern, with great facilities, based on Lantau Island, one of 260 islands which make up Hong Kong, which seems so much bigger than I imagined, with mountains, parks, rivers, masses of towerblocks and a business centre like the city of London.

We were allowed through the boarding gate early, as there were several security checks to go through, having to open our bags, laptops, etc. Once boarded the flight was further delayed as one passenger hadn't come aboard, so they had to take off all the luggage and make sure her case was removed from the baggage hold.

We were served a nice dinner of fish in tamarind sauce and Ling had braised chicken and rice and then the inflight video didn't work, so had to be switched off for half an hour while it was being rebooted. I watched a rather crap film with Ricky Gervais, called 'The Invention of Lying' and then tried unsuccessfully to get to sleep and was surprised that Ling didn't manage either. The Chinese guy next to me annoyed me most of the night with his elbows on my side of the arm rest and he kept fidgeting non-stop throughout the flight.

Lights were back on at 6.00 and we were served a breakfast of scrambled eggs, with bacon and baked beans. I wonder if the weight on board the plane is reduced at all, when 300 or so people have consumed all the in-flight food?. I mean, does their weight correspond with the equivalent of the intake of food, or is it in some way reduced? If the plane was weighed before and after?

With this weighty problem in mind, we landed in Sydney on time, at 8.10 am Tuesday, 02 March 2010 and so ended our travels in China, until the next time.

*Jinan Main Square.*

*Xian.*

*Crowds on the way to Terracotta Army Museum.*

*Xian City Wall.*

*Giulin.*

*Stone Forest, Kunming.*

*Park for 46 ethnic minorities, near Kunming.*

*Path in Yellow Mountains Anhui Province.*

*Art Factory 798 in Beijing.*

*Karaoke in Jinan, with some of Ling's friends.*

*Li Gong, ex pilot.*

*Su Bin and Li Gong.*

*Garden room for Ling's mum (3rd floor).*

*Computer room, where I write my diary.*

*Main Square in Jinan.*

*Ling's mum and older sister on way to shopping centre.*

*Ma's dining room and kitchen.*

*Off to the shops!*

*With Liu Lingsheng and wife Zhang Mei an Dr Ma-day out at Red Leaf Mountains on bus trip from Jinan*

*Treehouses in Red Leaf Mountain.*

*Red Leaf Mountain.*

*Ling with statue of Guilin, outside Weihai 2011.*

*Display model of flats for sale in Weihai.*

# About the Author

David was born in Ruskin College, Oxford, in 1944, to parents Thomas Colyer and Fred Olive Colyer (nee Gammon). He was educated at Holy Trinity Primary School, East Finchley and Woodhouse Grammar School, North Finchley.

He had several jobs in the insurance industry, including running an insurance brokerage in Glasgow for nineteen years. This had to close down in 1993, contributing to his divorce from his Scottish wife, two years later.

David met his second wife Ling while studying Chinese under Ma Tao, a lady teaching the language at the School of Oriental and African Studies in London. They got married at Westminster Registry Office in 2002, and have since then been travelling in China every year.

# Acknowledgements

The publisher would like to thank Russell Spencer, Matt Vidler, Laura-Jayne Humphrey, Lianne Bailey-Woodward, Leonard West, Janelle Hope and Susan Woodard for their hard work and efforts in bringing this book to publication.

# About the Publisher

L.R. Price Publications is dedicated to publishing books by unknown authors.

We use a mixture of both traditional and modern publishing options, to bring our authors' words to the wider world.
We print, publish, distribute and market books in a variety of formats including paper and hardback, electronic books, digital audiobooks and online.

If you are an author interested in getting your book published, or a book retailer interested in selling our books, please contact us.
www.lrpricepublications.com

L.R. Price Publications Ltd,
27 Old Gloucester Street,
London, WC1N 3AX.
020 3051 9572
*publishing@lrprice.com*